**Canadian Cataloguing in Publication Data**

Skumavc, Franc, 1926 -
On One-Way Path: A Life's Journey

ISBN 0-9696824-0-9

1.Skumavc, Franc 1926-  2.Catholic Church - Clergy - Biography.
3.Clergy - Ontario - Biography  4.Croatian Canadians - Ontario - Biography.  I. Title

BX4705.S48A3 1992     282'.09    C93-093186-6

## Acknowledgements

The Author expresses his gratitude to: Eleanor Doan of Ventura, California, for permission to quote the poem "What Will He Become?" from her book "A Mother's Sourcebook of Inspiration"; Division of Christian Education of the National Council of Churches of Christ in the U.S.A., for permission to quote passages from the Revised Standard Version of the Bible; all who in any way contributed to the production of this book: especially John and Loretta Kearsley of Beaver Graphics in Beaverton; Dave and Una Findlay of Indisys Computers in Pefferlaw; Carole Birss for typing the manuscript; John and Reta Stone for proof-reading the text; and Mike Watters (and his brother Tim, too) for just being so kind and helpful to everyone, including the Author.

Computer typesetting: Una Findlay
Graphic, Illustrator and Painter: Marta Brestovansky
Manufactured by John Deyell Company Limited, Lindsay, Canada
Published by the Author
Legal Deposit: National Library, Ottawa, Canada

# ON ONE-WAY PATH

A Life's Journey

Franc Skumavc

# Contents

Dedication

<u>Illustrations</u>

The book has a hard cover mainly in order to protect illustrations. It is hoped that they will be appreciated and enjoyed for many years to come.

Two of the coloured pictures are photos. The first one is a panorama of the Julian Alps in winter, taken from the foot of the Karavanke mountain range, from above Dovje. The more remote of the two houses at the extreme left is the home of my mother. The uppermost one at the extreme right, with three windows, the elementary school I attended. This view of the school is from the northeast; its snapshot in the section of black and white photos is taken from the west. The peak at the centre which seems to be the highest is Rjavina, 2542 m. The 2864 m high Triglav is seen to the right of it in the background, with a small glazier on its north side.

The hamlet Radovna is in the valley behind the mountain at the extreme left. Between it and the range with Rjavina at its end is a glimpse of the mountains on the south side of Krma valley as seen from just outside the courtyard of the Skumavc home (see the coloured photo "Springtime in Radovna"). The farthest area of the mountains on the second coloured photo is identical with the "glimpse" on the first one.

The area between Dovje and Mojstrana seems rather narrow and flat. In reality it takes a 10 - 15 minute walk downhill from Dovje to reach the river Sava, on the northern edge of Mojstrana.

I am especially grateful to Marta Brestovansky for her permission to include among the coloured paintings the two previously unpublished works of sacred art. They are truly beautiful!

The rest of her coloured paintings are basically true to reality. In her linear drawings, however, the artist took great liberty. My mother's laundry on the courtyard, e.g., is described in the text as it was done in snow and ice, while the drawing is a spring scene. However, by far the greatest liberty of creative artistic imagination is displayed in scenes of the prisoner of war camp and the life of its inmates. The romantic pastoral air of the drawings and the bitter reality behind them are poles apart.

Again, I wish to express my deep gratitude to Mrs. Marta Brestovansky for her beautiful artwork. I am sure everyone will agree that it is not only great art, but also very beautiful. (Franc Skumavc, Author)

# PART I

## THE JOURNEY

*What will he become, this little one?*
        *So innocent is he today!*
*What will life unfold for him?*
        *Open, O Future and say!*

*The baby answers in tones so clear,*
        *"What will you have me be?*
*I belong to you, your bidding to do,*
        *You may do as you wish with me.*

*I am so little, I know not the way,*
        *My life is all yours to mold.*
*O, parents, prayerfully plan for me*
        *That my life may in beauty unfold.*

*This life can be a lovely thing*
        *Like a flower that is wondrously fair.*
*Then train me lovingly dear ones*
        *With faith, and hope and prayer."*

AUTHOR UNKNOWN

# Dedication

There are so many to whom I would like to dedicate this work: my parents, family, grandma, teachers, and others who helped shape my life and nurtured my faith. There are the benefactors to whom I owe so much. There is Mary, the Mother of God, to whom I consecrated on the very day of ordination to the priesthood my remaining life and work, whole and entire. To anyone, or some, or all of these, and many more, this work could and should be dedicated. And so it is. However, if one plain individual person or group on this planet must be singled out, so let it be.

These lines are being written more than 50 years after the beginning of the Second World War, and well over 40 years after its end. My own life has been profoundly influenced by it, as were many millions of other lives, not to speak of the millions who perished in it. Much of this book is in one way or another related to that war.

The fears, horrors and agonies of those who suffered through that man-made global cataclysm and of those who died in it are beyond adequate description. No literary genius, no sound-track, no film can portray the reality of its intensity and magnitude. Much less has this writer been able to do so. Yet a little is better than nothing.

I am familiar to a small degree only with the war. There have been, of course, countless other wars and revolutions in the history of mankind; some are still raging this very hour. But no century had been as barbarian and murderous as our 20th A.D.

With my limited ability I tried to point out the enormity of war and godliness of genuine peace. Let the dedication serve to enhance my feeble effort.

Let this book be dedicated to the countless millions of orphans, widows and widowers, refugees, expellees from their ancestral homelands, civilians from infants to centenarians who were disembowelled by shrapnel of ear-drum-shattering bombs or barbecued slowly, alive, in air raid shelters, and those who are still dying of burns and radiation decades after the hellish atomic holocausts of Hiroshima and Nagasaki.

Let it be dedicated to the memory of all who suffered innocently in all wars, revolutions and holocausts, especially the most diabolical of them all: the ones of the "enlightened" 20th century.

Most specially let it be dedicated to the millions of soldiers who were innocent, both the dead and those still living, particularly to the unknown and forgotten ones, with utter disregard for the colour or fashion of uniforms in which they got stuck. I suffered more than enough, but most of them much more and much longer than I: indescribable pains of fear, exhaustion, loneliness, homesickness, vermin, and more. From the sizzling-hot sands of the Sahara to the vast frozen tundra of the Arctic they were marching, fighting, sweating, bleeding, freezing, hungering and thirsting, rotting and starving in P.O.W. camps - and dreaming of their homelands and dear ones: wondering if and when they'll meet again, if ever.

How many returned to burned-out homesteads, with no clue about the whereabouts of their dear ones: defeated, despised, dispossessed? How many never again saw their home and dear ones?

We do know that some perished after all the agonies of mind, body and soul on the battlefield or in camps. Some died in more mature age, most in their prime of life; some suddenly, others slowly; few peacefully, most violently: in mud, in the air, under the earth, in depths of the oceans...The exact number is known only to God. We only know that it is not legion, but rather legion times legion. It is not up to me to judge how many and to what extent some were guilty. That, too, only God knows. Personally, I am convinced that both the number of the guilty and the extent of their guilt are, all circumstances considered, much smaller than generally assumed. I am not judging their guilt, nor am I taking them into account here.

To each and everyone of the multitudes of the innocent martyrs this book is dedicated with sentiments so profound that they cannot be expressed in human language.

May my own humble story be a loving tribute to them, as well as a reminder and gentle invitation to all never to forget them and their agonies, but to remember them always, and pray for them and their bereaved dear ones.

May it also be a profound, even if small, token of gratitude to God who gives always enough strength to the weak to endure and overcome: if only they ask, respond, and cooperate with his grace.

And may it be an ardent invitation to all to strive, work, and pray for genuine peace and goodwill in the world. (F.S.)

Chapter One

# O Homeland, you are like Health

The great 19th century Slovenian writer, Ivan Cankar, expressed a profound truth in a touching sentence: "O homeland, you are like health."

This striking statement can be more fully appreciated only when we realize that its all-too-young author was dying of tuberculosis.

What earthly good could one in such circumstances put above health? Only by knowing the predicament of the author can the beauty and pathos of these few words be fully grasped.

"O homeland, you are like health..."

One's homeland includes not only one's land of birth, citizenship and childhood, but also its people. Parents, brothers, sisters and other relatives, and one's language and culture have a deep influence on us, in mysterious ways, somewhere in the depths of our subconscious.

My native land is Slovenia. I was born and grew up in its mountainous northwestern area, the majestic Julian Alps. We lived in a valley at the foot of the highest peak in what used to be Yugoslavia, the 2864-metre-high Triglav.

Before the First World War, Slovenia was part of the Austrian-Hungarian Empire; and after that war, most of Slovenia became part of Yugoslavia, a creation of the Treaty of Versailles. With its area of 20,251 square kilometres, it was the second smallest of the six republics or provinces of Yugoslavia. Slovenia, since 1991 an independent state, is bordered on the north by Austria and Hungary; on the west and south by Italy and the Adriatic Sea; and on the east by Croatia. Slovenian ethnic territory extends several kilometres into Italy and even deeper into Austria. In fact, the Austrian province of Carinthia has been rightly called the cradle of the Slovenian nation.

My forefathers, more than a thousand years ago, used to choose freely their own rulers in Carinthia, which is today the southernmost province of Austria. A throne, hewn from solid rock, still stands, protected by a high iron fence in a large field near the town of Maria Saal (Gospa Sveta). The Irish missionaries arrived in Carinthia long before the end of the first millennium. The Greek brothers Sts. Cyril and Methodius and their companions also preached there in the 9th century. Thus, Christianity was proclaimed in the area both from the East and the West.

But a nation that counts less than two million is not in an enviable position if it has giants as neighbours. While the Italian-Slovenian ethnic line remained almost static during the last thousand years or more, the German-Slovenian ethnic line is still moving steadily south towards the Austrian-Slovenian border.


The river Sava has its source in the Julian Alps, and flows close to 600 km eastwards where it finally loses itself in the embrace of the mighty Danube at Belgrade, the capital of Yugoslavia. The mountain range to the north of the Sava in the area of its origin is called Karavanke, on top of which runs the Austrian-Slovenian border. The mountains south of the Sava are Julian Alps. Both ranges are part of the Alps, although the Julian Alps reach greater altitudes than the Karavanke.

The Sava flows through my native parish. At that point, it is only little more than twenty kilometres from its origin. It is usually no more than a glorified creek, but towards spring, when warm southerly winds suddenly melt the mountain snow, like a warm breath, the creek can become a raging river taking bridges and everything else in its angry path. Fortunately, that happens only rarely. The village Mojstrana, the home of my paternal grandmother, is just south of the river. The village Dovje, which was my mother's home, is located just north of it, on the slopes of the Karavanke. In Dovje I attended both the church and the first five years of school. My home is a few kilometres to the south, in the next valley. Both the valley and the hamlet are called Radovna. Between the two valleys is a low area in the mountains, a kind of giant saddle.

In grade school I learned that the Julian Alps were named after Julius Caesar, who is supposed to have crossed them on his way to Gaul, today's France.

I have always had a hard time swallowing that theory. It

seems like reaching with one's right hand to get into the left pocket. One look at the map of Europe suggests that if he really chose that route, he must have been drunk, lost, or moonstruck. On the other hand, didn't Christopher Columbus sail west in the hope of reaching India?

My father's house, where I was born and grew up, was very old. Its thick walls were made of large stones of unequal size, held together with mortar and white-washed. The entrance faced east, and looked over the yard to the stable. Inside, from the large vestibule and to the right, steps went upstairs and down into the potato cellar, dug into the hill side. One door ahead led to grandma's chamber and, to the left of it, was a step down into the kitchen. On its left, another door led to the large living and dining-room, called simply the "house," from which another door opened into a small chamber where my parents, or for periods of time my father only, slept.

The kitchen, appropriately called the "black kitchen," had an open hearth and a huge built-in cauldron for cooking potatoes for pigs.

The hearth's walls and the massive arched ceiling were covered with thick black soot, stone-hard in spots, smooth and shiny. When the southern wind blew, the smoke refused to go up the chimney. Instead, it filled the kitchen, often down to mother's knees. From the vestibule I could see only her legs and the hem of her skirt. It is a miracle she did not asphyxiate.

Upstairs, a very large bedroom, co-extensive with the "house" below it, was hardly ever used. There were one or two beds in a vestibule-like room next to it, occupying the area above the vestibule downstairs. Yet, in the early 1940s my brothers John, Marijan, Tom, our mother, John's son Paul, and I used to sleep in one single room that was situated partly over the kitchen and partly above my father's "chamber." Our room could barely accommodate four beds: two along each wall, with only enough room in the middle to walk between them. We kept our clothing on the sills of the two windows or on hooks behind the door.

An old holy picture hung above these hooks. Its primary purpose, however, was not very holy but rather to cover an old stove-pipe hole left from earlier times, before some renovations.

More correctly, the picture hid the snuff tobacco that mother kept hidden in that hole before the Second World War. She had to hide it; it was smuggled from Austria. Although Yugoslavian snuff tobacco was available, she preferred the Austrian "vintage." I am tempted to think she liked it better precisely because it was smuggled; for even my mother was human... Her addiction to snuff tobacco started in her early teens when an old lady boarded at mother's home and was, herself, an avid snuffer. Later she committed suicide by drowning in the Sava river.

This tobacco was supplied by a good elderly friend of mother's. Allegedly, the lady secured the packages somehow between her knees and brought them across the border by train. Longer skirts, the fashion of the day, certainly helped in her "hobby." So did, no doubt, another circumstance: her son was the chief representative of Austrian railways at the border station on the Yugoslavian side of the nearly 9 km long Karavanke tunnel.

Other favoured Austrian merchandise for smuggling were lighters and the flint stones for them, but perhaps above all, saccharine. Sugar, at that time, was relatively more expensive in Yugoslavia than in almost any other European country.

Wine, smuggled from Italy, was brought over the border mainly by railway men who hid the bottles in the coal in the locomotives. The favoured smuggled goods going in the other direction to Italy were cattle. The Italian-Yugoslavian border, at one point, runs across a valley. Some farmers in the area had their opportunities tailor-made. It certainly did not require very much expertise to hay their fields across the border with two oxen and return with one, especially if you were on good terms with the border guards.

The Austrian-Yugoslavian border, running on top of Karavanke, did not offer such golden opportunities. Up there, one night border guards spotted a smuggler who was carrying a lamp. They ordered him to stop, and he by all appearances complied. But, coming near to arrest him, the worthy guards found to their chagrin only a lantern hung on a hazelnut branch. The smuggler and his loot had vanished into the night.

Around Christmas was the time to kill and cook one or two fattened pigs. An old farmer from the area presided over that ceremony which lasted from starry morning to a wonderful late night meal.

It was always a feast day for everyone, but especially us children. We would wait impatiently in the house with our ears plugged so we would not hear the angry pig fighting for its life in the stable. The pig was then brought to the house in a solemn procession led by my father with a petroleum lamp lifted high to light the way. (Until after the Second World War there was no electricity in the area). The rest of the ritual took place in the living and dining-room on a wide and somewhat concave table and in the kitchen.

In the following weeks large chunks of pork and dozens of the most delicious sausages I have ever tasted dangled from the bars on the kitchen ceiling. Having been properly smoked, they could last until next Christmas without any further ado or need of refrigeration. Cooking smoked meat was optional. All one needed to do was to wash a chunk to remove the protective cover of mould, and enjoy the most delicious *prosciutto* (smoked ham) with sour rye bread and milk.

I said "could last until next Christmas" because for various reasons they did not. Some were meant to be eaten before, especially during the very hard summer and fall labour. One occasion comes to mind when they were not meant to be eaten.

There was a nomadic band that came once or twice a year on its endless journey, and camped for a day or two near my home. Two of their ladies came once and one of them offered to tell my grandma her fortune. When they left, two choice items from the kitchen ceiling were missing. It seems that while one of the ladies was telling my grandma's fortune, the other helped herself to the hams. Thus, the good grandma's sin of superstition was punished right then and there.

Not only in my home but in Slovenian farm houses the living and dining room was the largest room. As a rule there was even a large bed in one of its corners. In the 1930s it was still the indisputable centre of home life.

The most prominent area in the "house" was God's corner. In it, near the ceiling, a crucifix hung in a tilted position: its horizontal bar from one wall to the other, the bottom of the vertical one in the dead corner. Beneath it, in most homes, a quarter-circular shelf was fastened with a little fence for small bouquets of flowers. For some reason there was no such shelf under the crucifix in my home.

Over the two windows, one on each side of the crucifix, there were various holy pictures and, further away, portraits of ancestors and relatives, as well as horns of mountain goats and deer. Still further away from the God's corner each of the two walls had a second window.

Between each of these two pairs of windows, a rather small cupboard was hidden in the wall, with a large rosary hanging on its side. Long ago, before petroleum lamps, these were the open niches for burning dry pine slivers to provide lighting. No wonder the tamarack ceiling was totally black. Then, for both brightness and easier cleaning, my parents decided to paint the "house," to the utter dismay of some visitors from the city who considered this action almost a mini-crime against the national heritage. With all due respect to my parents, I am tempted to agree.

In the corner with the crucifix, a large square dining table stood, with a bench along the walls and chairs on the two remaining sides. Opposite the "God's corner" there was a huge corner oven, operated from the kitchen and big enough to bake seven or eight very large round loaves of rye bread. It was built of large, square, light-brown ceramic tiles, each with a circular design in relief. Near the oven were two benches for people to warm themselves, while their fence-like back-supports prevented burning. One or two people could also lay there: pillows or coats stacked at each wall, feet meeting at the oven's corner. On one side my father liked to recline, smoke his pipe and look through the window, especially in winter. His bald head left a large greasy spot on the whitewashed wall. My oldest brother usually occupied the other side while we children loved to climb on top of the oven. One quarter of the square top was considerably higher than the other three quarters. This lower area, covered with boards and along the walls, was ideal for lying on, while the elevated quarter could serve as a table for games.

The floor and ceiling were of tamarack; however, the

boards on the ceiling were much thicker and every second one was recessed. I guess this was for better appearance. Across the centre of the ceiling, a massive tamarack beam had an artistically carved circle with the number 1764 in its centre. Near to one wall and right under the ceiling, a large shelf had been fastened to the beam and the ceiling. In my childhood large, wide, low bowls of milk were put there for a few days for the milk to sour. I remember my father putting a box of candy on that shelf, once in a blue moon. I got one candy a day, as long as they lasted, but only after begging in a special way: putting my hands together as in devout prayer and clapping them gently. If I asked for another one that same day, he said "The candies are sleeping now," which always caused great wonderment in my little mind: how can candies sleep?

Towards the opposite end of the beam there were several hooks for hats to hang on. They were close enough together to serve - if that is the right word - as suitable holders for a long hazelnut rod. Every year the good St. Nicholas brought one along with the other goodies: apples, walnuts, clothing, and the like. On the eve of his feast on December 6 the three of us young brothers would put round bread forms of straw on a bench next to each other. Very early the next morning we would rush with great anticipation to see if St. Nicholas had come. Every time he had filled each form with celestial delicacies - but on top and over all three there was invariably one long hazelnut rod, obviously meant for us all. Since the rod was from heaven, it was supposed to be kissed after each use - not by the user but by the one to whom it was applied.

Between father's bench at the oven and the foot of the bed in the corner across from it, there was the door to the chamber which was almost a holy of holies - what we would now call the master bedroom. In it my father and all of his children were born; my father also died there.

South of the house and the stable there was a lawn courtyard, with a wooden trough and running water in one corner. A shed, attached to the far end of the stable, formed with it one L-shaped building which together with the house formed the northern and eastern flanks of the courtyard.

The courtyard was enclosed by a wooden fence with

gates. On the outside and near it, a few isolated linden trees, elms, walnuts, and an ash stood. Beyond them lay both ploughed and grassy fields with some pine trees, tamaracks, and hazelnut bushes in patches or rows. Not very far away and beyond, the ever-present, steep mountain slopes led to peaks that reached up to the clouds, the moon, the sun and the stars.

The notion of the world as a "Global Village" is becoming daily more literally true. I would go so far as to say that it is becoming a "Global Farm."

However, on our farm we never worried about work, as long as we produced enough for our needs. In other words, the work was what it should be: a means to an end, not an end in itself, as it is on the "Global Farm." Nowadays we often hear politicians brag how many new jobs have been created thanks to their ingenious job creation programmes. How absurd! My father would have laughed into his mustaches if some self-styled genius had proposed to him a work creation scheme for our farm. I am not suggesting, of course, that some people should slowly burn themselves out by too much work, and others rust out because of none: which is precisely the situation in today's world with its robots and assembly lines.

I readily admit that the problems of economy on the "Global Farm" are incomparably more complex than they were on our little farm. Yet, I do not cease to wonder how come we were able to land on the moon, but seem utterly incapable to manage our economy here on earth.

A cartoon I saw in the mid-1930s describes the situation better than a thousand words.

There is a huge heap of wheat. On the top of it sits a fashionably clad, unusually fat man with a cylinder hat. He holds a revolver to his temple. His face is tense, eyes closed. He is wincing, in anticipation of the bullet which he is about to shoot through his brain. At the foot of the hill lies a man, turned in the opposite direction, with his feet horizontally stretched out on the ground and his upper body up the grain. As he is without shirt, his chest has the appearance of an old fashioned wash board: one could count each and every one of his ribs. He, too, has eyes closed. Utterly emaciated, he has a striking resemblance of an inmate in the Tushino P.O.W. camp during the 1944 - 1945 winter. By all appearances, he will not outlive very long the fat man on the top.

Isn't this a perfect mirror of our world society and economy? Surely, between the extremes of the Utopias of Communism and *laissez-faire* Capitalism there must be a better way: probably not ideal, and certainly not perfect, but the best available to us mortals. Indeed: if we had enough brains, money, and determination to construct the most incredibly complicated and ingenious devices for landing on the moon (and are already getting ready for Mars!), why are we seemingly unable to solve the problems so vividly illustrated by the cartoon? Granted, I can offer no adequate solution for world's economic problems. On the other hand, while I could offer even less help to reach the moon, there were others with enough know-how and material resources to reach it.

Perhaps we are like the star gazer in ancient Roman times of whom we heard in our Latin class in high school. Walking over the fields by night, he fell into a pit. His slave maid overheard his cries for help and dragged him out with a rope.

"Did someone throw you into the hole?" she asked him.

"No, I fell into it while looking at the stars."

"Serves you right! You are nosy about things way up in the skies, but do not see what is in front of your nose."

Something to meditate on...

Whenever I think of my home, the title of the book *How Green was my Valley* comes to my mind. But in winter "my valley" was white, wrapped in deep, virginal snow.

Before skiing became popular, only snowshoes were known. My parents recalled how, towards the end of the First World War a very heavy storm kept people snowed in for two weeks. At that time there were rumours of how Swedes and Norwegians used boards to go over the snow. Not long afterwards, my father and a friend of his were the first ones in the area to have skis. By late 1930s, most of the champions of Yugoslavia, some of international fame, came from the area. During my grade school days, the highest ski jump in the world (and may still be), Planica, was in a nearby valley of the Julian

Alps.

In spring, after the snow has melted, the valley turns from white to green, enriched with a variety of colours.

The crocus appears first. Impatient to see the sunlight, it often pushes its bowed head right through patches of snow, usually around hazelnut bushes and near the edges of the forest.

Gradually, other flowers appear all over the fields, in waves, one after another. Among the trees and hazelnut bushes alongside the dry river bed there are so many lilies-of-the-valley that people come from far and wide to pick them. The fields turn from predominantly purple and pink, to yellow, then blue, then after a week or two some other colour. Much of what turns to hay is, in the Alps, actually flowers of various kinds. Many have medicinal powers. Long experience has taught the inhabitants what disease can be cured by this or that flower and which herbs are good for which organs. On the other hand, cattle and sheep know with even greater precision than humans which are poisonous and avoid them while grazing on the slopes where hay cannot be cut.

The mountainsides around the nine small farms are very steep and rocky but are nevertheless covered with forests; the flatland in between is basically gravel. Through the ages the gravel was brought from the mountains down the two valleys that meet to form a triangular flatland. Near the middle of it the two river beds also meet to form a single one leading into the long and narrow, winding valley to the east. It is only further down this valley that a small creek originates and soon becomes a fairly strong, crystal clear, cool, fast running little river, rich with delicious trout, and a flour mill or sawmill here and there along its shores.

Near my home, the waterbeds are usually dry. However, some years in the fall after long rains, and more rarely during spring thaws, the water comes rushing down these beds. It was a great day for us children when in the morning we could hear the water rumbling in the river bed. It was a thrill to watch it winding its way around the bends and carrying leaves and dry branches. Our parents, though, were very reluctant to let us go to watch these delights. For in some places the water would undermine the shore, and the ground above could break off.

In a few days the water would vanish and all the thrills come to an end for another year or two. However, once in a rare while that happened only after the water overflowed its shores and covered fields here and there along the river bed with gravel. Hundreds of years later, rotted leaves and small plants would bring about some semblance of land suitable for farming.

This is how all the farmland in the area was formed. As a result, the top layer is very shallow and heavily mixed with gravel. It is so shallow that if the plough is pressed too hard, pure gravel is turned up with a rattling noise.

Much work is needed to wrest a living from that miserly soil. Freshly ploughed fields look almost black, but when rain washes the earth that clings to the stones (the average size of which is that of walnuts and beans, with some of them like potatoes), the ploughed fields look almost white.

In my youth, of all the nine local small farms only ours and our neighbour's had running water. During the winter water supplies usually ran dry, mainly because cattle used up much of it. Then most of the farmers had to turn to shovelling snow into the cisterns and, when that was not enough, haul water in large barrels on sleigh from our or our neighbour's courtyard troughs. One farmer, however, even though he lacked running water, never ran short of it, thanks to an unknown ancestor.

His house with its adjunct buildings stood alone near the southeastern edge of the small plain. Much of the year it was without sun because it lay close to a high perpendicular wall in the mountain side, called "Kitchen."

That farmer's well was a real tribute to the daring and diligence of its digger.

On its surface was a roof, a horizontal round shaft with rope wound around it and bucket, and a metre-high circular wall all around for safety. The well was 36 metres deep, round and certainly not much more than one metre in diameter: otherwise, how could anybody get down or up? For the only known way is by stepping on, and grasping with hands, stones on the perimeter.

But why should anybody want to go down?

Well, the person who dug this well (what a daredevil!) had to lay stones in a circular position, one round beneath the other, as soon as a few shovels of gravel were removed. No mortar or anything else was used to hold them together and, in all likelihood, the work was carried out in winter when farm labour was not pressing and the water at its lowest level, near the clay layer which is beneath the gravel brought down from the mountains by glaziers and water long ago. All building stones had to be somehow lowered down, and gravel taken up by hand. And right over the digger's head!

When water was reached, the work was deemed completed. However, several stones at the bottom got loose over the years and the only way to do repairs is obviously to descend. The odd one who dares to do it is considered very courageous indeed. It is said that, from the bottom, stars can be seen at noon. While I did not test that "theory," I did throw pebbles into the well. Thrown a little sideways towards the wall they bounce from one side to the other, causing a sound almost like a tinkling bell before finally splashing into the water.

There are many things that could be told about the "green valley" and its inhabitants. It is only after a long absence that some of them begin to be appreciated and cherished. But some I enjoyed profoundly even while still living there.

One night, near midnight, I was walking home from Mojstrana over the wooded saddle behind our house. Coming downhill through the forest I stood on the narrow road and looked enthraled over the wooden fence, the steep grassy slope fenced in for the grazing of calves between the road and the stable, over the roofs of the stable and the house, over the fields and up on the mountains on the other side of the plain.

Not a single leaf moved; not a single sound could be heard, anywhere. Even cattle in the stable below must have been sleeping, for no chain rattled. The fields beyond the home and the mountain slopes on the other side of the plain were in darkness, although trees, bushes and other large objects could still be seen dimly. But the even higher mountains farther west were bathed in the light of the full moon. Formed of solid lime rock, with partly wooded gravel slopes running from their foot towards the bottom of the valley, these majestic mountains appeared to be made of pure silver.

I stood there long as if enchanted, hearing nothing but my heartbeat, drinking in the heavenly beauty of the Alps.

Spring in the Alps is much longer than elsewhere. It is interesting to watch "green branches go over the mountains," to transliterate the local saying.

The first to awake from the winter sleep is the bottom of the valleys and the plain. Then the leafless trees and bushes higher up the slopes slowly turn freshly green. The dividing line between the green area and the still brownish one above is quite sharp, and this line climbs slowly up the mountain slopes. It seems as if an invisible water is filling up the valleys until, finally, "green branches go over the mountains."

One of the most delightful sights - and smells - in the late spring and early summer is a field of buckwheat in blossom on a breezy, sunny day. I still remember very well such a glorious day in 1937.

My mother and I knelt at the very edge of a gorgeous buckwheat field, admiring the beauty of buckwheat in blossom and the thousands of busy bees, butterflies, and other "flying objects," going from one cluster of buckwheat to another in search of honey. The next day a violent hailstorm changed the field into an area of broken stubble. It was the only hailstorm I recall from my early years, although quite severe thunderstorms occur at least a few times every year.

In the Julian Alps clouds usually move in a more-or-less northerly or southerly direction. Sometimes dark grey, thick, heavy masses of them appear from the direction of the Adriatic Sea, the plains of Northern Italy, and Friul. Sometimes it seems as if an invisible volcano is spewing these clouds, or as if a sea was churning its mighty waters and spilling them over the mountains, for they appear to be rising almost straight up from behind the mountain peaks before passing over the valley. In spite of their massiveness they move very fast, and their advance is accompanied by a continuous rumbling, like a distant sound of the Niagara Falls.

The phenomenon is an infallible sign that heavy rains will come. However, if a strong and cool northerly wind blows, at the same time, from the Austrian Alps over the Karavanke, trouble is inevitable. The two giant forces clash and sparks fly. Everything turns dark, clouds churn, and lightnings accompanied by almost simultaneous thunder begin to strike.

The danger of hail now becomes real, although it rarely materializes. Hail is much more frequent over the wine-growing hills east of Ljubljana, towards the Croatian border.

Hurricanes and tornadoes are unknown in the Alps, at least in their "giant sizes." There are, however, "mini-tornadoes." They are small and harmless and usually happen on a pleasant, sunny summer day when hay lies drying on the field. Suddenly, at the edge of such an area, the hay begins to turn around swiftly in circles whose diameter is, at most, one or two decimetres.

As the hay is sucked higher and higher, the circles become wider and wider and slower and slower, reaching perhaps a diameter of a hundred metres. Finally the hay begins to fall over the fields, or is dropped into the forests on steep mountain slopes. Usually the "mini-tornado" travels slowly, in an irregular path, and disappears without any further sight or sound once it crosses the drying hay.

The phenomenon can be a delight for a child and a "mini-upset" for the farmer who has to watch helpless as precious hay is carried "up, up and away..."

A storm in the mountains can be an awesome experience. I have listened to many a mountaineer's stories about sparks flying from every metal object and lightning bolts striking all around and dangerously near.

Such storms can come suddenly and unexpectedly. Some years ago, a group of tourists was caught on a sharp, high ridge halfway between the top of Triglav and the saddle some 300 metres below. When the storm struck, it unleashed enormous electrical energy in the form of thunder and lightning, killed several climbers and wounded others before it was over. One survivor told reporters of how he lay down and how at each close strike he jumped up, or rather was thrown into the air. The group had to be rescued by helicopter and doctors were airlifted to treat the victims. One is tempted to agree with a saying, expressed in rhyme in its original Slovenian language, "Mountain is not crazy, crazy is he who goes up."

This little piece of popular wisdom notwithstanding, mountain climbing can be a delightful and literally uplifting experience. But if you ever intend to go climbing - Alps, Rockies, whatever mountains - please do remember one thing: consult an experienced person beforehand about all the relevant details and follow the advice. Then enjoy every minute of it!

Nobody did more to open the Julian Alps to tourism than Jakob Aljaž. He was the pastor of my native parish and died in 1927. Through his passion for mountains and his efforts, many paths were opened and dangerous spots made secure, by iron cable or spikes driven into solid rock. He constructed buildings for sleeping and eating, and even built a small iron "tower" to provide shelter for about up to five people, which was firmly fastened on the very top of Triglav. There is an even larger cavern for the same purpose hewn into the solid rock just beneath the top. He completed most of these works just before the First World War. He also wrote some poems about mountains, especially Triglav, and composed music for them.

It seems natural that as a devout spiritual shepherd he did not forget the souls of the mountaineers. He built a little chapel about 300 metres below the very peak of Triglav. Vandals destroyed it in 1952. My mother wrote me then: "The little bell fell silent in the abyss." The chapel has been rebuilt in 1992, larger and more beautiful than the first one, with three bells.

It is said that when he became unable to climb, he would sit for hours behind a telescope at the rectory window in Dovje and watch the top of Triglav and the other Julian giants. The view of the Julian Alps from Dovje over the Sava valley and the village of Mojstrana below is unusually beautiful. This dedicated priest certainly deserved to enjoy it in his old age.

The Rev. Jakob Aljaž appreciated and enjoyed to the fullest the beauties of God's creation. He strived to share the joys with others and helped them to appreciate and enjoy nature. In this, he is a shining example for all to imitate.

"How green was my valley!"

It was and still is, but not quite as it used to be. Now there is electricity, running water, and the road has been widened though not yet paved. People own cars, and many cottages are scattered throughout the area. There is much more dust and noise, although the air is still quite fresh and pure.

With machines and tractors, work is almost like play compared to toil from dawn to dusk that I remember. But I still have a nostalgia for the valley as it was in my childhood - and never will be again...

Chapter Two

# I will not forget you

The words just quoted above are in the opening verse of a beautiful devotional song which expresses in poetic form God's message in Isaiah 49:15-16 to his discouraged people: "I will not forget you. Behold, I have graven you on the palms of my hands." Since we are created in the "image and likeness of God" (Gen 1:26), it seems natural to have similar sentiments, especially about our own near and dear ones.

My father's father, John (Janez), was born in 1850, and his mother, Mary (Marija, b. Košir), in 1853; my mother's father, John, was born in 1840, and her mother, Maryanne (Marijana, b. Pintar), in 1843. I only knew my father's mother. She lived with us and died in 1939. The other three died before my birth. All toiled as farmers, "like cattle," to use the local expression. The farms were small, the earth poor, and families large. My father was the oldest of five children, my mother the youngest of ten. Except for one of the four boys in my mother's family, all the children grew to adult age, which was unusual for that time. It is curious that my mother and her five sisters all married men named John. My father had one brother and three sisters. Apart from my mother's mother who hailed from the hill country a good fifty kilometres to the east, all were born and grew up in one or another of the villages or hamlets within my native parish.

Fifty kilometres in those places and in those days was very far away. Most people never travelled that far in their whole lives. I do not know how my maternal grandmother came to marry someone so far away; often such happy "accidents" happened on pilgrimages to one or another of the several shrines in Slovenia.

My father, John, was born in 1878 in our home. He never attended school, yet learned on his own to write, and play the accordion and the zither. He was to marry a sister of my mother, but when he returned from military service, (1899-1902) in the

Austrian-Hungarian army, she was married to someone else. Later he worked in a factory in Switzerland, then as a labourer in a mill-and-butcher shop in Mojstrana. He was not interested in becoming his father's successor on the little farm, although that was customary for the oldest son.

My mother, Christine (Kristina, b. Lakota: her maiden surname means in Slovenian famine), was born in 1887 in Dovje. By the time she was of school age, the law required everyone to attend school for five years, which she did. In 1906 she had a boy out of wedlock; I believe he was a half-brother of mine. He drowned as a toddler in the large trough near the middle of the village, used primarily for watering cattle. Later, she was employed as a farm worker by her brother who took over the home farm, which is considerably larger and more fertile than ours.

Thomas (Tomaž), my father's brother, who was to inherit the homestead, got himself into some complications regarding an illegitimate son he had with a lady who had children by several different men. Mainly on account of that problem, he emigrated to America where he worked in a western gold mine. He died very tragically: a woman put poison in his coffee. Rumour has it that she later visited Slovenia and that when my father heard of it he looked for her with a gun. Knowing dad's nature and his love for his only brother, I have no doubt about what could have happened, had she not escaped somehow just in time.

As a child I was puzzled during the daily family rosary. At the end, among other prayers, an Our Father was always added "for the late father, for the late Tomaž: Our Father who art in heaven..." Why did he mention both of them the first time and then only the father? For some reason I never asked him to explain.

His father died in his fifties, of pneumonia. With both his father and Thomas dead, my dad took over the homestead, and marriage became almost a necessity.

If it is true that some marriages are made in heaven, then my parents' was one of them.

Shrines, especially the ones dedicated to Mary, and pilgrimages to them played a very important role in the lives of my ancestors - not only in their religious lives, but also socially and even recreationally. There were no holidays as we know them nowadays.

When the "acceptable time" came for my father to ask for the hand of his future bride, things were done in an indirect way. It was not he, himself, who went to see the bride's parents to ask for their daughter: his mother went on that errand. At the same time, however, my father was making a pilgrimage for the same purpose to the main Slovenian shrine dedicated to Mary, the Mother of God, in Brezje.

Whatever modern sophisticated grooms-to-be may think of such unorthodox pre-nuptial procedures, one thing is certain: it worked for my dad, and it worked very well indeed.

Of course my parents did not always have heaven on earth, even in regard to their personal relationship! Did not St. Paul himself very cleverly and realistically say to forgive one another as soon as a quarrel begins, rather than "never begin a quarrel"? (Cf Col 3:13).

According to their customs, they never expressed their mutual feelings before their children. I never heard them saying "I love you" or "honey" to one another, let alone see them kiss. Calling one another by their first names was as far as they would venture in front of others. Yet one knew there was much more there than could be seen. We, their children, always called them "ata" and "mama" and the "you" was always in the plural.

Whether or not this marriage was made in heaven, I don't know. That it was at least ratified there, we can piously presume. No wonder God blessed the spouses in many ways, including a priestly vocation of one of their children for which I say: thank you God, thank you Mary, thank you dad and mum! Lord, I am not worthy, but because of it, I thank you even more for the unspeakable gift.

The marriage was celebrated in 1908. By 1914 three boys and a girl were born of this union: a boy was stillborn, John arrived in January 1912, and the girl in December the same year. She died in her infancy, and John in 1987. Rudolph (Rudolf) who is two years his junior, died at Christmas 1991, so that at the time of this writing I am the only one left.

After a ten-year break, four more boys followed. Frank

(Franc) died a few months after his birth, to the great sorrow of everyone, not least the two boys. John, twelve at the time, is said to have just stood at the crib repeating "he is not dead, he is only asleep." It was almost natural that when I came on the scene in 1926 they just had to have another Frank.

My maternal grandmother's name was Marijana and, as there were no more girls to inherit her name, the next boy, born in 1930, was named Marijan. He drowned in 1950. The stork came around once more and brought Thomas in 1931. While my father had absolutely refused before to have any of his children named after his murdered brother, this time he insisted, with a stronger-than-usual closing of a cupboard door for emphasis, "Let him be Tomaž!" - just before he was taken to the church for baptism. Thomas died very suddenly and unexpectedly of a heart attack or stroke at only 35 years of age.

Indeed, not all was heaven on earth for my parents. They buried five of their children.

I was not at home for any of the seven funerals during my lifetime: neither my brothers', nor parents', nor grandma's.

In September 1939 I entered high school, (College of St. Stanislaus), near Ljubljana, the Slovenian capital. Returning for the Christmas holidays I missed my grandma.

"Where is she?"

"We buried her in October."

"Why didn't you let me know?"

"We thought we would disturb your studies."

What could I say to that?

My parents had other heavy crosses too.

There was the question of who would succeed them on the little farm. John was, as the oldest boy, by custom, the heir apparent. However, he fell in love with a girl who for various reasons was not acceptable to either of our parents. She bore him a son but they never married. While he would have loved to marry her and inherit the home, my father never gave it to him. Otherwise my father seemed to have a slight predilection for John. Rudolph became a forester, got married, and had three boys, but he was not interested in the farm life. Since boyhood, I had always wanted to become a priest. Although both my parents were happy about this choice in principle and in theory, in practice they wanted me to get married and carry on their tradition. Marijan was in the middle of a six-month truck-driving course when he drowned. Thomas - the "Benjamin"- was an excellent cartwright. Since nobody else was left, and my parents were too old to carry on, he got married and reluctantly took over the hearth to keep the farm going. His boy and girl were nine and six respectively at the time of his very premature death. He had built a shop on the premises to work as a cartwright, especially during the winter time.

Some part-time revenue was a necessity for the nine small farmers in that "green valley," because of the small acreage and the poor quality of the soil. The forests all around provided work for loggers. Some were specialists in the art of producing charcoal from beech wood, for the iron works in the Sava valley on the other side of the mountain, before coal replaced charcoal. In modern times, some from our valley with cars even work in that factory.

My father, too, had to work in the woods. Soon after his marriage, he became a game warden, with just enough time to look after the land and the few head of cattle on his little farm. He became one of the very best and most experienced game wardens ever in that area.

In the lower lying forests of the Julian Alps there are fox, deer, partridge, and the like. The really precious game is high up, around the tree line, especially chamois (a species of mountain goats), and also two kinds of wild hens with their roosters as the prize trophies. Most coveted are the horns of chamois, shaped like an inverted letter J. Their long, beautiful shoulder and neck hair is also quite precious: it is used as a noble decoration for men's hats.

My father approached the work of binding the hair with a real sense of importance. Hairs were put, upside down, into a narrow glass cylinder and shaken so that they fell even on the piece of cardboard held across the open end of the cylinder. Then he would lay it carefully on the edge of the table and with utmost care tie with very thin thread the root ends which protruded from its opposite end. That caused the "blossom" end of the hairs to fan out beautifully. The small bundles were then carefully arranged, for stability, around a rather short piece of wire. Finally, starting at the very bottom, green thread was tightly wound around the whole thing up to about the end of the wire, in gradually wider and wider spirals, for both stability and beauty. The finished product, fanned out wider and wider towards the top with its "blossom" - a rainbow of various shades of grey and brownish colours - was the pride of its wearer. Depending on the length of the hair and the beauty of the "blossom," these decorations were worn on special occasions, on Sundays, or even daily after they became a little worn out by rain. The object could be worn on a hat in one of two ways: if relatively short, in a slanted position over the left ear; if truly gorgeous and long, at the back and straight up.

Hunters: kings, generals, government ministers, aristocrats, and foreign ambassadors would usually leave the chamois - minus the horns and possibly the neck and shoulder hair - to the game warden. The meat was quite good and its soup excellent, reputedly even medicinal, but the tallow hardened very quickly. It had to be eaten very hot; even so, one soon began to feel tallow gathering around the mouth.

There are two varieties of wild hen, one larger than the other. When killed, the rooster was often stuffed and fastened standing on a strong branch, mounted on the wall.

The small wild hens like to play in the snow covered slopes, formed by falling gravel beneath the rocky mountain heights and running towards the valley bottoms. They live in the low, thick fir bushes at the sides of these mostly bare slopes. The rooster has a short, very peculiar tail: wide, flat, upright, with feathers curved beautifully, in a semi-circular way, to the right and left. The tail's back side is padded with considerably shorter, softer, snow-white feathers. Half of the tail can be worn on the hat over the left ear, the whole at the back straight up. While the chamois "bouquet" used to be worn straight up mainly by married men, especially older ones, the wild rooster's feathers, worn straight up, used to be the pride of bachelors of marriageable age.

The peculiarity of the large wild hen is the rooster's singing. In the morning he flies somewhat lower down from his hideaway high up in the mountains and sits on a branch, preferably of a dry, weather-beaten tamarack. While he sings, he seems to see and hear nothing. His song is regular and predictable. One who knows its rules can approach very close, undetected, by moving forwards during the singing and not budging during the silence. One *faux pas* and goodbye rooster.

The game rights in the Julian Alps were owned, during the Austrian-Hungarian era, by the aristocracy of Vienna and Ljubljana; during the Kingdom of Yugoslavia by the royal court; during the Second World War by the Germans; and after the war by the Federative People's Republic of Yugoslavia. Most of the area of the Julian Alps is now a national park. My home is just outside its core area, in the secondary zone of the park.

In 1929, the kings of Yugoslavia, Rumania, Greece, and I believe also Bulgaria, lunched together under the large linden tree just outside our courtyard on the occasion of a hunt for chamois.

On similar special occasions, the hunters accompanied by the game wardens would take up positions on strategic points roughly in a line up the mountain side. Several local men then formed a similar line a long distance away. At an agreed time, the second group started to move slowly, all the while whistling, shouting, and blowing horns to scare the chamois towards the hunters. Of course, since there were many steep and dangerous spots to cross, these men had to be not only courageous but also know well the invisible paths. Just after the war, I helped in one such hunt in which some ministers of Tito's government took part. Because of too little experience, I was sent to the top of the mountain ridge to stop the poor chamois from escaping to the other side of the mountain.

Most often, though, only an individual hunter used to be accompanied by a game warden who, through earlier daily observation, had discovered on what spots the chamois appeared. Towards the evening, they usually come from the bush to the middle of the gravel slopes, stand on some grassy island and bask in the setting sun or graze soon after the sunset. The warden would have cleared a path, at the end of which a simple place was readied to sit and wait, hidden by branches through which the trophy could be seen and shot.

My dad led kings, ministers, generals, ambassadors and other dignitaries to hunting adventures.

He could handle both the Serbian and Croatian languages because they are almost identical and of the same Slavic family of languages as Slovenian; he could also manage German, which he learned during his military service, and even some Italian picked up during his service as military gendarme during the First World War in northeastern Italy; but he had no clue about English. On one occasion he led the grouchy British ambassador (according to dad's English, either Anderson or Henderson) on a "solo" hunting expedition. For some reason, dad got a hefty slap in the face before the adventure was over. Knowing him as I did, I am glad this untypical Englishman didn't have to pay the price of his soul for allowing his "Irish" to come up.

I was told, and still vaguely remember, that around 1930 king Alexander I of Yugoslavia came into the little chamber where I lay sick to change his shirt. I didn't know then who he was; but he had a peculiar cap which caught my attention. Later I saw a picture of him with it and recalled the occasion.

An anecdote worth recalling here is the "hunt" of an aging Yugoslavian Minister of Defence. He longed to get a chamois but could never hit anything. I cannot recall the exact details of the shrewd stratagem the game warden concocted: the warden either shot a chamois and set it up so that a pull on a rope would make him fall at the sound of the gun, or tethered an ordinary goat in the well-founded hope that the minister wouldn't know the difference. The end result was that the man was happy when the worthy game warden brought him the "trophy." But he must have had at least a suspicion of foul play, for he is said to have quipped, "it looks like a sheep!"

On a fateful August day in 1914, the shots in Sarajevo killed the Austrian-Hungarian crown prince Ferdinand and triggered the First World War. The nature of the "game" changed drastically for my father as it did for so many millions of others. At first he served as a military gendarme in Mojstrana, within the parish limits, but later he was stationed in northeastern Italy, just behind the front line, until the end of the war.

Mother remained alone on the farm, with her two little

children, father's mother, and a teenaged girl as farm hand. Practically alone for all the work, not only in the house and the stable but also in the barn and in the fields, she had to count the steps (to find out which way between two given points was shorter), in order to save time. She often reminded us of it, particularly when any of us were affected by laziness.

On top of that, the Austrian-Hungarian and Italian fronts were dangerously near much of the time. During the bloody Isonzo offensives, named after the uniquely beautiful, green Alpine river Soča (its Italianized name being Isonzo) the very powerful Italian artillery played a decisive and murderous role. The cannonade could actually be felt at our home. My grandma and mother, sitting in the evening at the oven or on top of it, could distinctly feel explosions of heavy shells through the ground. In one single military cemetery on a hillside just across the present Italian-Slovenian border are the names of nearly 60,000 Italian soldiers. The hill named Doberdob (Italianized to Doberdo) is called, in a most moving song, "The grave of Slovenian youth." The war, thank God, was over before my family became refugees like so many thousands to the southwest who had to flee only to find nothing but ruins on their return.

After the war and until his old age, my father continued to serve as a game warden as well as till the land, although my mother and at least one or more of us brothers, also worked on the farm during that period.

Yugoslavia was attacked by the Axis (Berlin-Rome) powers on Palm Sunday, April 6, 1941, in the early morning. Both my older brothers were in the army but both were home by Easter Sunday: for various reasons the country collapsed like a house of cards. One bright spot in the gloom was the fact that for the most part, including our area, there was no fighting and thus hardly any damage at all.

The whole country was occupied within a week. The occupation forces arrived at Dovje and Mojstrana on Good Friday. A German soldier with rifle across his back - not even "at the ready" - followed by a few others, strolled through Mojstrana, and that was it. A much larger Italian contingent arrived later. After about three weeks of the Italian administration, German forces moved in to stay to the end of the war. One Sunday, coming from the church in Dovje, we saw truckloads of helmeted German soldiers driving eastwards on the main road through the Sava valley below. The end result was the division of the province of Slovenia into two almost equal halves: the southern half, including the capital, Ljubljana, was occupied by Italy; the northern half by Germany. The border ran, quite unexpectedly, through the very suburbs of Ljubljana.

As the war dragged on, things became progressively worse in every aspect. People used to say, "By Christmas the war will be over," but four times such beautiful dreams proved vain. Very soon, there was not only an international war, but also a guerilla war and a revolution. While war sets nation against nation, revolution sets brother against brother.

The greatest mistake the occupation authorities committed was to assume that brute force was the easiest way to conquer a nation.

Within months of the occupation, resistance fighters appeared, operating mainly from mountain hide-outs.

Before long, Marshal Tito's forces became dominant in this resistance movement. There is little doubt that the victory of Communism was their main goal; the war against the occupation powers was not much more than a means to that end. The ones who suffered most were the innocent people. Failure to report partisans could mean death from one side; reporting partisans could mean death from the other. The same fate befell God knows how many from both sides for simply saying a few wrong words.

Soon after their arrival, German authorities deported or incarcerated most priests, lawyers, teachers and other educated people, in addition to Jews, partisan sympathizers, and suspects.

Most were held as hostages. If a German was shot dead from an ambush, a number of hostages would be brought near that spot and killed. Their names, along with the reason for their deaths, were always published numerically on lists posted on buildings, bulletin boards, and trees. For a long time, lists of 10, 25, 50, even 75 new names appeared almost every week: more or less, according to the number of Germans killed or the importance of their position.

On one occasion a special announcement was posted in

both German and Slovenian; I read it carefully and with utter astonishment. It stated unequivocally and explicitly that if such attacks continued the entire Slovenian nation could eventually be totally wiped out of existence.

Due to the ruthless and plainly stupid policies, hatred grew against anything German. In a kind of vicious spiral, more and worse atrocities were perpetrated in return for more and more attacks; the partisans poured gasoline on the flames in order to get more support and more supporters. The only way for many to escape certain death was to flee to the mountains and join the partisans. The occupation authorities, incredibly, seemed to believe that the wrath of the population would turn on the guerillas. In fact, it returned like a boomerang to their own heads. As the situation was in varying degrees similar throughout all the occupied Europe, one can imagine the enormity of the problems the occupation authorities created for themselves by their haughty, insane policies. And the more their military manpower and supplies dwindled and at the same time those of the opponents grew towards the end of the war, the more unmanageable became their situation.

Behind our house was a "partisan path." During the last months of the war, whole groups of partisans dropped in looking for bread and milk. On the same day, a German patrol could also "visit" with the same request. My mother told me later - for I was away from home after August 1943 - that she was convinced the sour rye bread somehow multiplied in her hands as she cut wedges off huge round loaves.

I also learned only after the war that my mother's "partisan name" had been Olga. Supporters were given fictitious names in order to hide their identity, especially in case any lists of them were captured.

It was little short of a miracle that my family survived the war. One piece of bread given to a guerilla was punishable by death, yet on top of bread and milk my parents more than once during the war had to give them also a calf or pig, while "the law of the land" required all animals to be registered to prevent such "deals."

In the eventuality that the buildings were destroyed, a pile of beams and boards was prepared hidden in the bush so that emergency shelter could be set up. It was never needed. Within my native parish, there were no major battles. Allied planes on their many flights of hundreds at a time from Italy over the Julian Alps dropped only a few stray bombs into some forests and fields. And in the first days of May, 1945, the Germans simply drove through the Sava valley much as they had arrived some four years earlier - from the opposite direction. My cousin whose house is on the main road told me that this time they were shooting wildly from their trucks. But they aimed at the mountain slopes, deliberately missing the buildings. They simply wanted to escape over a pass farther west across the Karavanke into Austria before Tito's forces, advancing from the area around the Adriatic port of Trieste, cut off their escape route.

A unit of 25 German soldiers retreating by foot on the same road surrendered to the partisans just east of Dovje on or about May 8, 1945, the very day the war in Europe ended. A courageous girl in her late teens, a classmate of mine from elementary school, was sent by the partisans to meet the unit as a mediator to suggest and arrange the surrender.

Arms were laid down without a shot. Then the soldiers were led to a small meadow near Mojstrana and killed. One tried to flee but was hit just before reaching some bushes. In the spring of 1946, I saw their common grave on the spot where they were executed. It looked like a burial ground for cattle after some epidemic disease.

One could meditate a long time at such a grave.

Where did these soldiers grow up and play as innocent children? Were their parents or spouses still alive and waiting to embrace them? Or were they simply spared finding their homes in ruins with their dear ones incinerated beneath them: in Dresden? Hamburg? Berlin...? Did some of them commit war crimes in their more glorious days? Or had perhaps one or another put his very life on the line to spare or save an "enemy"? In war time, all military orders had to be obeyed under pain of death, including the ones judged in retrospect as war crimes. Could it be that he was now killed by the very person spared or saved at the risk of his own life? One thing is certain: these soldiers survived more than five bloody years only to meet their doom literally in the last hours of war. There is much food for thought here but little need for comment.

Much the same could be said of the following case.

There was a hamlet one hour's walk in the valley east from my home. Its inhabitants also supported the partisans, willy-nilly, but were either betrayed or caught in the act. In the early morning hours of September 20, 1944, the hamlet was burned to the ground together with all its inhabitants. Only a woodworker who lived in a temporary tent-like shack under a beech tree escaped, apart from those who were in the mountains with the partisans or possibly elsewhere. It is not known if the people were shot first or burned alive. An elderly farmer's bones were later found in the large oven in his house: nobody knows whether he tried to hide there or was thrown into it. The youngest child was nine months old, the oldest woman in her eighties: she was the grandmother of this child and, ironically, an immigrant of German origin. In all, 23 people perished in that holocaust.

These are only two of many similar tragedies.

More than once my mother sighed: "Would that someone could give to all the soldiers everywhere, at the same time, the thought to turn back and go home!"

Looking from the courtyard across the silent fields, up the mountains, to the starry sky with its Milky Way, she would exclaim: "O, how beautiful God created the world, and such crazy fools on it!"

During the war, peace seemed like a beautiful dream. With the war over, some of it came true. But much turned out to be just that: a dream. My parents, like just about everyone else, had to learn that basic lesson by experience. They also had to taste the bitter truth of one of my mother's favourite sayings: "Ingratitude is the reward of this world." Some of those for whom they sacrificed and risked their lives bit, more than once, the very hands that fed them. Moreover, after a life of hard work and diligent saving for their five children's better future, they found themselves in their old age with no savings left.

In 1918 the Austrian-Hungarian empire disintegrated, and Yugoslavia was created by the Treaty of Versailles. Whatever my parents were able to save until then went, along with the empire, down the drain.

From 1918 until the invasion of Yugoslavia in 1941, we all worked hard and saved carefully. Allowances were unknown; we worked at home for no money. Our family lived modestly: there was enough of everything, but no frills or luxuries.

By 1939 they had saved enough to pay with the bank interest my tuition in a Catholic boarding school. I enroled one week after Germany invaded Poland. They also judged the principal in the bank adequate to give a good start in life to the one who was to stay at home and the four of us who would sooner or later have to leave. And they decided to take things a little easier and to enjoy, for example, some better food.

The dream turned into a nightmare in April 1941. With the onslaught of the Axis powers, all the money saved became worth only a few German marks.

The "new" Yugoslavia that came at the end of the war was, for all practical purposes, a truly new state. German marks and any pre-war Yugoslavian money became almost valueless.

After a life of hard work and saving my parents faced old age with little in the line of material goods.

But life went on...

Chapter Three

# The Dawn

On a starry night in the late spring or early summer of 1925 in the Julian Alps, God summoned a little angel: "Listen, my little no-body: get ready! Herewith you are appointed guardian angel of a baby boy, just conceived, whose soul I have created this very moment. Like yourself and like all the other creatures of mine he is created out of nothing, but let that not make you complacent or careless: he will be quite a bundle for you to take care of. Now off you go, and Godspeed!"

In the next moment the angel became present near my mother, sound asleep after a hard day's work in the fields, stable, and house, in the little chamber at home. It did not take very long before my guardian angel got the chance to put his expertise to good use: probably not the first time, certainly not the last.

The circumstances of the first moments of my existence will remain a deep mystery, of course. But shouldn't everyone be granted, once in a while, a little flight of imagination: even about the most profound realities?

As a child I had a horrible fear of darkness. In my early teens I once overheard a conversation between my mother and a bricklayer who was doing some renovations on our home and boarded with our family. He wondered: "Why is your Francek (little Frank) so scared of darkness?" Mother explained how, not long before my birth, she was returning from Mojstrana. Near home she took a less travelled path over a meadow where there is nothing but little knolls and valleys, very irregular in both shape and size.

There was deep snow, with a solid crust on top. A foot would go more or less unexpectedly through the crust now and then into the deep snow below. That's what happened to my mother. She fell so badly that she thought I would never be born alive. It was to this mishap that she attributed, rightly or wrongly, my awful fear of darkness.

In any case, the happy day of my birth was Monday, March 8, 1926.

The local midwife, my mother's sister, lived one-and-a-half hour's walk away in Dovje. With no telephone nor any other fast means of communication or transportation, the two women and their brother devised a clever plan.

They agreed that as soon as it was known the birth was imminent, my two older brothers would be sent to the uncle in Dovje with the message that the mother was not well, and that they had come to get some walnut oil for her.

The trick worked: all went without a hitch.

In the 1920s there were no "family-life" programs in schools, and certain facts of life were taboo between parents and their children of pre-marriage age. Yet it is hard to believe that a 12 and a 14 year old boy did not have at least some suspicion about the nature of the "walnut oil" which they were sent to fetch.

All of us seem to have some traces of superstition: a black cat crossing one's path, knock on wood, number 13, and so on. In fact, often people who claim to have no faith are more prone to believe astrology and horoscopes than are most others. A cousin of mine, a leading Communist whom one would expect to be immune to superstition, during my visit home, gave me his "little Tony," a tiny statuette of St. Anthony. He carried it in his pocket all through the war and, in all earnestness, attributed his survival in many incredibly dangerous military operations he described in great detail, to "him."

Sometimes, strange things happen with such extraordinary regularity that it is hard for anybody not to become superstitious.

My mother used to dream about a certain lady. This woman and her husband lived in my mother's house when she was a child. The lady introduced her to snuffing tobacco - a habit my mother never abandoned. Later the lady took her own life by drowning in the Sava river. Whenever my mother dreamed about her, some mishap followed: someone cut himself with an axe, an animal died, or one of us fell ill.

In one dream she approached my mother as if looking for something, and all the while repeating: "You must give me something; you must give me something!" Suddenly, my mother heard her late mother whisper, as it were from behind the shoulder, into her ear: "She wants your Francek!"

We used to say that after a bad dream one should say a prayer to St. Christopher to carry it over the ocean, which she did. Perhaps the good mother prayed too hard. Twenty years later not only the bad dream but the "little Francek" also went over the ocean.

There is the story of an old lady who gathered dry branches for the winter. With her loaded two-wheeled cart, she struggled uphill and prayed: "All saints, help me!" Coming over the hill, she just couldn't keep the cart back and exclaimed: "Half of the saints away!"

The lesson? Even in prayer moderation is needed!

Between our house and the stable there was a pile of square wooden beams for a new roof. They were of various lengths and provided ideal spaces for playing. (I had to play alone, because the nearest houses were too far away for little children to meet).

One day as I played in my favourite pile, I saw mother coming from the trough in the courtyard; I ran towards her. In the same moment, a heavy board on the old house roof became loose, rattled down the roof and struck my former place in such a way that, had I still been there, it would have probably decapitated me. I can still see my mother lift up both her arms, shout something, and run towards me.

That is one of my earliest memories; the incident probably occurred in or before 1930, the year the new roof was put on the house.

Even though I am supposed to be a "Piscean" - born under the sign of the fishes - I loathed nothing more than bathing. Whenever the little oblong wooden tub was readied, tears flowed sooner than water.

One of the earliest "lucid intervals" in my memory is a precise spot near some hazelnut bushes at the corner of a ploughed field on our little farm. My mother, probably on her way home from the work on the fields, was leading me by the hand. Just as we were coming around that corner, the neighbouring farmer's little boy cried as if somebody was pulling him out of his skin. Although their house was on the other side of the long fields, his screaming echoed from the mountain slopes just behind it. I still remember how, at that point, I remarked very philosophically: "Mum, do you hear how the neighbour's little Louis is crying? Certainly they are washing him!"

About 30 years later both mother and I still recalled that little episode, quite understandably with some amusement.

In spite of the fact that we were five brothers in the family, my place was somewhat lonely. On one side there were two, 14 and 12 years older; on the other there were also two, four and five years younger, so that I really had no playmate.

We all went along quite well, except for Rudolph and me. He and I were in a continuous state of war for most of my childhood years, and even into the teens. There may have been a connection between that unfortunate state of affairs and my supplanting him after his only shortly interrupted, almost 12-year long reign as the baby in the family. The interruption was only a short one, because the first Frank did not live very long although, according to my parents' account, both my older brothers were thrilled with his arrival.

Whatever the reason, Rudolph and I just couldn't see eye to eye. I couldn't count the number of times he pulled my hair, beat me, or locked me into the dark cellar: he knew I was scared to death of darkness.

On two occasions he nearly drowned me. The nature of my real or imaginary offenses escapes my memory: the punishment probably never will. On both occasions I was grabbed in such a way that I could not move my arms and was carried under his right arm straight to the large trough in the courtyard. By a single upward turn of his elbow, he held me feet up and head down in the water. I can still vividly recall the agony of not being able to move or breathe, and the terror I felt on the way to the trough the second time, when I knew what to expect.

Had these two traumatic experiences occurred before my aversion to water, it would easily explain why water and I just don't seem to be compatible. But these incidents only added fear to the already ingrained repugnance. The situation is even more inexplicable because I am, as already said, supposed to be a "Piscean": born in the sign of fishes. So, shouldn't I be expected to love water?

We have a tendency to be fascinated by things like the Zodiac: the mysterious, the unusual, the sensational. This is natural, and I see nothing wrong with it. But too often we take for granted things or people that are familiar and ordinary, even though it is they that really matter. Usually we realize their value and importance only when we lose them.

Perhaps no people are as often taken for granted as parents, with the possible exception of grandparents. Although I loved and appreciated mine, I also learned only through experience the truth of my mother's often repeated saying: "When my eyes will close, yours will open."

Superstition is against the very first commandment of the Decalogue. I like to think that I am not superstitious, and God forbid me to tempt you to so become!

Allow me here to digress a little and share with you my thoughts on the Zodiac and horoscopes, without giving a lecture on the subject. Many of you probably know more about it than I do, anyway, for many people are interested in it nowadays. It seems that the more people abandon genuine religion, the more they turn to superstition and the occult.

There is little doubt in my mind that the heavenly bodies exert some influence on us. However, and this is important, I do not imply for one moment that they have some magic power; rather, it is quite natural.

The influence of the sun and the moon is beyond doubt. Tides are the most obvious phenomenon. Not only the sea level: even the earth's crust is raised a little by their gravitational pull.

Our bodies are very delicate and sensitive. A very small change in blood temperature causes us to fall sick. Changes in weather have also a notable influence not only on our bodies, but even on our moods. Many people can predict accurately changes in weather many hours ahead by their rheumatism or other ailments.

Especially since our bodies, including brains, are made mostly of water, it takes no genius to see the very real probability that heavenly bodies have a notable influence not only on oceans, but also on people. Nurses, especially those in emergency wards or in mental hospitals, agree that around the full moon there is usually a rash of accidents and other emergencies. This is not superstition: it is fact.

The sun, moreover, emits various kinds of rays, especially during sun flares. If they affect so strongly radio communication, is it not to be expected that our so delicate nerve and other body systems will also likely to be affected?

Planets, though, are rather far away and I doubt we can detect any real influence they may have on our lives, at least not at this stage of human science. Therefore, I believe that not the planets and the signs of the Zodiac under which we are said to be born, but rather the seasons have some real influence on our lives. Probably not so much in urban societies as in rural ones, especially in the past when most of the work had to be done by manual labour. A child born in summer, for instance, had quite different pre-natal experiences than one born in winter. An expectant mother had to work much harder in the fields and at home and had less sleep in the last stages of her pregnancy in the first case than in the second. Surely that, together with differences in temperature, sweating, etc., must have some influence on the baby to be born, although I have no idea about the nature of it.

Since the 12 signs of the Zodiac are always in the same seasons, it is easy to see how any general differences in character or personality, due to seasons of Europe, came to be attributed to the signs of Zodiac.

In any case, these are my personal views on the subject.

My father was a strong man in every way, a caring provider, a man of solid faith. In winter evenings he often played the zither, the sweetest sounding string instrument. He laid it on the table in "God's corner" and allowed us children to sit around, listening. I liked to put one ear on the table and put a hand over the other ear. The sound of the zither came through the pinewood table as a beautiful, zooming vibration.

My father rarely used corporal punishment, but when he did, it was severe. As soon as he began to untie his leather belt and the rattle of the buckle was heard, tears began to flow profusely. Nobody ever dreamt of trying to escape; it was unthinkable. Punishment deserved had to be endured.

My mother also applied the rod when needed, but more frequently and less severely than my father. Both of them followed the Biblical advice faithfully - even too faithfully for my youthful taste: "He who spares the rod hates his son, but he who loves him is diligent to discipline him" (Prov 13:24).

One of my fondest memories of infancy and early childhood is the way mother used to lay me to sleep.

We had a special little bed for small children, which literally translates to "little garden." It was made entirely of pinewood boards, like a box set fairly high on four wooden legs, with moveable bottom boards. On top of the four sides, a wooden fence of thin, narrow, vertical boards was spaced close enough to prevent a child from putting the head through. The fence had a horizontal bar on the top to keep it solid and to allow for comfortable leaning. The mattress was a hemp fabric filled with dried corn leaves. The bottom sheet was also usually made of hemp but the top sheet, the one under the blanket or quilt, as a rule of flax and thus not so coarse and lighter than the bottom one.

Mother put me into that "little garden" very gently. She unfurled the top sheet high over it, holding it at the two side corners so that it fell down slowly. A gentle breeze was created by the descending sheet. I just loved that gentle breeze.

A blanket or quilt was placed over the sheet and tucked in. Then my mother signed me on the forehead, the mouth, and the breast with three crosses: "In the name of the Father, and of the Son, and of the Holy Spirit. Amen. Now you are good; now you are mum's." In the original Slovenian this was said in verse form with "Amen" and "mamin" rhyming.

After that she leaned a little farther over the "little garden," turning her upper body slightly leftwards so as to bring her face more into line with mine, and looked, smiling, into my eyes. She teased or tickled me a little under my chin, kissed softly on the forehead, straightened up gently smiling at me a few more moments, turned slowly, and left.

I loved this simple ritual which has stayed with me since the first dawning of memory.

In 1982 I had a gallbladder operation. It was my first and,

at least so far, the only one. As I woke up from the anaesthetic late in the afternoon, I had an unusually happy feeling of peace. No doubt it was an aftermath of drugs; but I knew there was something more to it. Only gradually I became aware that the whole reality of my mental vision was filled with my mother's smiling face: very indistinct and formless, yet unmistakably the very one that shined on me lying in the crib, the "little garden," so long ago in the dim past, at the first streaks of the dawn of my life. I am convinced that it had been brought from the depths of my being closer to the surface by the drugs used for the operation.

That blessed face, so indistinct and formless, yet so real and all-pervasive, hovered over me for at least the next two or three days as I lay in the hospital bed, evoking in my whole being a feeling of heavenly peace and joy. I am absolutely convinced that even after that, having receded back into the unfathomable, mysterious depths of my being, it still imperceptibly warms and enlightens my life and always will. Not only that: I am inclined to think that even those around me, and those around them, are warmed and enlightened at least a little with that glow whose ultimate origin is, I believe, God Himself.

Besides my parents and brothers, my father's mother also has a special place in my heart from the very dawn and childhood of my life. If she had a special chapter in this book, it would probably have the title: "A truly grand grandma."

When my parents married in 1908 both my father's parents were still alive. His mother had, for many years, serious stomach trouble. She would cry for her husband: "Janez, what are you going to do alone when I die?" However, she outlived him by about 30 years. Grandma attributed her complete recovery to the blueberries she picked and ate while looking after the cattle.

She had a special chamber next to the black kitchen, with the entrance from the vestibule; complete with a bed, a small table, and a small iron stove so old-fashioned that it belonged no doubt to one of the first generations of iron stoves.

Grandma and her chamber served more than once as a "refuge of sinners." One or the other of my two younger brothers, or I - or any two or three of us together - often found a sympathetic ear and grandmotherly solace after a serious fallout with mother, father, or brother Rudolph. On such occasions, or evenings, especially in winter, she would have any of the many kinds of herb and fruit teas ready in no time; just the right one to suit the need. For colds, stomach aches, cuts, bruises, slivers, or bee stings there was a supply of salves made from fox, rabbit, or chamois fats. There was just no disease that could not be handled with the proper salve, combined with the right kind of tea.

Never mind that the light in that chamber was very poor. While we in the rest of the house used normal petroleum lamps, grandma had an "owl" - a flat medium-sized green bottle with petroleum and a wick through a metal gadget that sat on top of the bottle. Grandma's smile and goodwill more than compensated for the scarcity of light.

Now and then grandma opened her special treasures: hazelnuts, or slices of dry apples or pears. On special occasions she would fry, on top of her stove, a fresh apple or two: a real delicacy!

I once pulled her laundry which hung drying on the courtyard fence right into the trough full of water. In that moment she appeared from behind the corner of the house, saw what was happening, and dashed in hot pursuit of the villain. She was then in her mid-seventies and I about three. The chase raced over the whole courtyard, with grandma scolding me all the while but seemingly enjoying the whole thing. My mother, standing in front of the house, laughed so heartily that she had to hold her head with her hands. Instead of escaping to the open fields I veered, in my inexperience, into the storage for leaves, which were daily put under the cattle - a real trap. With a wall of hard-packed beech leaves in front and grandma catching up with me from behind, my fate was sealed. She was so delighted with her victory that all I got was a few shakes and pulls of my golden curls, along with some scolding. I have the feeling that she had to try very hard to appear angry and restrain herself from laughing.

Occasionally, we set out for a visit to the other side of the valley where one of her married daughters lived. When my two younger brothers were old enough to join us, she took one or both with us; she carried the youngest one much of the way on piggyback, led the other one by the hand, and let me run all around. However, it was only for a year or two that all three of us were able to go for such visits. At about the age of seven I had to start helping with the work in the fields, at home, in the stable, and around the barn.

On the way through the bushes near the dry river bed in the middle of the valley we picked berries or hazelnuts. The choicest hazelnuts were usually high up, but grandma used her cane to bring the branches within reach.

Her daughter always served us the choicest tea and delicious rye bread. Every housewife baked bread, and at every house the bread had a different taste. But everybody else's tasted better than one's own. It was a well- established custom that visitors were always given a big wedge of bread to take home.

An old holy picture in this house that hung among others in "God's corner" fascinated me. It depicted the death of the just man and the death of the sinner: one scene on the upper left side of the same picture, the other on the lower right.

The just man looked peaceful and angels hovered around his bed. The sinner appeared scared. No wonder: beside his bed there were bags of money, piles of coins and change from torn bags scattered all around them, and a large snake winding its way through it all. What's more: one or two devils were pulling the sheet and quilt from his bed. That was my *pièce de résistance*. I was so fascinated with the devils and their "work" that on every visit I just had to stand on the bench to get a closer view.

Referring to my grandmother's efforts, my mother used to say: "I would never do for my own children what you are doing for them, even though they are not your own: in my seventies carrying them piggyback, and putting up with them the way you do." However, when she herself was the same age, she was no different. On pictures sent to me in Canada she usually held or carried her grandson, looking at him with a big smile on her face.

My grandma died in 1939 at the ripe old age of 86. In her last few years she was afflicted by a stroke. Several times the parish priest came to strengthen her with the Sacraments of Penance, Holy Communion, and Anointing of the Sick.

The priest's visit was always a special event, in which

some other people from the area also took part. The church caretaker brought the priest with horse and sleigh or ordinary wagon, depending on the season. From time to time he rang a small bell: it was a sign to kneel and adore Jesus in the Holy Eucharist passing by. We waited in front of the house for the sound of the bell from the forest behind the house: the sign to get ready. Father and mother met the priest at the door with a burning candle and led him into the vestibule. He closed the door to hear the Confession; meanwhile everyone prayed in the vestibule. When the door opened we all went in, gathered around the bed, and watched the priest administer Holy Communion and the Sacrament of the Anointing of the Sick. Anointing the eyes, he prayed: " May the Lord forgive you by this holy anointing and his loving mercy whatever sins you have committed by the use of your sight. Amen." Anointing the ears, the nostrils, the mouth, the hands and the feet followed - in that order - in a like manner. Though Latin was obligatory elsewhere, in Slovenia vernacular was allowed for administration of Sacraments. After one or two such occasions I knew all the formulas by heart.

The priest and his caretaker were always served a good meal before returning home.

Regardless of whether our grandma was able to lead us on hazelnut "safaris" or had to lie sick in bed, she was an inspiration and inexhaustible source of courage and optimism.

"Were you scared by night," she was asked more than once, "when as a girl you looked after sheep, and had to sleep alone in that log cabin in Vrata, with forests but no living soul for kilometres around?" "No! Why be scared?" she would answer; "Nobody can take my soul, and with these bones he will not go very far."

When she was going on 87, she joked even about death: "Last night," she said once, "I heard a bang in the chamber; so I called out 'Death, if it is you, come here so I can give you a slap!' - but there was no answer. I expected to die long ago; I think Death forgot me." But I was told that shortly before she died someone asked her: "Mother, would you still like to live?" "Yes, I would," she whispered and nodded, with a smile.

My mother, in spite of her overwork as the only other woman in the house, with care not only of five boys, three of us still small children, and work in the fields, in the stable, and in the house, always found time to take good care of her mother-in-law. Towards the end, after a stroke two or three years before her death in 1939 she fed, washed and clothed her with a mother's loving care of a baby.

How much love and joy did our good grandma give us when we were young!

And the more she gave, the more she received in return.

Chapter Four

# The Sunrise

We had a shepherd, Ivan, a boy several years my senior, to look after the cattle during the summer in the forests. In the fall the cattle grazed in the fields, but the shepherd had to go to school at least three times a week. Ivan used to tell me stories about the school. One of the most incredible was that it had windows bigger than doors!

The school was situated in Dovje, my mother's home village, and where our church was. The church stood in the midst of the fields, just outside the orchards surrounding the village.

The school was in the middle of Dovje. My mother showed me this mysterious building once. Indeed, the windows were just about the size of doors - something I had a hard time believing. She told me then that soon I would be going up the few cement steps with the peculiar iron railing. I would have to sit quietly for long periods of time, all the while holding, with both hands, the edge of the table in front of me as a sure way to achieve quietness.

To me that seemed quite impossible and incredible. As it turned out by the time I began school, the solution for restless hands was to hold them across our backs. Usually the whole class had to do it with military speed on the command: "Hands on the back!"

The school had three fairly large classrooms and could accommodate six classes a day because they were held either from 8:00 a.m. to 12:00 noon or from 1:00 p.m. to 5:00 p.m. six days a week. There was also a room for a single teacher, quarters for the principal and his family, and, in the basement, dwelling for the elderly janitor and his wife. He was also the church caretaker and sacristan.

There was a crucifix in every classroom near the picture of the king. As far as I remember, all the students were Catholics, and every Tuesday and Friday the local pastor came to the school to give each class one period of religion. Our parents made sure that, if at all possible, we never missed these two days of school.

The pastor was very pious, and mother held him in high esteem. In her view he had only one imperfection: from time to time he scolded mothers for their alleged neglect of their children's proper education at home.

"I have five of you pantbearers to contend with," she'd wring her hands, "and then the pastor descends on us poor mothers..." Usually she added, though, that she was happy there were at least no girls in the family: "Thank God I at least don't have to wage war with girls. They'd want to follow the world and have permanent ventilation. I would insist on braids. There would be an eternal war." (She had in mind the permanent undulation: permanent waves, but could not distinguish between the two words of Latin origin).

Come on, mum, take it with a grain or two of salt: I know you better...!

The pastor was very kind in class. If one of the students was doing things under the desk, he'd quip, looking askance, halfway over his shoulder, "Are you skinning a cat? Are you shearing a sheep?" I was one of the few who was at least once sent to kneel in front of the blackboard for causing mischief.

There are millions of refugees in the world today. Practically the only ones we knew before the Second World War were some Russians who lost their struggle against Bolshevism during the October Revolution. Most of them found refuge in France and Yugoslavia. Yet, both our school principal and grade one teacher were refugees.

The principal was a Slovene from the southern part of Austria, the province of Carinthia. In a plebiscite after the First World War he favoured the province's predominantly Slovenian district joining the new state of Yugoslavia. His side lost and he became a refugee.

The grade one teacher was a lovable, elderly widow from that part of Slovenia which, during the two world wars, belonged to Italy. Her husband had been a mayor. The outcome of a plebiscite in this case would have been a foregone conclusion, but none was held. The good lady fled, with her son and daughter, and settled in Dovje.

In spite of her kindness she nevertheless held a small

grudge against Italians.

In the fall swallows gather to fly south. For a time, they sit tight to one another on electrical wires. Then, after flying once or twice around the church steeple, they take off over the Julian Alps towards sunny Italy. The good lady told us that "the wicked Italians" try to catch them in their nets and eat them. We first-graders didn't feel as much anger towards the "wicked Italians" as sorrow for the poor little birds.

My native parish, in the extreme northwestern corner of Yugoslavia, bordered Austria on the north and Italy on the south. Thus, both these two refugees were only a few kilometres from their homes - yet so far away! They were forerunners of the millions of refugees in the wake of the Second World War throughout Europe and the rest of the world.

I was already in my eighth year when I started school.

Motor vehicles were such a rare sight in my valley that whenever a car or motorcycle appeared I fled into the bush if unable to make it to the house or stable. My parents knew that something had to be done, for I was about to begin school in Dovje. The way to the school led through Mojstrana, and in both villages cars appeared almost daily, often more than once a day. During my grade school years a person in Mojstrana even bought an old Ford: the first car owned by a local resident.

So I was sent to spend a few months with my cousin's family, within the year just prior to my starting the school.

Their house, in a hamlet a little west of Dovje and Mojstrana, was an ideal spot for purposes of my sojourn. In front was the main road; across a fence the railway; and not far beyond, the Sava river: at that point not more than a glorified creek.

Each of these was for me a wonder in itself. The three together were a bundle of delights!

I was fascinated with passing cars - as long as they could be observed from a safe place, preferably through a window. And I hardly ever missed running to see the trains go by.

Often it is the little things that make a big difference: a spark can cause a huge forest fire; a smile dry up someone else's tears.

One day a simple event occurred that had a tremendous influence on my whole life. I recall it as vividly as if it happened today.

My cousin and her husband were working in the hay barn. All of a sudden she paused and asked point blank: "Franc, what are you going to be when you grow up?"

I had never thought of that and had no clue.

My spontaneous reaction was to show off with a joke.

"I'll be a pastor because he just eats and drinks well."

Both she and her husband burst into laughter, and I felt tickled pink about my joke.

A day or two later she asked: "Do you really mean to become a pastor?"

This time I was embarrassed to tell the truth. So I told what today I would consider at least a grey lie: it may not have been quite black, but certainly not lily-white, either.

"Really!"

Almost 60 years after that decisive event, I am sure that that was the origin of my vocation.

Let nobody say God has no sense of humour!

As time rolled on, the idea of priesthood slowly took root in my soul, gradually maturing and blossoming.

At first it had selfish alloys: good food, easy work, a chance to play the organ, and more. With time, though, it was purified, like a good wine, of its more selfish admixtures, and I began to see gradually also its thorns, as on a beautiful rose.

My parents were happy with the prospect of having a son priest, but they wanted me much more to take over father's little farm some day.

In our area at that time, perhaps two or three out of a class of 20 or 30 used to go beyond elementary school. The others continued to work on their family farms, in the bush, or at the iron works in the not-too-distant town of Jesenice. Some became apprentices in various trades. A few even emigrated to Western Europe or overseas.

To continue higher studies was looked upon by many with a good deal of suspicion, except for the priesthood.

Doctors were few: if for no other reason than they were

not very busy. A person would go to a doctor only for very serious sickness: usually it was the doctor who came to the patient. Children were born at home with the help of midwives; and there were popular remedies, salves, and teas for just about every known sickness, and probably for a few unknown ones. If a person was sick enough to require a doctor, he had to be fetched usually by horse and buggy, or sleigh, according to the season.

Lawyers were all looked on as crooks - and with some justification. There were many cases where farmers would litigate for years over a few square metres of field. Some went bankrupt in the course of such foolishness - while the shrewd lawyers became richer and built villas. They were referred to, with a fair amount of disgust, as "tongue doctors."

Small wonder I had to struggle for years before my parents finally yielded.

Students who left high school supplied an additional negative factor. People looked on them as lazy bums and good-for-nothings. To make the measure full, many ceased practising their faith and became radicals. This did not sit well with the generally faithful rural population.

Elementary school lasted eight years, but the last three were low key - only three times weekly, and in the winter when farm work was not pressing.

High school also lasted eight years: four for junior, then four more for senior matriculation. One could enter high school after completing only five years of elementary school; even four, if one had really good marks.

High schools were of two types: "Classic" and "Realistic": the former for professions like doctors, lawyers and priests, the latter for more "practical" ones.

I lost one year at the start of elementary school on account of the initial letter of my surname. The 1926 crop of babies was too large for one class, so all with their surname initials R to Z had to wait one year. By grade four I had not succeeded in swaying my parents to send me to high school. By grade five they yielded to the point of sending me the following year to the "City school" in Jesenice which offered a two and a four-year course. "Even a farmer nowadays needs some mathematics," mused mother, and father gave in: "Some German also helps. Let it be. Let the boy go for two years."

And so it was.

As it turned out I only went for one year.

My thirst for study was still not quenched, and the desire to become a priest still unabated. I did not rest on my victory, but kept busy mobilizing the support of my uncles, aunts, and my elementary school principal; he had been also my grade five teacher. The barricades came down when the pastor entered the struggle. He was the last straw to break the camel's back or the ram that penetrated the fortress of my parents' resistance.

Only God knows with what ecstatic joy I took the train - accompanied by mother - to the College of St. Stanislaus on the outskirts of Ljubljana in September 1939: a few days after the start of the Second World War in Poland.

Later, in military barracks in Germany, in the P.O.W. (prisoners of war) camp in the Soviet Union, in military barracks in Yugoslavia, and finally as a refugee in Austria and Canada my night prayers included regularly the petition: "That I may become a good priest, if that is God's will. Hail Mary, full of grace..."

In Germany and in the P.O.W. camp in Moscow the only yearning in everybody's heart was to be home some day, even though it seemed impossible. In my wildest dreams I never dreamt of coming to Canada, let alone expected my childhood dreams to come true in this blessed land: truly blessed, even though still within the confines of the Valley of Tears.

But I am going ahead of myself and perhaps even a little off the track; let me pick up again the thread of the story.

My school days and years, starting with grade one, were a mixed bag of joys and sorrows.

I loved school. I cried more than once because I had to miss a day.

The thirst for learning and the heavy labour during the summer, combined, caused me to consider the opening of school each September as the beginning of my annual holidays.

My brother Rudolph also loved school, but John, the oldest, had the opposite view: he wished that lightning would strike the school, so that it would burn down. There were times when he cried because he had to go to school.

Of course, I do not remember my older brothers' school days. It was my parents who told me about them.

Although there were six school days in the week, we went only three or four times from Radovna, allegedly on account of distance: a one-and-a-half-hour walk, first uphill, across a saddle between the two mountains, downhill towards Mojstrana, across the Sava river, and then again uphill to Dovje. Most of the road wound through forests of pine and beech, with some meadows here and there; the rest led through Mojstrana, then over the Sava river, and uphill towards Dovje. This last stretch was cut through beautiful fertile fields arrayed in step-like terraces on both sides of it, then along one such terrace eastwards, and again up through some more terraces. The last few minutes greeted the traveller with the rich orchards that surround Dovje. The village is situated on the beautiful, sunny, southern slopes of the Karavanke where the soil is very fertile. Farmers in Dovje used to be relatively rich; but they had to work "like cattle," as the saying goes. The inhabitants of Mojstrana, on the other hand, were predominantly labourers who commuted to Jesenice, where the second-largest ironworks in Yugoslavia was situated.

While the children from Radovna attended school only three to four times weekly allegedly because of the great distance, the main reason was without doubt the need of the parents for a labour force. Between them and the principal there was a continuous tug of war: he wanted us to be at school every day, but the parents always managed somehow to have their way.

Some students were quite happy to exchange attendance for farm work. For me it was quite the opposite, and never more than when I had to stay home when the class had a "school exercise." For some subjects the teacher held a special notebook for each student. One day each month, with advance notice, these notebooks were brought to the class and distributed to us for writing the test. These exercises were important for marks at mid-term and at the end of the school year.

Marks were given in Latin numerals from one to five, with one the worst, and five the best. In my mother's school days - she attended the same school some forty years or so earlier - five was the worst and one the best. It sounded strange, if I was dawdling or working in a sloppy manner and she said with a mixture of humour and scolding: "O, playing one!" For my ears "O, playing five!" would have sounded more appropriate.

After the "school exercise" the teacher collected the notebooks. In a few days they were brought back, corrected and marked, for a review. Only at the end of the school year they were returned to the students for good.

The usual subjects for such tests were mathematics and Slovenian, both grammar and composition. In grade three Serbo-Croatian - the main language in Yugoslavia - was added. Serbs and Croats generally hold that they are two separate languages, not just dialects of one. The writing, however, certainly does differ. Serbs use Cyrillic characters while Croats use Latin ones. It was the language (or languages) used by the army, and everybody had to learn it (or them) two hours a week all through elementary and high school, starting in grade three.

In high school, of course, other subjects were added as material deemed suitable by the authorities for the "school exercises." The teaching methods, though, as well as the tests and examinations, remained pretty much the same.

The road from my home to the school was very poor, especially through the forests. It was really no more than a glorified cow path with two ruts for horse or ox-drawn wagons with iron-clad wheels. In such a wagon that rambled over gravel and potato-size stones, the ride was so shaky that one was afraid, as the saying goes, to lose one's very soul.

Whenever two wagons met one had to pull to the side and wait until the other passed by. Many stretches were cut into the ground, or so narrow that even that would have been impossible.

In winter, with very deep snow, the road turned into a kind of ditch: two sleigh ruts with horse or ox path between and snow piled high on both sides. This scenery provides the stage for a winter's tale - a true one.

In January 1931 my younger brother, Marijan, was born and shortly after baptized. On the way home from church, his godmother sat on the plank put across the sleigh, holding the baby all bundled in blankets. Suddenly she realized, to her very understandable dismay, that she was only holding a blanket: the baby had mysteriously vanished. The only reasonable thing to do was to stop the sleigh and go back in search of the baby. Thank God, he was found: not in swaddling clothes and lying in a manger, but bundled in his warm blanket, lying peacefully on the soft snow at the edge of the road.

Towards spring, when the snow began to melt, the road turned into a path of slush. In many stretches water flowed through cavities underneath packed snow and ice. From time to time a foot would break through, turning walking into a real penance.

During the winter we school children liked to take a small sleigh with us. Naturally it could only be used downhill, but pulling it across flat stretches, and even uphill, was fun.

In early spring when snow still lay only on the road over the saddle, the sleigh was used as far as it went, then hidden behind some bushes to be picked up on the way back.

How many times I arrived in school with shoes full of water, and clothes soaked through to the knees. In the school they dried slowly, only to get wet again on the way back home.

In any mountains, nights seem longer than elsewhere. Traces of sunlight may still linger on the peaks in the east while the stars already begin to appear and dusk falls in the valleys. In the morning an orange breath of sun appears on the snow-capped mountains in the west almost simultaneously with the first streaks of dawn.

All this seems more pronounced in winter. For weeks some farm houses in valleys do not see the sun. These periods were usually described in terms of saints' feasts: this or that house gets no sun from the feast of this to the feast of that saint.

My home, set on the north side of the valley, always enjoyed at least some sunshine. For a week or two in the fall and in the spring the sun rose and set twice a day, passing behind the mountain between the valleys of Krma and Kot. For most of December and January it appeared at least for an hour or two as it crossed the fairly narrow valley Krma to the southwest of Radovna.

There was no electricity in Radovna until several years after I left home for good. As there was not much point to linger around in the evenings, in the misty twilight of a petroleum lamp, the rules were: milk the cows, feed the cattle and pigs, eat supper, say the rosary, then to bed for a rise at the early dawn.

In spite of early bedtime there were occasions when we stayed up longer, especially when winter brought long nights, less pressing work, and much more opportunity for visiting.

Neighbouring farmers exchanged visits with one another. Their conversation included many topics and often lasted late into the night.

During the Depression our home frequently offered food and overnight shelter to beggars. Most were veterans of the First World War who had served in the Austrian-Hungarian army. In summer, they slept in the hay loft. In winter, they preferred the stable because the cattle kept it warm and cosy. Father sometimes looked a little stern, twisting with one or the other hand, or even with both hands, his gorgeous mustache. But mother was always impeccably kind and patient.

The beggars liked to stay overnight at our home because the next house, in Mojstrana, was a good hour away, by foot, on their journey.

The veterans, and above all the crippled ones, had really no need to say anything: everyone was his own living, walking story. But they all recounted most vivid histories of unspeakable madness, of war's cruelty, and of man's inhumanity.

Some beggars came on crutches; some had a leg missing; others had only one hand. Everyone spoke about sufferings of trench warfare in Northern Italy or on the Russian front, battles in burning heat and freezing cold, fear, thirst, hunger, exhaustion, wounded and dying comrades, sickness and much, much more.

These miserables had been simply drafted by the Austrian-Hungarian army and sent off to the front. The idea of conscientious objection to military service was still unknown: refusal to answer the call would have meant death by firing squad.

The poor Slovenian veterans had returned, in effect, to enemy territory. That is why the cripples received little or no support from the new authorities. Some said, "We get too much to die and too little to live."

In our innocence, we children were unable to grasp or feel

the gravity of the tragedy and pain. The war stories were fascinating and the missing limbs a cause of curiosity rather than compassion.

In a few years, many of our generation would experience a similar fate.


The dim light of a petroleum lamp standing on the large table in "God's corner," and the warm oven in the opposite one, together with the dark, cold winter night, and the deep snow outside, provided a near perfect setting for the stories of war, ghosts, and wild hunts.

Adults usually sat around the oven, nursing their rheumatic limbs. The children sat on the floor or took a position on the top of the oven, with eyes and ears - sometimes even mouths - wide open. The respectful awe of the youthful audience seemed to have had a stimulating effect on the imagination of the venerable narrators. The picturesqueness of description, sharpness of detail, and gravity of the presentation was noticeably enhanced.

I could never compete with their skills. Their fare may have been less true than imaginary, less wise than otherwise, but it had an air of wonder and awe.

Here is a sampling.

At the cross, where the forest road reaches the plain, night travellers had often seen a light. From afar it appeared like a huge glow-worm, then it moved past the large crucifix at the roadside and disappeared into the dark night. Anyone who saw it had to say a prayer and some magic words.

Most of the spine-chilling stories, of course, dealt with nocturnal phenomena.

On the road about 15 minutes' walk uphill through the forest behind our home, near a plain meadow close to the southern edge of the saddle, there is a soft stretch of roadside that is always wet. When walking over it one has a distinct feeling of going over a huge water-bed.

Once upon a time, a lady carried a large, wide basket of food on her head through that mysterious area. In summer, the women often carry huge wicker baskets placed on small, doughnut-shaped cushions on their heads and filled with food, to workers haying in clearings in the midst of forests on the mountain side, or in meadows close to the tops of mountains. (Usually such meadows have wooden fences: it is exciting to watch deer gracefully jump the fence in the evening to graze on delicate mountain grass and flowers, often with a small fawn).

The lady in this story is said to have disappeared without a trace. Presumably she had sunk into the ground, and all that was found was the basket, which did not sink with her because of its width.

Near the northern edge of the saddle, a narrow road branches off the main one into the heart of the thick, dark pine forest. Here, on occasion, a casket is supposed to have been seen coming down the path all by itself, gliding slowly and silently through the air near the ground.

A little further on, where the road begins to descend gradually towards Mojstrana, there is, near the road, a huge solitary boulder the size of a small kitchen, and a fountain of fresh, drinkable water next to it. In that general area, boots without anything or anyone in them have allegedly been seen by lonely night travellers.

This is but a sampling of the strange stories told by visitors, veterans, and beggars on long winter nights around a warm oven. These few have been chosen mainly because of their association with the road I travelled for several years to school.

There is another horrible story: about the wild hunt.

On a dark night a traveller through these mysterious Alpine forests - with no living soul for kilometres around - might have to deal with the wild hunt.

It is an extremely dangerous and frightening experience.

All of a sudden, in the darkest night, all kinds of animal sounds - of bears, pigs, cows, cats, dogs, wild goats, chickens... - are heard from afar, usually accompanied by the clangour of cowbells, both big and small ones, such as little calves or lambs wear.

The noise of the wild hunt comes closer and closer through the darkest forest and along the road. Soon one's fate will be decided!

One could be ground to a pulp. The only way to escape unhurt is to lie down as quickly as possible in the right rut - or is it the left one? There was a conflict of opinion on the point. Almost as distressing was my confusion as to which rut was the right and which the left one: it all depends, of course, from which direction one looks down the road.

Nowadays, when driving longer distances, I usually say the rosary and meditate for a while; then I listen to the radio or cassettes.

In my school years, I was more devout. Many times on some beautiful spring morning or evening I prayed all the way to school or back, if I went alone.

From late fall to early spring, though, about half of the trip was in pitch-dark, especially on overcast days. As every classroom was used by two classes, the younger students' school day was 1:00 to 5:00 p.m., while the older went 8:00 a.m. until noon. That meant that those from our valley either had to leave home at 6:30 a.m., or return around 6:30 p.m. In mountain valleys the dawn broke in winter time much later, and the dusk fell much earlier. Often long stretches of the road could be travelled only by memory, and I had no light.

Sometimes two or more of us students went together; often I was alone.

Only God knows the agonies of horror and fear I went through on such days in these pitch black mountain forests with no living soul for kilometres around.

The wild hunt might appear any moment, but I was not sure in which of the two ruts to lie down.

Some snow-covered pine would look from afar like a strange creature, and you could take an oath it moved.

Are the boots going to appear on the usual spot? And the spine-chilling casket...?

From the dark of the forest I imagined bright spots peering: burning greenish eyes of monstrous, spine-chilling, charcoal black, ghost-like bodies that blended with the darkness itself.

The situation was aggravated by my regularly recurring dreams. I would go down into the dark cellar. Just before reaching the last step, an indescribably terrible monster, like a giant bat and even more horrible than the forest phantoms just described, appeared always from the same spot in the open space behind the boards on the opposite wall (which were there to prevent potatoes in that large compartment from touching the humid stone wall). Its most agonizingly fearful features were the angry, hostile, burning eyes fixed on me, and its black, ghost-like body, hovering in the air. The creature then flew towards me and I literally disappeared in it, devoured in supreme horror. The moment I lost consciousness, having died mainly of fear, I suddenly woke up.

The dream was so agonizing that at bedtime I often vowed not to fall asleep.

On pitch-dark winter evenings, returning from school, I used to bite my lips to convince myself that I was not dreaming. Then I felt a little more secure that fiery-eyed monsters would not immediately fly to devour me.

There were occasions when I went almost berserk. I began to run, run, run... even uphill, as fast as I could, crying all the while to the extent I could with the little breath left for it.

Once I ran unexpectedly into a couple of border guards on patrol.

"Why are you crying?" they asked.

"Because I am scared."

"Don't worry, you have nothing to fear; we just came from Radovna and there is nobody on the road."

A most useless piece of information! It was not people I was afraid of but the dark and its elusive monsters with glowing, threatening eyes.

The guards spoke Serbian or Croatian and we had a hard time communicating. They came around a day or two later, recounted the episode to my parents, and asked how I was. They thought that somebody had beaten me up badly.

In higher grades when I attended school in the morning, things were not quite as bad. The morning darkness was not quite as frightful and the forest seemed not quite as monster-infested as in the evening. Also, my brother John often accompanied me to the top of the saddle: usually with an old-fashioned petroleum storm-lamp. If fresh snow fell overnight, he would go ahead to break the path. Towards the top of the saddle the amount of the snow usually rapidly increased, becoming knee-deep or even deeper across it. By then the dawn broke and John could turn back home. Towards Mojstrana there was less and less snow; it was a downhill walk; and frequently I met a horse and sleigh which broke the path: a farmer on his way to haul logs.

What a relief when days became longer: snow disappeared, birds began to sing again in the forests, and mountain flowers appeared in the small clearings.

For some time, of course, there was still a lot of slush, or a foot would break through the ice now and then into the water standing or flowing underneath it. I would come to school with leather shoes full of water and heavy woollen stockings wet to the knees.

The sun shone along most of the road only to a certain distance down from the mountain tops on the east or west side, depending on whether one was on the forenoon or the afternoon shift. Late in the spring, though, and in early fall, most of the road was in sunshine, at least those portions where it could penetrate through the trees. Big tamaracks, pines and beeches grew on both sides of the narrow road, and in many places their branches met over it.

More than once, on a sunny, fresh, heavenly beautiful Alpine spring morning, mother would send me off to school with the remark: "O how I envy you. The birds will sing to you all the way. It will seem as if a choir of them will greet you just up the hill in the forest behind the house and accompany you all the way to Mojstrana."

I knew so well she didn't envy me. On the contrary, she rejoiced with me and only wished I'd realize how fortunate I was.

From a date in the spring to a date in the fall, I travelled all the way to school and back barefoot. Both the beginning and the end of the "barefoot period" were determined by the feast days of certain saints whose names I have forgotten.

In my youth the majority of important activities in the house, the stable, and the fields were determined by feast days, much more than by other factors, including weather. The reason for bare feet was to "save soles." During the "bare-foot season" children and some adults walked and worked without footwear to save money. Shoes were worn only to church. Until the soles of the feet became hardened, gravel felt very sharp, especially right after a rain when leaves and dust were washed off the sharp gravel.

Also tough were freshly harvested fields, most of all rye fields. The stubble was hard on the soft spots between the toes and the foot. It also pricked the skin on the lower side of the ankle joints. While working on such fields, one tried to step on the stubble in such a way as to move it sideways as soon as the sole touched it.

At about seven years of age many children had to start working in the home, in the stable, on the fields, or guarding cattle.

Forests owned by individual farmers provided their main and in many cases only revenue to pay taxes, and buy clothing and some foods. Only a few areas were owned in common by municipalities. However, for grazing purposes all forests were common property. The cattle would sometimes travel very large distances through the valleys - and at times got lost in spite of bells. It was distressing to find oneself far from home, with night approaching, and no herd to take home.

There were two special problems: one was swarms of gadflies and particularly, on very hot days before thunder-storms, a so-called "stampede fly."

When this fly appeared, the cattle lifted their tails up and took off as fast and as far as they could, with the poor shepherd left behind. Quite naturally, the herd would instinctively run through the thickest bush in order to get rid of the unbearable gadflies.

The other problem was "mushrooming."

At a certain time some mushrooms appeared that seemed to bewitch the whole herd: oxen, cows and calves travelled all over the woods in search of these mushrooms. It was a nuisance, but at least one could keep up with the herd.

In the fall cattle grazed on fields, but even that had its problems when the cattle headed for some late crops or the neighbour's property. There was common grazing only in the forests, not on the fields.

The good times were when two or three neighbouring shepherds - and usually some "helpers" - met, baked potatoes, or played: when the cattle's *Wanderlust* was at a low ebb.

# THE SUNRISE

My parents were firm believers in the "work ethic."

Father was a game warden, so the rest of us had to work harder, although he also joined us for some of the farm work. In 1933 both my older brothers were away: John served in the army in Macedonia near the Greek border, at the other end of the country; Rudolph attended a forestry school.

A cousin who had already served in the army helped us. He seemed to expect me to work like an adult. If he thought I was not moving fast enough he pointed to the large, white corpus on a cross that stood at the edge of the forest across the fields, and remarked: "You are like the one on the cross."

Starting that year (age seven) I had to work full time around the house as well as in the fields, in the stable and in the barn. From early morning to dusk I was often leading a pair of oxen up and down the fields, ploughing - barefoot, of course. The oxen had leather-clad cushions and wooden yokes fastened to their heads with long leather straps, which went several times around the horns and all around the head. Each ox had its own yoke to which were hooked strong chains for pulling the plough. A chain from under one ox's chin to the other kept them going in more or less the same direction.

One of the pair was usually older than the other. The younger one now and then began to twist its head trying to escape. Occasionally one would step on my bare foot. Fortunately the oxen too were barefoot, in summer, and the furrows soft.

Of all the work, haying was the hardest. I liked to rake freshly cut grass or even carry loads of it, in my hands or in small toy-like wagons, to areas where it would dry. This was usually necessary because there was not enough grass to simply leave it all over. Many Alpine meadows produce hay of high quality but very little quantity: much work but little produce.

I did not mind the raking and carrying, but pressing hay standing on a wagon was not my cup of tea. Above anything else I loathed pressing hay in the barn - which, by some yet-to-be-discovered Slovenian equivalent of the famous "Murphy's law" was usually my lot.

As the barn was relatively small, the idea was to tramp down the hay, and to put it into every available space, especially when the heap began to reach the roof. There were beams everywhere, cobwebs packed with dust galore, and a sun-baked wooden roof just overhead.

To make full measure, brother Rudolph delighted in throwing forksful of crumbling-dry hay, often with thistles in it, behind my sweat-drenched neck.

We never suffered hunger, but without hard work most people in rugged, stony Alpine environments would starve to death. More than once my mother made remarks about the toil of my native people, quoting her mother: "To suffer is not sin."

In my valley it was impossible to cultivate the steep mountain slopes. Further to the east, though, where the Julian Alps become hills and where her mother hailed from, cultivated fields were also on the hill sides. Too steep for horses or oxen, they had to be hoed, obviously downhill. But when the whole field was hoed, the furrow at the low end had to be carried in baskets on people's backs up to the upper edge to prevent the whole field from eventually being brought down into the valley. All produce and manure also had to be carried in baskets. Women and children worked at these tasks just as much as men. Small wonder that women from that district were highly favoured as farmers' brides.

There was hard work, simple food and clothing, practically no luxuries, very little money - but never starvation or hunger in my native land.

Only towards the end of the First World War did the spectre of hunger loom seriously. Fortunately, in the neighbouring province of Croatia, "corn opened up" as mother used to say, and hunger was averted.

Weeding was another important occupation. For days, from morning to dusk, we slowly moved up and down the fields picking weeds, on our knees. In spite of heavy potato bag aprons, knees began to itch, especially when the ground was humid.

Potatoes were planted in rows like nowadays. Men worked the ground between rows with triangular spade-like hoes; the weeding was strictly women's and children's work.

Carrots were sown and had to be weeded when still very small. Since the ground couldn't be hoed ahead as with potatoes, each weeder used a small two-pronged fork-like tool to loosen the ground in small patches. Then the weeds were uprooted and piled in small heaps. As both were green, one needed eagle's eyes to distinguish the tiny carrot plants from the weeds.

Most people would think mothers cannot do farm work because of their children.

Not so my mother!

She regularly took the three youngest of us along to the fields, and simply placed the younger two on some empty bags while I ran around; although very soon I also had to work. She would then help with haying, weeding, spreading manure, or other work.

She also devised an ingenious way of cooking the meals on such days. Potatoes, carrots or whatever meal was on the stove was first brought to a boil before she left home. Then some fairly large, hard, knotty beech logs were used to make the fire burn slowly. Perhaps once before noon or evening she would go to check things. On the next trip she prepared the meal and either called us home to eat or brought it out to the field. However, if grandma was in good shape, she usually took care of us children and if we didn't go for an outing she also looked after the fire.

I remember as vividly as if it happened yesterday a special occasion of weeding carrots with my mother. Although I must have been only about six at the time, I even recall the particular area of the field.

Mother took a wide swath and I, on her right, a narrow one. That one afternoon she taught me the Ten Commandments by heart so well that I never forgot them.

She had, without any doubt, lots of ingenuity, diligence, and the  kind of love that "moves the sun and the stars," as the great poet Dante Alighieri put it in his *Divine Comedy.* For, in the midst of almost uninterrupted toil from dawn to dusk, six days a week and much of the seventh as well, and never any holidays, she always found time for her family and especially us, her children.

Always!

She found time to teach me how to pronounce R, for example, on her way up the steps to the barn, with an empty basket under her arm. I said something to her but pronounced L instead of R. Like Italians and some other people, Slovenes roll the R, and children are unable to do it until they reach a certain age. So she stopped halfway up the steps, bent a little down towards me, and showed me again and again how to pronounce it properly.

On the very same spot, but at the foot of the steps and probably some years later, she taught me in a like manner even how to whistle.

Once I came from school and during the snack I worked on a crossword puzzle. I must have been really addicted to it, for in the middle of the meal I ran out to the field where mother was weeding to ask what was the name of the "Turkish God." She knew it was Allah.

On one occasion she led me by the hand on the way home from Mojstrana.

"Mama, what is that?" I asked, pointing to the roots of some pine-trees near the road, felled by the wind.

"That is God's fence."

I objected that cows could easily go around at each end of the area, and so the fence didn't make much sense.

No doubt she had an appropriate answer to my objection, but unfortunately it escapes my memory.

With only five years of grade school, she gave me, way back in the mid-1930s, an answer to the question what an atom was that perfectly satisfied my thirst for knowledge about atoms for the time being.

In a newspaper I saw the photograph of a contraption referred to as "An American machine for smashing of atoms."

"Mama, what is an atom?"

"An atom is something so small that it is almost nothing."

I understood perfectly that it was the smallest thing possible.

This is only a sampling of many similar anecdotes.

The limitless availability in the midst of an incredible amount of work is one of my fondest memories of my mother. The very thought of it thrills my heart.

Cars were a rare phenomenon in Radovna around 1930. One happened to go along the two-rut road down the valley among the fields and left a small valley-like tire mark in a softer spot on a tiny slope. While mother was haying she put her baby

Frank in that little valley. It seemed to her ideally fit for my little body. From then on the spot has been referred to as "Franc's valley."

This last story, of course, is not told in order to be imitated in our times.

While my father was more conservative in his approach to matters of economy, my mother came up with quite a few progressive ideas. One of the most "revolutionary" ones was the moving of winter laundry from the trough on the courtyard to a new addition to the kitchen, constructed specifically for two purposes: cooking of fodder for pigs, and winter laundry. As an afterthought and luxury, a primitive bath-tub was also installed in one of the corners: constructed of cement, with no faucets or shower. Hot water for any purpose had to be prepared in a large cauldron. The tub was like an evolutionary leap forwards, for until then all we had for bathing was a large bowl put on an ordinary chair.

From times immemorial women washed the laundry outsidè. I remember watching my mother through the window on some cold winter day. Dressed in heavy and old men's clothes, with baskets full of laundry nearby, she worked in snow and ice at the trough on the courtyard for hours. Sometimes she would call me to help her wring bed sheets. I would hold coarse hemp sheets at one end, she at the other, twisting them around. Then we folded them and mother took them to the attic to dry.

Moving the laundry inside was for my mother like a foretaste of heaven. Later she would recall how sometimes things were literally freezing in her hands. No wonder she suffered from rheumatism.

The "outhouse" had been relocated in the warm stable already before my time. Washroom in a house was still unthinkable. I recall the talk and wonderment when the first such case appeared in the area. Even the fact that it was called an English washroom, water-flushed, did not convert the diehard traditionalists.

The purse strings were in mother's hands. My father handed regularly all the earnings to her, but that did not mean his abdication as the head of the family. He refused to agree to a radical but almost necessary renovation of the stable, nor to a new roof for the house. So, at the advice of mother's beloved brother Rudolph she simply ordered the necessary bricks and other material. "When the message arrived that the rail car of bricks was at the railway station," she used to reminisce later, "and had to be unloaded in 24 hours, I thought I was to suffer a stroke." Well, she suffered no stroke, but I understand that there was a lot of scratching of the neck, twisting of mustaches, and grumbling on the part of my father, to put it in mildest possible terms. However, when all was completed, he showed with great pride any visitors the work done: "Lately I have put a new roof on the house, modernized the stable, and moved the pigsties into it to keep the animals warm..."

Ants were my great fascination: from big red ones that lived in the stumps of large pine-trees, to the very small yellow ones that lived in mounds of earth, with grass usually growing right through their dwellings.

Between these two varieties were two more kinds. There were the fairly small, brown ones, and my favourites: reddish coloured, quite similar to the largest kind, but somewhat smaller.

My favourites had their anthills mainly in the grassy fields, with abundant grass around but not on top. They were expertly built from pieces of dry straw and grass stems, pine needles, very small pebbles, chunks of earth, and crumbs of pitch, which serves as the most aromatic incense for divine services. In the Holy Saturday liturgy there is even a special reference to the "diligent ants that gathered the incense."

If such an anthill is cut accidentally by a scythe, the levels of well-planned storeys and rooms can be seen. The first concern of the ants is to carry their larvae to safety; only then do they begin to rebuild their dwelling.

From the anthill, paths lead for dozens of metres in all directions. They are very smooth and dug not only among the grass but now and then also under grass roots.

On a hot summer's day, these ant highways were almost as busy as the modern super-highways. For me they were an inexhaustible source of sheer fascination. I admired the busy ants hauling pieces of straw, dead insects, and even pebbles as large as themselves. And no matter how many or how busy, every ant greeted each and every other ant by momentarily touching at least one if not both antennae as they hurried past one another. I do not remember whether they had any rules as to which side of the road they used but, in the days of my childhood in the Julian Alps, not even the people cared about that.

I would have loved to watch ants for hours, but usually the voice of my mother reminded me that this was a time for work, not ant watching.

There was one mystery I was never able to solve: the hotter the day, the more lazy I felt, while the ants, on the contrary, were faster and busier. On such days we children loved to play tricks on them.

One trick was to move the hand up and down, with the palm alternatively turned up, then down, as close to the anthill as possible without touching it while repeating "vinegar, oil; vinegar, oil..." The ants stopped, twisted their rear ends under their bodies forwards and upwards, and turned into a mighty sprinkling brigade. Tiny thread-like jets appeared rising high over the anthill.

Soon the hand smelled like vinegar. Ants seemed to give vinegar only: no oil.

Another trick was to touch the anthill on one spot and watch the ants run with utmost speed. Within seconds the commotion spread, with ants pouring out of their holes.

Having completed five years of elementary school, I attended one year of "city school." Because of the long walk home to the railway station I stayed with the family of a cousin of mine in Dovje, travelling daily by train to the school in Jesenice.

At the age of 12 or 13, I had some vague and confused ideas about the "facts of life." A girl in the family I was living with was far more "enlightened." Moreover, she knew that her mother had certain books on the subject. The trouble was that these mysterious works were kept in a chest of drawers in a room that was always locked. Fortunately it had a window that could be reached from the outside with some daring and ingenuity.

The whole situation was just too tempting for two adventurous youngsters full of thirst for knowledge - at least the kind under our consideration.

Once, when everybody else was away, we succeeded in climbing through the window. Our sense of expectancy must have equalled that of Howard Carter and his entourage entering Tut's tomb. Ours must have been even greater: for while they were discovering mysteries of a tomb, of death, we were exploring the mysteries of life itself. Our struggle through the window and our curiosity about the "forbidden fruit" no doubt added substantially to our fascination.

With the greatest anticipation we opened the chest of drawers and found the prize: *The Mothers' Helper*. It was a book so elementary that most twelve-year-olds today would find it utterly boring.

But those were different times. I learned that my parents also kept certain similar books under lock and key. The irony is that our parents were very religious people, and these books were published under the auspices of the Catholic Church! My mother often used to say, "Most expensive is ignorance," but on this subject our parents somehow didn't succeed in putting their wisdom into practice.

A few times this same girl hid my railway student pass which caused me serious trouble. Some train conductors were very strict: no pass, no ride! A few times I had to walk the 11 km to school as a result. For her it was sheer fun; for me a serious penance.

She and I had beds in an unfinished attic with the usual junk and our two beds. More than once I found in my bed thistles or nettles. I guess we were slowly but surely coming into those mysterious years of adolescence. The girl was a year or two younger in physical age but surely more mature in other respects.

A few days after the beginning of my school year in the "city school" a skinny, sick-looking boy arrived. He tried to sit in several benches, but nobody could stand his literally rotting breath. In spite of my natural repugnance, I invited him to sit next to me, in order to make him feel welcome and at ease. On December 17, 1938, my new friend Boris died.

"Remember not the sins of my youth, or my transgressions..." (Ps 25:7). Heaven knows, and I too, that there were both of them galore, although God in his infinite mercy gave me the grace of repentance, confession and forgiveness. If I were another Aurelius Augustinus (St. Augustine of Hippo), I could write a book of *Confessions* of my own. As I am neither a genius, saint, or writer of his stature, this short paragraph will have to suffice on this point, for better or for worse.

But whenever I recall Boris Kristan and what I did for him in the last weeks of his life, a soft, warm feeling of peace and joy fills my heart.

During my sojourn in Dovje, situated on the sunny southern slopes of the Karavanke mountains, a group of us students made an excursion to the top behind the village. Although the adventure cannot be considered mountain climbing, the ascent was quite steep and strenuous. All one could see was the mostly rocky ground in front of the nose and the sky above the trees. Not a very exciting trip. But I will never forget the moment we reached the top.

The last 200 metres or so there is a somewhat less steep meadow, with hardly any trees and few rocks. Again, all one could see was grass, cattle grazing on the meadow, and the sky above the horizon on the top of the mountain.

Then, suddenly, after one last single step, the whole of southern Austria (Carinthia) with its fields, forests, rivers, lakes, roads, villages and cities, appeared deep below and beyond the precipice on the north side of the Karavanke.

A breath-taking sight: a truly unforgettable moment. At the spot where we reached the top, the Austrian-Yugoslavian border stones stood, a considerable distance from one another, along the very edge of the precipice. Further to the east, the top of the precipice ran more northwards, and the border across the meadow. We hurried across the border, and in a fairly deep depression in the plateau on the Austrian side found even some snow.

That was my first small venture outside my native land. It was by no means the last...

Apart from these little anecdotes the "City school" year was a relatively quiet and uneventful one in my life - the calm before the onslaught of the storms: both storms of adolescence through which every normal boy (and perhaps to a lesser degree girl, I guess?) must pass on the way to adulthood, and storms of the Second World War.

The summer of 1939 I spent at home working as usual.

In early September I took the train, accompanied by my mother, to enter the College of St. Stanislaus on the outskirts of Ljubljana. After years of struggle my parents had finally given in: "If Franc really yearns with such longing to study, let it be. After all, he wants to become a priest; so let him go in God's name."

The glorious victory almost turned into a Pyrrhic one: the entrance exams had been held in early summer and I had missed them!

I am still in possession of a precious souvenir: a note which the rector of the College wrote to my pastor - I believe they were classmates - who then gave it to my parents. The rector, Dr. Anton Breznik, was the greatest modern authority on Slovenian language. But he was a lousy typist, judging by the appearance of his note; and his typewriter had to be one of the first ones ever made. In translation, the letter read:

> Št. Vid near
> Ljubljana
> August 21, 1939.

> Dear Reverend Pastor!

> With entrance exams in the fall are great difficulties. However, I am taking that upon myself if thereby I can be useful to the boy and our College. In agreement with the Reverend Spiritual Director, who besides the Reverend Bursar and myself, accepts the students into the College, I am letting you know that the boy should come on Saturday, August 26, at 8 o'clock to make his entrance exam, but only on condition that his father will pay for him Din 400 monthly. If he does not do that, the College does not accept the boy, nor do I accept the difficulties for his

exam.

Heartfelt greetings, your

Dr. A. Breznik

If he comes, he must, of course, bring with him all papers, i.e., birth certificate and his last school report.

It was with great anticipation, my heart overflowing with joy seasoned with a good helping of apprehension about the exam, that I woke very early that Saturday morning, got ready, walked with my mother the one and a half hours to the railway station, and took the two-hour train ride to Ljubljana. The only memory from the trip itself is the red sun rising through the early morning mist, and a teenaged girl standing in a field with her hands on top of the handle of her hoe, chin resting on her hands, and looking at the train as it was pulling out of one of the stations. When my mother and I sat in the beautiful, almost grandiose college lobby anxiously awaiting the exams, she noticed in the bright sunlight a thin thread hanging from the nicely decorated ceiling. She quipped: "Look, there are cobwebs even here."

It turned out that another boy had also come to make the entrance exam. I believe he had been sick earlier. Both of us were conducted into the classroom by two or three professors. I only recall that we had to analyze a sentence and solve a mathematical problem: how many shingles of a certain size will be needed for a roof that has so many square metres. I did not take into account the fact that there is some overlapping, but apparently the good professor did not expect such cleverness in a 13 year old boy. We both passed!

There are no words to describe my joy when the happy day finally dawned to take the trip again to the College: this time to stay. My mother accompanied me once more and helped carry my baggage.

The College of St. Stanislaus had the distinction of being

the first Slovenian high school. Until the end of the First World War Slovenia belonged to the Austrian half of the dual Austrian-Hungarian empire. The monarch in Vienna was officially titled Emperor of Austria and King of Hungary. Although my mother tongue was used in elementary schools, the official language in high schools was German.

Dr. Anton Bonaventura Jeglič, the bishop of Ljubljana, saw the need for a high school for boys that would be both Slovenian and Catholic, and an institution for education of both clerical and secular leaders and intellectuals.

The College was solemnly blessed and opened in 1905 after four years of building and great financial sacrifices and other difficulties of the bishop, priests, and people. It was a beautiful and very imposing building which housed over 20 professors, some sisters, other workers, and well over 500 students, with all the necessary rooms a large boarding institution the size of "Collegium Sancti Stanislai" needed. Basically, the first floor was classrooms, the second held large common study rooms, and the third, common dormitories. The front rose five storeys and was topped by a cross. The college title was inscribed immediately over the main entrance, and high above it, between the third and fourth storeys, in much larger letters: "To Christ, the Redeemer of the World."

In those days there were many priestly vocations in Slovenia. So the bishop sent the brightest students to study in Vienna, Graz, Innsbruck, Paris, Rome, and other European universities. Many of the teachers were, themselves, graduates of the College. No wonder that they dedicated their lives so enthusiastically to the education of the new generations of students. Just before the Second World War, the College of St. Stanislaus was recognized by state inspectors as the best high school, academically, not only in the province of Slovenia, but in all of Yugoslavia.

I studied very hard, but with great eagerness and joy, and having been gifted with a good intellect and memory, I was always first in the class. My ambition was to become a priest and professor in that College.

Our education took great care of the whole person: "Spirit, soul and body," to use St. Paul's words in 1 Thes 5:23.

# THE SUNRISE

There were eight grades of high school: four for junior matriculation, and four more for senior, but one could enter after grade four or five of the elementary school. In the very first year there were about twelve subjects, among them four languages: Slovenian, Serbo-Croatian, French, and Latin. In the third year Greek was added. In the first years, grammar and vocabulary were strongly emphasized, to serve as a tool for the study of literature in higher grades. I remember that in my first year the students from the higher grades staged the French drama "Athalie" which was attended by the French consul in Ljubljana. I learned to play the harmonium in music lessons as a preliminary step towards learning the organ. (The latter had to be pumped by another person and there was no point learning fundamentals on it when they could be learned just as easily on a self-pumped harmonium or on piano). I also joined the school choir which sang mainly at Sunday Masses, but also at Christmas concerts. It was an excellent choir, led by Matija Tomc, one of the greatest Slovenian composers, who was also a priest, professor, and a consummate organist. However, before the end of my stay at the college I had to quit the choir because my voice was changing.

We attended Mass every morning, and one day a week there was the opportunity for Confession. Besides the professors, we also had priests who took the place of our parents in all other areas of life. Each of the common study rooms, perhaps eight or more in all, was the home of a real community or family, called "Division." Each was supervised by a young priest titled "Prefect." He was with us and available at all times outside the classes: for study, prayer, chapel, recreation, walks through the fields, and sports. His suite was adjacent to the common study room, with one door to the corridor and the other (complete with a peep-hole!) to the common study room.

All our books were kept in our desks, which could be opened only by lifting the top. However, one was allowed to open the top only before each study period. Now and then somebody tried to open it sneakily, but he was never sure whether or not the peep-hole was "active" or not, even when the prefect was not around. Talk during study periods was strictly forbidden.

Discipline was strict but seasoned with genuine love, thus quite palatable to most of us - most of the time. The one exception happened to me in the very first days after my arrival.

In the beginning, every day for about half an hour, the prefect explained the house rules and related matters. Among other things he pointed out that we must escort visitors to the visitors' room. In the Slovenian language, "visitors' room" and "visitors' slaughter house" sound almost alike, to my misfortune: the former is *obiskoválnica*, the latter *obiskoklávnica.*

I sat very near the front, with a genuine city-slicker as my desk-mate. He leaned over and whispered in my ear: "When my mother comes I'll lead her to the visitors' slaughter house." Both of us giggled, but the harder I tried not to giggle, the more I did. The prefect gave us a long, serious look. No words were needed to convey the message. The other boy stopped laughing but try as I might, I could not. The prefect stepped into his room and in seconds appeared with a bamboo reed. The end of this episode is predictable: a red line the length of my right palm. I had the dubious distinction of being the first to experience that medicine, in that school year, in that "Division." But it worked: I was effectively healed of laughing about the visitors' slaughter house.

Our souls were well looked after, but neither was the body neglected. We had simple, healthy food, sufficient sleep, recreation, and sports. Every afternoon we went, in "Division," two by two, for a walk in the nearby fields. In winter we were even allowed now and then to engage another "Division" met on our walk in a lively snowball match, with our prefects taking full part, goading on their troops. My favourite game was a ball game called "Between Two Fires." Two teams threw a volley-ball-sized ball at each other, confined in their respective rectangular areas on the field. The ball could either be dodged or caught. If it touched the ground after hitting a player, he was out; he had to retire behind the opposing team. However, he was allowed to take part in the game from there. The team that had all its members knocked out first, lost.

Saturdays we had studies only until noon. And every Thursday we spent the afternoon on the meadows near the Sava river. We used to play "Between Two Fires," bake potatoes under the ashes, and have a really good time. Once we came upon a curious scene along the road: two men had, by all appearances, just finished making a huge barrel and were obviously celebrating their accomplishment. They were sitting high atop its flat end, trying to sing, and swaying dangerously in all directions. Their guardian angels must have worked hard indeed to keep them on high, for they were "high" indeed in another sense of the word.

One afternoon in the middle of December 1939, I began to feel pain in my ankles during the walk through the snow-covered fields and returned to school, limping. By evening I couldn't walk at all. It just happened to be the one day when the doctor was on his regular weekly visit. Two of my classmates carried me sitting on their joined hands with my arms around their necks to his office. Diagnosis: rheumatic fever.

I spent a week or so in the college sick-room. Every day for about three hours I was wrapped in cold, moist sheets and covered with a number of blankets, with only a small opening left for breathing. The idea was to sweat somehow the sickness out of the body. There were a few others in the same room, and every morning a priest brought us Holy Communion. During the day, we followed daily newspaper reports about the encounter between the German battleship *General Graf von Spee* and British warships, which ended with the scuttling of the German ship near Montevideo in South America.

Nobody felt much pain. There was peace in the land and in that cosy sick room, and Christmas holidays were only a few days away. Little did we suspect that in not quite 16 months our native land would be dismembered and engulfed in both war and revolution: that the majority of us would never live to see the end of it, and that most of the few survivors would be dispersed throughout the world.

I was released just in time to go home for Christmas holidays. However, at the medical exam at my release, the doctor suddenly lifted his hands into the air and in a gesture of deep disappointment told me, in a voice full of regret, that the rheumatic fever left my heart damaged.

At the time I did not feel any different; but a year or two later my health was notably worse.

At the end of the first school year in June 1940, I returned home for the summer. That same day afternoon I was already working with an iron rake: shaking earth from weeds on a freshly sown buckwheat field. My hands were so soft that I got four blisters: three ordinary and a bloody one. But my hands soon hardened and there were no more blisters that summer.

Next fall I returned to the College, but the school year was never completed. It ended on March 31, 1941. However, the mayor of Dovje, whose son was a classmate of mine, somehow managed to get my successful annual exams report smuggled later that year from Ljubljana, which was under Italian occupation.

Chapter Five

# Through Raging Storm

In order to stay out of the war, the Yugoslavian government concluded a non-aggression treaty with the Axis powers in March 1941. Soon afterwards, there was great dissatisfaction which resulted in demonstrations in Belgrade against the treaty; the government fell; and the treaty was repudiated. After that it was only a matter of time...

On the afternoon of March 31 the students were in their common study rooms. As usual, there was almost perfect silence. Suddenly, the prefect opened the door of his suite, stepped into the room and said: "Get up and go home on the first train!"

In a matter of seconds the scene resembled an anthill on a hot summer's day. Some thought the war had already started or was about to break out. Everyone was looking for empty boxes, bags, and anything else to pack books, blankets, or underwear from the cupboard at the foot of his bed in the dormitory upstairs. I took most of my books and left practically all my clothing behind. My mother felt, most of all, the loss of a blanket for which she had a great sentimental attachment: it was the gift of her mother on the last visit to my home.

By the time everyone was ready for departure it was already dark. The college had a farm attached for eggs, fresh vegetables, and milk. From that farm, and perhaps from some friendly neighbours' farms, several wagons were brought to the school yard. Our belongings were loaded and off we went towards the not-too-distant railway station. The horses trotted much of the way and we ran beside and behind the wagons. I can still see the sparks flying from under the horses' hoofs as they struck the cobblestones. I caught the train that evening. Those travelling eastwards had to wait until the next morning.

Thus my beautiful dream ended in a nightmare. Like a rose trampled into mud.

Six days later, on Palm Sunday, April 6, 1941, Yugoslavia was invaded. My native parish area was occupied on Good

Friday. Someone once said that our country fell apart like a house of cards. The one consolation, at least in our area, was that there were no casualties or destruction. Yugoslavian forces were withdrawn before the occupying armies marched in. Then, when Croatia declared its independence on April 10, the country's defences disintegrated.

My two older brothers got civilian clothes from some farmers, just in time, and were home on Easter Sunday. The older one was given a hoe or rake to take along so that it appeared as if he was on the way to work on the fields. One of our neighbours, however, was not so fortunate. He was caught in his uniform and spent years as a P.O.W. in Germany, but he worked on a farm there and was not too badly off; he and his "hosts" even became good friends and he visited them after the war.

The Germans, finding little or no resistance, simply marched - or more correctly, drove - through. Although they were the first to come, the whole district west of Ljubljana was occupied by the Italian forces for about three weeks.

The College of St. Stanislaus opened again and most students returned with the intention of completing the school year, but I learned about it only months later. It is possible that my parents knew about it, but they probably wanted me to stay at home, for more than one reason.

The resurrection of St. Stanislaus, though, turned out to be a short one.

About three weeks after the invasion, the Germans took over the whole district west of Ljubljana. The border between the two Axis powers was drawn almost exactly through the middle of Slovenia and ran right around the outskirts of Ljubljana which fell under Italy. The College of St. Stanislaus happened to be one or two hundred metres from the border - on the German occupied side.

A student later told me that everybody was called to assemble in the large hall where concerts and plays used to be held. An officer stepped on the stage and shouted *Auf und raus!* (up and out!); and everybody had to run out.

Most students of the College had been from the Italian occupied half of Slovenia. As the Italian rule was, at that time, less ruthless than the German, the majority of students reassembled in Ljubljana where the College and its professors continued their work.

Today, the imposing building still stands: a vivid image of a chaste virgin, ravaged. (However, in 1992 the government of independent Slovenia returned it to the lawful owner, the Archdiocese of Ljubljana. After 51 years it will hopefully soon again serve its original purpose). Germans used it as a concentration camp. Soon after the war it was one of the places where Slovenian soldiers, who had defended their villages against Tito's partisans, were herded together, after their unfortunate extradition by the British authorities, from Austria where they sought refuge after the war. Even the bishop of Ljubljana was saved only by being literally snatched from the British occupation zone by Americans and taken to Salzburg into their zone.

The majority of these men: the cream of Slovenian youth; the pride, joy and hope of both the Church and the country, were handed over to their executioners like lambs for the slaughter. Some were executed in the very bosom of my alma mater: in its basements. Many thousands of others perished in large forests where they lie buried in underground caves. The delay of my return after the war was in all probability a blessing in disguise.

On the afternoon of March 7, 1946, I saw the school again through a train window: the first time since March 31, 1941. The inscription "To Christ, the Redeemer of the World" was gone. On the pinnacle above the main entrance a large red star had replaced the cross. And in the field where we used to play "Between Two Fires," a scattered crowd of German prisoners of war, with their distinctive green caps and mantles, looked more like statues than living people.

The time between the stormy events in the spring of 1941 and my draft into Hitler's war machine on August 1, 1943, was for me a kind of twilight zone. Mother used to say, "Let us snuggle to this mountain." She meant that we should do our work and not get entangled with war and revolution. And in our district, although both were horrific, revolution was later by far the worse of the two.

My heart, damaged by rheumatic fever, was giving me trouble. On one drizzly evening I happened to be upstairs and my heart began to beat faster and faster, weaker and weaker. I leaned on the window sill, looked at the wool-like edges of the low-hanging, heavy fog on the mountain across the fields and thought I was about to die. Instinctively I began to breathe deeper, and things returned to normal.

I was living and working at home then, and rumours soon began to circulate that there were "foresters" in the mountains: a term people first used for partisans. Before long, gun or mortar fire could be heard occasionally. Then the real existence of partisans was proved by their attacks, usually from roadside ambushes, on military patrols, and by occasional liquidations of important persons. I only remember seeing two partisans during the war. On a foggy, melancholy, fall evening, they came into the chamber, took two of my father's hunting rifles hanging on the door, and disappeared into the forest.

The reaction of the German occupation authorities was miserably mistaken, totally miscalculated, and deadly wrong. Instead of concentrating on flushing the partisan guerillas from their mountain hideaways, they retaliated against the general population and provoked an even greater hatred. As the German-occupied territory increased, especially after the invasion of the Soviet Union, the price for their blunders became exorbitant indeed. I heard that towards the end of the war, for example, when they urgently needed soldiers on the main fronts, about sixty divisions were tied down in Yugoslavia alone.

Some people saw at first the occupation as a kind of restoration of Austrian-Hungarian empire; quite a few old-timers still had a soft spot in their hearts. After all, it used to be their "home and native land." They had fought for it in the Great War less than a quarter century earlier, and had a certain nostalgia for it. Although the population in general loathed the occupation troops, most people were inclined to wait for the end of the war and the defeat of the Axis powers by the Allies, without doing much about it. The perpetual rumour, no doubt a child of wishful thinking, was: "By next Christmas the war will be over."

The new authorities decided to Germanize the German-occupied half of Slovenia. The Italians pursued their own policies in their half, which included the former provincial capital Ljubljana.

# THROUGH RAGING STORM

The German-occupied territory of Slovenia was annexed to Germany in such a way that it became an integral part of the Third Reich. All towns and villages, mountains and rivers were given German names. German became the language in schools, in offices, and in public institutions.

In a whole district near the Croatian border, all the people were "transplanted" to Silesia in today's southwestern Poland; German-speaking people replaced them.

The day of my draft was fast approaching, and I was blissfully unaware of it.

I had received the draft summons for *Reichsarbeitsdienst* (State Labour Service) in Germany, only hours before departure. I would rather have gone to the mountains to join the partisans. It was either Hitler's State Labour Service or Tito's partisans; there was no other possibility except certain execution. Departing from this life seemed very uninviting to a youth of 17.

I had been ordered by the doctor not to lift any heavy objects, climb mountains, swim, or perform any other strenuous activities. Although I had not felt sick for perhaps a year or more, symptoms of heart disease reappeared, and I was put under the doctor's care with daily medication. So I took the train. I had no real doubt that on account of my poor health, I would return home with the train later that day. My mother was of the same opinion, for I learned later that she had coffee ready to serve.

It was not meant to be.

My father, mother, oldest brother John and I got up at about 3:00 a.m. that Sunday morning. We did not awake the two younger brothers.

After a good, hot breakfast I was ready to leave with my wooden trunk, packed with clothing and personal belongings. It was the same one my older brothers had used in the army.

My mother stood in the kitchen, holding the door into the vestibule half open - or was it half closed? She held the door handle, slightly bent forwards, her face mild and peaceful.

My father stood behind her, looking over her shoulder towards me on the vestibule side of the door. That was nothing unusual. What was unusual were his tears and his trembling voice. My father was a paragon of strength, of diamond-like hardness:

hard, but naturally good as home-made farmer's bread. Just plainly strong and genuine. A Slovenian poet described such men: they seem not to have been born of women, but rather that they pried themselves off the mountains' hips.

Yet there he stood: that rock, with tears. Neither he nor my mother stepped into the vestibule, nor even opened the door to it more than half-way.

I turned and left, trunk in hand, through the vestibule, the house door, through the forests up the hill, over the saddle, down into the valley, through the dreamy village of Mojstrana, and over the Sava bridge towards the railway station.

With a few of my peers in the same dire predicament, a 15-minute train ride took me to the small industrial city of Jesenice. There we were at once placed under armed guard. At the local elementary school, the perfunctory medical examination, classification, and other formalities of draft took place. It seemed like I was falling into a trap, but there was no going back. Whoever drank the coffee my mother made that afternoon was not me.

I was classified *Ersatz Reserve II* (Substitute Reserve II), whatever that meant. One thing became clear: anyone able to walk was considered fit.

The same Sunday evening about 70 of us, all born in 1926 in the district, were escorted back to the railway station and shipped to a camp on the outskirts of Kranj, a city farther east, half way to Ljubljana. It was made very clear to us that the camp was well guarded and that there was no point trying to escape. There is little doubt that everyone believed the sincerity of these "friendly" assurances.

Next morning it was back on the train towards Jesenice. Needless to say, we were well "protected" in our two or three special cars. Yet in spite of it, at a station between Kranj and Jesenice, one man escaped. I saw him jump through the window of the car next to mine just as the train began to move. He almost sat on the ground, got up, ran through the people who were on the platform, escaped down the slope, and disappeared into some bushes and trees. I learned later that he made it to the partisans, but just before the end of the war he was killed. From then on we were forbidden to open the windows.

# THROUGH RAGING STORM

After a short stop in Jesenice, the train pulled away towards the almost 9-km-long Karavanke tunnel into Austria.

It was a trip to an unknown destination and to a totally unknown, certainly uncertain, unmistakably threatening future.

That was Monday, August 2, 1943. My next trip through that tunnel took place on Saturday, March 11, 1950. It was in the same direction but under very different circumstances.

We travelled through the beautiful Alpine valleys and the next day arrived in Vienna's *Südbahnhof* (South railway-station). We changed trains there and travelled north-west to Gmünd where we transferred to a local railway with narrow tracks and smaller cars. Our destination turned out to be the last of the several small stations on the line: a village by the name of Litschau, situated in the midst of the Bohemian Forest, on the former Austrian border with Czechoslovakia.

We arrived at night, which was the case from then on whenever we transferred. Unknown places can look different at night. During the war, that was even more true: there were no lights burning because of air raids.

The camp was on a slope, at the edge of a forest, about a quarter hour's walk from the village. The ground on which the camp was built used to be forest, and there were still some pine-trees and stumps. Behind the camp, up the slope, were some ploughed fields.

On the night we arrived there was a violent storm and clouds glowed with a pulsating red from a barn set afire by lightning, just beyond the horizon on the top of the slope.

Wooden, one-storey barracks, all prefabricated, had been assembled, along with a kitchen and dining hall, an assembly hall, a coal storage, and two or three other general purpose buildings.

The living quarters consisted of four barracks, each of which had three fairly large rooms with bunk beds along two opposite walls: heads at the wall, feet towards the centre of the room. Each of the other walls had one window. Near one of the windows there was a table with two benches; near the middle of the room, an iron coal oven; and near the entrance, a storage place for the omnipresent shiny spades used for exercises instead of rifles. In the dead centre of each room a square post, with beams radiating from it, supported the gently inclined roof: there was no real ceiling.

Between each pair of bunks four narrow cupboards, mainly for clothing, stood against the wall, although everybody also had his own trunk shoved under the lower beds.

The stools at the foot of the beds served one purpose: every evening our pants and the jacket had to be carefully folded into an exact square with the jacket on the top of the pants and put on the stool. The boots or shoes were placed under it.

On a few occasions we used the stools for snow removal. Men formed a line in front of the barrack, set stools on the ground one next to the other, and pushed the snow off the yard and over the edge of the hill.

Behind the barracks, up the slope, a large exercise yard had been made level by digging out some of the ground of its upper part and filling the lower area. After a rain the terrain became mud.

Below our quarters was the barrack housing the kitchen and the large dining hall, and in front of that building was another area for assemblies and for orders from the camp commander, given to men standing at attention. Every morning the flag was hoisted ceremoniously on a high pole. Every evening it was taken down in a similar manner.

Some other smaller buildings were still lower down, with the guards' quarters and the exit to the road at the lowest spot. At the entrance, a guard stood day and night, with a spade held almost vertically on his left shoulder as if it were a rifle. Except for the leaders, everyone in the camp was officially titled *Arbeitsmann* (worker).

Every morning the commander, who lived in the village, arrived by foot, and the whole guard was called out for a solemn greeting ceremony.

A narrow gravel road ran along the lower edge of the compound. From the main entrance, one could turn left and, in five minutes, uphill into the woods, or a small artificial lake; or else turn right and walk down the gently winding road to the village of Litschau in about 15 minutes.

On the way to the village one was accompanied by a murmuring brook departing now away from the road, then coming closer. Over the brook gently rolling hills with fields, meadows, and forest stretched as far as the eye could see.

There was no running water in the camp. We had to go down to the brook after every meal to wash our dishes. Those higher up the creek had to take care not to muddy the water, which ran here and there over what could be called mini-rapids, from one pond to another. On the very first such visit one of my countrymen named the brook Frog Creek: a name it still has today, if it is still there, at least among its Slovenian friends of long ago.

The "campers" were from two relatively small areas.

We were the first to arrive: about 70 Slovenes from northwest of Ljubljana. All were of 1926 vintage, but one had the dubious distinction of being born on the very last day of that year. Had he been a few hours younger he would never have been drafted. I don't know whether he survived the war or not. From our area we were the youngest to be conscripted, although in some other areas of the *Reich* younger men were called to military service before the end of hostilities.

Upon arrival we were lined up exactly according to height, from the tallest to the shortest. In that order we were assigned rooms in each of the four barracks with the tallest ones in the first room of the first barrack and the smallest in room twelve of the fourth one.

The bunks stood two and two together. One of us had to take the lower left bed, and the next the top right one. The reason became apparent. Two or three days later a group of Germans arrived from the city of Znaim (Znojmo) and its surroundings, in Sudetenland, a district of what had been Czechoslovakia. They were also all born in 1926, and occupied the empty beds. God alone knows how many, or more likely, how few of them are still alive. One thing is certain: wherever they may be, they are probably not at home, for Germans from Sudetenland were expelled from Czechoslovakia after the Second World War.

The other camps in which I had the dubious distinction of residing were pretty much the same. There may have been some "cosmetic" differences but hardly any substantial ones.

Later, in army barracks, even the "mixing of races," for

example, was devised in a similar way, but not with such precision. The ratio of Germans and Slovenes, of course, was never again 50-50. As the group of us became dispersed wider and wider, our percentage dropped accordingly.

The camp was a unit of *Reichsarbeitsdienst* (State Labour Service): in reality, a pre-military and paramilitary outfit.

We wore brown uniforms. The left arm was "adorned" with a red arm-band, with a black swastika on a round white background. Footwear was either shoes or leather boots, and for exercises we carried a spade, which always had to be shiny.

As a rule, exercise and work followed one another on alternate days.

Exercises, as with any military infantry training unit, consisted of marching, running, making turns, creeping on our bellies, fooling around with spades as if they were rifles, and other similar "vital" activities. Like any true soldier, every *Arbeitsmann* had the ever-present gas mask. We kept them in green, cylindrical sheet-metal containers on top of cupboards. We trained in a tear-gas-filled chamber, changing filters and even the mask itself, but I do not recall ever training with them in the open spaces. That "privilege" was only given in the army.

Singing was considered an integral part of marching. Many a time nail-studded boots on cobblestones coupled with a rousing song caused windows to open all along the route. They did not open shyly or stealthily, but widely and quite deliberately, with both hands at the same time. The hands usually belonged to no one else but beautiful *Mädchen.*

The sight of their smiling faces, some embraced by gorgeous braids, likely caused many a young heart (behind the rectangular pouches with folded anti-gas protective paper) to speed up its beat. It certainly seemed to give the boots just a little more punch and the lungs more power.

Returning from strenuous exercises and long marches, wet from sweat or mud, practically exhausted, a rousing marching song always mysteriously brought pep to our tired limbs. Unlike the marching songs of the Yugoslavian Army, the German ones, with a few notable exceptions, had hardly any political or fighting content. For the most part they were love songs of nostalgic, patriotic poems.

One of the exceptions was a song urging: "Put the red rooster on the cloister's roof!" It dated from the farmers' revolts in the Middle Ages. My company commander often had us sing it when passing by the only church in Litschau. I did not sing that song: I pretended to sing by opening my mouth in unison with the others.

Another song went something like this: "When I return home again, early in the morning just as the sun is getting up, I will look down into the valley where in front of every door there stands a girl. Then I will stop and whisper silently: 'My homeland, my (here everyone mentioned his own particular "land"), we will see each other again on the banks of (whatever river flowed through that land).'"

My nostalgia on such occasions became all-consuming. I imagined myself coming back from the military, downhill through the forest behind my home and looking down on its roof, across the fields, and up the mountainsides beyond it. The valley was always, in my imagination, bathed in morning sun and covered with flowers, the air filled with the smell of honey from buckwheat fields and linden trees, and deep peace hovering over it all. But I knew that even a furlough was out of the question, let alone a return home.

Our chief work was logging. Early in the morning we picked up our tools, took the local train to a station perhaps some 20 km away, and walked into the forest.

After the branches were cut off the large felled pines, we peeled off the bark with our sharpened spades, and cut the trees into long pieces which were hauled away by large trucks. In the evening we returned to the camp.

After about a month, the unit was sent to the vicinity of Wiener Neustadt, an industrial centre south of Vienna. There, in a place called Grossmittel, near Felixdorf, we worked in a large ammunition complex.

In the middle of the night during our trip, a railway worker opened the sliding cattle-car door and shouted: "Italy capitulated." A half-awakened leader, lifting his head drowsily from the floor, replied, "I thought that would happen." He then huddled back under his blanket and everything was quiet again. History tells us it was September 9, 1943.

We were allowed visitors on weekends, not only before in Litschau, but even here in spite of so much ammunition in the general area. My mother, although in her mid-sixties and reluctant to leave her beloved Radovna, came once to visit me.

Later she also travelled all the way to Litschau, which was considerably farther. A mother like mine would go to the ends of the world and beyond to see her child, even if only for a day.

During my stay in Grossmittel I once had a most beautiful dream - and a most disappointing awakening.

I dreamt that I arrived through the area in the middle of Radovna, walking through meadows, some small groves of trees and hazelnut bushes, down into the dry bed of the brook, across its round, white gravel, and up the bank nearer to my home. At the top, I leaned against the slope and looked across the fields. A heavenly view presented itself to my eyes.

It was a balmy, beautiful day, to be enjoyed only in the Alps during the late spring. A most gentle breeze kept kissing softly my cheeks and face as I drank to the point of inebriation and rapture the beauty of the sun-bathed plain. In the middle of the field were about ten reapers, mostly women. They had just finished their work of reaping the rye and were leaving the fields, sickles in their hands, peacefully chattering with one another and quietly laughing from time to time.

It was a sight so familiar to me in happier days!

They were on their way to my home for a little party and a good meal to celebrate the happy conclusion of the rye harvest. They were walking, scattered through the field, about one or two hundred metres from me.

My eyes drank in this beauty, and I felt a profound happiness in my breast as I looked over the plain and beyond the reapers to my home, snuggled below the forest. From there my gaze went up the forest-covered slopes of the mountain saddle, across it towards the Austrian border on top of the Karavanke, and the blue sky above. Only a few scattered cloud formations, like grazing flocks of sheep, floated slowly over its vast expanse.

Looking in my dream over the mountains, I got a mildly

melancholy feeling mixed with nostalgia. I felt rather than knew that I would have to pass by my home and far beyond the mountains into the unknown.

Suddenly I woke up.

The scene changed completely.

I was in the midst of that far-away "unknown" and my first realization was that the war was on. Outside was an unusually dull autumn morning. Only a few nearby rows of small, bushy fir trees could be seen. Behind them a few more rows just barely. Everything further away was lost in heavy, dark grey, drizzly fog.

The whole area around Grossmittel was very dreary: flat land with a lot of gravel, here and there patches of grass, some shrubs, and large sections planted with small fir trees row on row on crests between wide furrows. These thickets were ideal hiding places for the many small rabbits who had their burrows there.

Our task was to build a narrow-gauge railway from the train terminal, in a round about way far through the area, and then back to the terminal. At intervals along the line, tracks branched into huge hangar-like storage buildings, which were being built from large prefabricated parts. One branch went left, the next right, off the main tracks, and so on all around. From the air it must have looked like a long twig bent into a loop, with large square leaves.

On October 1, 1943, we experienced our first air-raid.

We were busy at work when suddenly sirens sounded all around. Soon, squadrons of planes appeared. The thundering roar of their motors was a sure sign that there were many and heavily loaded. Bombs began to fall in clusters here and there through our area but to my knowledge did not hit any ammunition dumps, at least not any full ones. A nearby town got the brunt of the attack, with quite a few casualties.

We were working in groups scattered along the rail line. One group sought shelter in a nearby gravel pit. A few airplanes separated from the rest of them and dropped some bombs narrowly missing the pit. The only casualties were one or two rabbits in the fir thicket at its edge.

The reason for the "mini-attack" was, no doubt, the

shining spades. Every day we brought them simply for exercise, as if they were rifles, lined them up, and laid them on the ground - all under command, of course - in perfect order. As they had been regularly polished with sand paper, they must have practically blinded the airmen in the sunny skies above.

From that day on we stored the spades in a shed that stood behind an ammunition depot, the hub of a whole complex. It was the terminal of the regular railway as well as the terminal of the narrow-gauge railway we came to build. Behind it was the area for our assemblies both upon our arrival in the morning and before the return "home" in the evening.

During the air raid my group sought shelter under some bushes; I huddled behind a small mound of large gravel and small stones.

The anti-aircraft fire was ferocious but not very effective. Thousands of tiny black clouds dotted the path of the high-flying squadrons. Most of the shells seemed to have been fired too late, too high, or more likely too low for any hits. The customarily very inflated reports had it that sixteen *Fliegende Särge* were shot down in the general area of Wiener Neustadt. "Flying Caskets" was the name Dr. Joseph Göbbels' propaganda machine gave to the "Flying Fortresses." Perhaps two or three came down: one of them dangerously close to where my group sought shelter.

There was no point in trying to flee, so I glued my face behind the mound of stones and prayed very fervently.

When I lifted my head a huge, bulging pillar of thick, black smoke rose into the air, perhaps no more than about 100 metres directly in front of me. In the hellish noise of airplane motors, anti-aircraft artillery, and exploding bombs I could not even distinguish the noise of the crash of the doomed fortress. It had probably unloaded its goodies before its end, but it did turn out to be a flying casket: only one man came down with a parachute. The commander of our group, always armed with a pistol, apprehended him as soon as he touched the ground. Ironically, he was a Dutchman: literally a "Flying Dutchman" until his landing.

Not long after the first air raid came the tragic end of the ill-fated ammunition depot mentioned earlier.

THROUGH RAGING STORM

We were having lunch in one of the storage buildings along the track. Our leader taught us, usually during the noon hour, to sing; he accompanied us with his violin. In the midst of a folk love-song such a violent blast occurred that the leader-musician dropped the violin. For a few moments we were all petrified. I thought we had not heard an air raid alarm and a huge bomb had fallen in front of the building, for the gigantic doors opened wide.

The food pouches, which we carried attached to our leather belts, lay in orderly lines and rows on the ground in one corner of the large building. After a few short moments the command *an die Brotbeutel!* (to the bread pouches!) was given and was carried out in a big hurry.

Coming through the doors we saw a large pillar of smoke and objects like black, square sheets of paper falling from high up in the air. The blast was so powerful that it bent edges of the large prefabricated sections of the walls. Parts of a similar building nearby were sucked out of its walls and were lying, pulled towards the blast, on the ground.

Besides our paramilitary unit there were also the so-called *Ostarbeiter* (Eastern workers), men and women from the occupied Poland and from areas of the Soviet Union, whose status was somewhere between that of prisoners and ordinary labourers, as well as groups of lively German girls who also worked in the area. Apparently the *Ostarbeiter* must have accidentally dropped a box of ammunition and caused the disaster. About 10 of them were blown up; some toes and pieces of a foot was all that was found of them.

One of our groups was having lunch near there in a hollow. A few of them were only wounded by flying debris. It seemed like a miracle, considering that an iron axle from a railway car, with its wheels still attached, flew over their heads and landed on the other side of the group.

We returned to the Litschau camp sometime before Christmas in 1943.

Among the European nations that are still at least nominally Christian, Christmas is a feast that evokes deep feelings. It is a religious and family solemnity that everyone

89

yearns to celebrate at home.

A few days before Christmas 1943 our camp played host to the families, primarily the ones with small children, of local servicemen who were far away: perhaps at the front, in a submarine in the middle of the stormy Atlantic, in a P.O.W. camp, or dead. We prepared a party for them in the dining hall and they came in force. What stands out in my memory is the song *O Tannenbaum,* sung by children of pre-school or kindergarten age as their expression of appreciation. With some syllables longer and others shorter than expected, and peculiarly accentuated, their angelic voices brought about a truly charming performance.

The other memorable event was the first of my four jail sojourns: up to the time of this writing, at any rate.

On Christmas eve we were allowed to go to the village. On the far side of it, by the bridge across a little brook, was its only movie theatre. On Christmas eve it showed *Ein altes Herz wird wieder jung* (An old heart becomes young again): a silly comedy about an old executive in his eighties or thereabouts, flirting with his young secretaries. The film was quite innocent in itself, especially judging by modern standards, but hardly appropriate for Christmas eve.

The movie started at eight, and everybody had to be back in camp by ten. I had no watch; there was none in the theatre itself; and it never occurred to me to ask anybody about the time. I had the notion that no movie lasted more than two hours, and time flies when it's enjoyed.

My seat was in one of the first rows of the theatre, and I thoroughly enjoyed the antics and plots of the jolly old fellow flirting with his young ladies, without realizing how late it was.

After the show the clock in the lobby showed 10 minutes past 10:00 p.m. There was no point in hoping to break the time barrier: I knew I was in trouble.

I sped through the sleepy village, then to the right up the gentle slope beyond and through the snow-bank-flanked road, taking a short-cut among tree stumps into the camp in order to avoid the guard at the gate. The camp had no fence; it was not a strictly military camp and there were no guerillas nearby. There was only one guard and he was more ceremonial than real: he had only a spade as his "weapon."

The path led right to my barrack, but I arrived from one end and the officer making the *Zapfenstreich* (final rounds), from the other.

Shortly after everybody was to have been in bed, the officer in charge went through all the rooms in every barrack. Usually he simply stepped in, turned the flashlight in all directions and continued on. I thought I could slip into the room and into bed: boots, mantle and all, in hope that the officer would not try to check if, or at least how, the clothes were piled on the stools at the foot of beds. Occasionally their folding was imperfect. If so, then it depended on the officer's mood: he may have thrown the pile off the stool or simply asked the culprit to get up and make things square and neat. I had hoped that at least on that holy eve nobody would be too punctilious.

As it happened, the officer and I met on the courtyard right in front of the entrance to my room. He flashed his flashlight into my face and told me to get ready for jail: put on shoes without laces, remove any knives from my pockets, and take off my suspenders. These measures, aimed at preventing any inmate from committing suicide, were, like the camp guard, mainly ceremonial.

No camp would have been complete without a jail, no matter how small. However, on that Christmas Eve there was an unusual number of "sinners": mostly late arrivals from the village. So, there was no more room in "the inn." What to do? The inventive, practical Teutons found a solution even to that "momentous" problem: turn the gas chamber into a jail! And that is where I did my penance.

The chamber was a simple, tightly closed room with cement floor. It was designed for only one purpose: to train in "the real thing" - tear gas - to change gas mask filters or the gas mask itself. Usually these exercises were held before lunch, and although we were in the open air after for a while, there was so much gas left in our clothing that while we were in the dining hall everyone shed tears.

That gas chamber, mercifully totally free of gas, was my inn or stable at Christmas 1943 for four nights. I was released very early on the fourth morning just in time to join the rest of the "campers" and fetch the train which took us to work in the forest.

Time went by: one day at exercises, the next at work in the forest.

How mysterious is the reality called time!

It is, like water, one of those simple things that are most extraordinary, yet so common that they are taken for granted. I can grasp the meaning of the past and the future, to some extent. But what is the present? For as soon as any given moment arrives it is already past forever. It seems to me that the present is nothing more than the shortest of all imaginable moments, or tiniest of all imaginable gaps, between the past and the future. I would go so far as to say that they are unimaginably short or tiny. Light or electricity, for instance, need only one second to travel around the earth's equator seven and a half times. Yet between two no matter how close points on the path one is in time before and one after the other...

And how relative is time, in a certain sense! When we enjoy something - a holiday, a friendly visit, a movie: anything! - the time "flies." Yet when we suffer - pain, loneliness, boredom, or whatever - it almost seems to stand still.

I used to stand guard many a dark winter night, from midnight to 2:00 a.m., or from 2:00 to 4:00 a.m., later as a soldier with a rifle, but in this camp with a spade, of all things. The post was often in a forest covered with snow and sunk into deep silence and darkness, or sighing under icy winter winds. One stood there or paced up and down a few steps each way, dragging huge straw shoes: not unlike a child playing with grandpa's boots or mother's high-heeled shoes. After an eternity one would learn from the hands on his watch dial that not even an hour had passed.

The time in the camp dragged on, seemingly without end. Finally, in the middle of February 1944, the Slovenian "campers" were taken for a tour of Vienna, and the *Sudetenländer*, the German-speaking half of our unit, went home for a short furlough. The different destinations were due to differences in conditions in our native lands. The situation in Sudetenland was more or less normal, in so far as anything can be normal in wartime. For there too, like anywhere else, one wrong sentence overheard by the "right" ears could mean execution.

In Slovenia, conditions were much different. There were partisans in the mountains. The authorities were afraid that either we would be picked up by the guerillas, or, more likely, escape to their ranks. Those who came on furloughs from the fronts were allowed to travel only as far as the southern border of Austria. The wounded in combat alone had the privilege of going all the way home: and even then not always.

Our tour of Vienna and the Sudetenlanders' home visit over, we returned to Litschau, but only to exchange our brown uniforms for the green ones: we became full-fledged soldiers.

On February 16, 1944, some time after midnight, our transport took us to a town called Mistelbach, about 30 km northeast of Vienna. It was a bitterly cold night and we had to wait, freezing outside, until dawn. Finally we were assigned to our barracks and informed that everyone was now a *Grenadier.*

The Mistelbach military compound was fairly large, and we stayed there until the early summer of 1944.

Not long after our arrival, there was a great ceremony: the *Vereidigung* (taking oath) with a general or some other "big shot" present for the occasion.

On the large square in the military compound we "neophytes" lined up in perfect formations. We had to repeat loudly, in unison, a few words at a time, the oath: *Ich schwöre bei Gott diesen heiligen Eid...* (I swear by God this holy oath, etc.). We swore solemnly to be always faithful to our fatherland and to the *Führer,* Adolf Hitler.

To me the whole affair presented a serious dilemma: I had already decided to desert or give myself up to "the enemy" at the first opportunity. And now I had to swear by God to be loyal to Adolf Hitler! Not only had the words to be shouted, but the right hand, with its index and middle fingers extended, had to be raised high.

I was in a multiple dilemma: mortal sin of perjury was out of the question; so was taking the oath; but neither did I want to be put before a firing squad.

93

What to do?

I happened to have an oversized jacket or mantle, so I pulled my left hand into the sleeve and made what we call at home "a fig": placing the thumb between the index and the middle finger. It is a sign of ridicule or denial. Sometimes this configuration of fingers is made with the thumb pointing towards the person for whom it is meant; sometimes it is turned upwards, meaning: "Sit up here and you'll see Venice." In my case, of course, the thumb pointed to the ground, but that didn't change the meaning: what my right index and middle finger did in the air was repudiated in my sleeve with the left ones. Hitler could "see Venice" even with my thumb pointing down. And to avoid any doubt about its nullity, I also explicitly contradicted it by adding a fast *nicht* (not) after the verb *schwöre*. I hope my guardian angel heard it, for it was pronounced very fast and very quietly.

Some "oath" - some circus!

Our main training took place on machine-guns, although rifles, pistols, and hand grenades were also included.

The invention of the machine-gun changed armed combat forever. It was one of the most deadly weapons in the Second World War. German machine-guns were, at that time, of two kinds: MG 34 and MG 42. Each type was called a heavy machine-gun if it was used on a tripod, and light if used without it.

The tripod could be set up so that the machine-gun became an anti-aircraft weapon. To increase stability, a second soldier was to put his leg through the two straps used for carrying the tripod and hang there, not unlike a monkey.

There were few differences between MG 34 and MG 42. The former had round holes in the pipe that encased the actual barrel; the latter had oblong ones. The encasing was round in the MG 34, and almost square in the MG 42. Tripods were the same for both types.

The main difference was in the speed of shooting: the MG 42 was much faster - so fast that there were three bullets in the barrel at any given moment during firing.

The procedure for changing the barrel was also different for each model. It was a frequent chore, because of either jamming or overheating. In the 34 model, a button had to be pressed to release the lock, and the butt rotated half way in order to shake the barrel out. In the 42 model, all one had to do was to hit a knob. The encasing opened sideways and the barrel slid out.

After every use the barrel was so hot that special pads were needed to hold it: a luxury that time did not always permit. One of our trainers, who had been in action, had burned his whole palm while changing a boiling-hot barrel, because there was no time to indulge in using a pad.

The machine-gun has a very cleverly designed mechanism, but it would take too long for my purpose here to explain it in greater detail. Let me only say that the reason for the greatly "improved" performance of the 42 model is a very simple, small gadget which brings every bullet to the barrel in two short moves rather than a longer one, as the 34 model. The result is that the girdle with cartridges practically flows, smoothly, from left to right through this hellish machine.

God only knows the number of those who perished in the fire of this deadly weapon. Soldiers who survived the hell of *Massenschlachten* (mass battles) of the Eastern Front tell how the masses of the attacking Soviet infantry were literally mowed down so that semi-circles formed before the German machine-gun nests, for one of the deadliest features of the machine-gun on a tripod is its ability to shoot over a wide horizontal angle with hardly any variation in height.

A word or two about a grenadier's personal gear.

The gas mask was the number-one nuisance among all our paraphernalia. On exercises it was hard to breathe through it, and on hot summer days sweat would drip profusely through its filter. The mask was kept in a cylindrical box made of sheet metal, corrugated for added strength. It was carried on the back, attached to the leather belt, but the jumble of straps, buckles, hooks, and buttons was too complicated to describe in brief. On top of it all, a very awkward rectangular pouch containing some kind of heavy, folded green paper, hung in front of the chest on the strap which led from the mask over the left shoulder and under the right arm back to it. In case of an attack with mist-like gas, such as first used at Ypres in the First World War, one was to put on the mask, turn the back to the wind, unfold the paper, throw one end of the sheet back over the head, step on it with the heels, crouch down, and hold the other end in front of the breast.

The mask "windows" were treated with a delicate grease on the inside to prevent fogging, and those who wore glasses had to have special frames held with narrow strips around the ears.

The gas mask was a constant, although very unwelcome companion, except when one was off duty: usually at the movie theatre or in a restaurant on a Sunday afternoon. It had to stand always ready during the night near the head, and along with the rifle and the steel helmet it had to be taken to the air raid shelter or trench during every *Fliegeralarm*.

Standard equipment included a cap, either a canoe-shaped one or one with a shield. The latter had a fold all around, which was fastened in front with two small buttons. In winter the flap could be unfolded and buttoned under the chin: a very good idea. Of course, everyone also had a steel helmet.

The heavy leather belt had a buckle with the inscription *Gott mit uns* (God with us) or *Blut und Ehre* (Blood and Honour). The belt was not meant to support the pants; for that, one only needed suspenders or else an ordinary belt. The heavy leather belt was designed to hold or suspend all kinds of junk. There were leather pouches for cartridges, fastened together in rows of five; a bayonet and its scabbard; a leather casing with a small spade; a felt-covered coffee bottle; a food pouch; and last, but not least, the hated gas mask.

With all that weight, something had to keep the belt from slipping. A simple device did the trick: two straps, woven of strong threads, one over each shoulder, under the jacket. At each end of them, strong and fairly long hooks were fastened; they came through the holes in the jacket and held up the leather belt. The two front hooks could also hold two egg-shaped hand grenades; the ones with handles had to be tucked under the belt.

One Sunday afternoon I went to an amusement area in which there was a heavy wire cage, suspended on iron posts. Standing in it and holding the inside bars on the opposite sides of the cage, the aim was to rock it back and forth so that finally it would begin making complete circles. I had almost made it when one of the two hooks at the back caught the wire fence and tore out the whole back of the jacket.

Our uniform was the well-known green *Wehrmacht* (Army: literally, "defense might") outfit, and we wore either ordinary high shoes or leather boots.

An ordinary "working" day began quite early with the sound of a whistle, a bell, or a trumpet. In each garrison either one was used at all times. One thing, though, was always the same: in the German labour and army camps, as well as later in the Yugoslavian army we had to jump from our beds into our pants and shoes and gather outside for about 20 minutes of calisthenics - rain or shine, snow or hail!

After that, beds had to be made with consummate perfection. To achieve it, boards were often used, sometimes in teams of two, although it was nearly impossible to make edges and corners perfectly square when the straw in the mattresses had become like oats.

Then came the scrubbing of the floors which were usually made of pine planks. Only after that were we permitted to line up for breakfast. All the activities before breakfast had to be carried out in a feverish hurry, as if time was running out.

After breakfast there was the ceremony for hoisting the flag, the review by the commanders, the receiving of orders for the day, and then the usual military exercises for about three or four hours. Drills resumed again after lunch.

More than once our whole unit or smaller groups of soldiers were transferred to some other place. Wherever we found ourselves, it did not take very long before we had marched or trained through all the villages, fields, and forests within a radius of about 20 or 30 km of camp. Rivers were crossed using three ropes: one under the feet and one under each armpit. By night we learned how easily and far away a spoon tap on a pot can be heard, or a single drag of a cigarette seen. The lesson was, of course, to avoid such mistakes in real war.

Naturally, our training would have been deemed quite incomplete without some gas-related activity, besides the mere changing of filters or masks in a gas chamber. So we learned how to cross misty-gas-infected ground and mark it with yellow streamers to alert others.

Exercises could be quite strenuous: long marches in sweltering summer heat; running or crawling with a rifle, machine-gun, or with heavy cases of ammunition in each hand tied together with a broad belt around one's neck, or with a tripod which alone weighed about 20 kg; plus all the other standard gear, while wearing a steel helmet and gas mask. One usually tried to partly unscrew the mask filter in order to breathe easier. Sometimes we were caught, but it was well worth trying.

The hardest sessions were those held in early spring, over the muddy, ploughed clay fields with the snow just melted. After crawling on our bellies, handfuls of wet, sticky mud clung to us and all our gear. There were times on our way back through the town when people would stop and shake their heads in disbelief.

This "training" usually took place before noon. After lunch we went to a large room with a number of troughs and taps, and one or two hours later stood on the courtyard clean and ready for review. Don't ask me how this was possible: I don't know. I only know that it had to be done and that it was done.

During my sojourn in Mistelbach we had quite a scare during one of the air raid alarms.

On a beautiful, sunny day, the sirens suddenly began to squeal. As usual, we took to the trenches between the barracks. Being close to one of them, I only heard the planes until they could be seen over its roof. It was a sunny day and when I looked up huge formations of planes were approaching like flocks of birds, and they flew directly overhead. The "enemy" must have known there was a large military compound on the edge of Mistelbach, or at least the pilots must have seen soldiers in the trenches, presuming they were not blind. My feelings as I looked and waited for the hundreds or thousands of bombs to begin their deadly descent cannot be described adequately. The anxiety was compounded by a feeling of utter helplessness. I felt a mysterious force in the upper front of my shoulders which seemed to pull me, like gravity, to some safe place far away.

Not a single bomb fell anywhere near. It turned out that the planes flew in from Italy over Hungary and were completing their U-turn over Mistelbach to attack some suburbs of Vienna from the north. The rolling thunder of the bombardment could be heard distinctly; and later, a huge black cloud hovered over the southern horizon.

The countryside around Mistelbach was rolling farmland. Cherry trees grew on both sides of most roads between the fields and over little hills. It was a beautiful sight to see cherry trees in blossom, and good to taste some of their abundant fruit later on. One or the other of my companions invited himself on a free Sunday afternoon to pick some cherries fresh from the trees. Usually, though, we could only look at them as we marched through alleys of cherry trees on our exercises around the town, or all the way to the large oilfields at Zistersdorf in today's northeastern Austria. For the main task of our garrison, in addition to training, was to protect these vital oilfields. There had to be enough soldiers ready for any eventuality at all times, and there always had to be a fire squad ready in case of air raids: the Allies never announced their weekly or monthly schedules.

Next spring, in 1945, I recalled the beautiful and tasty cherries of Mistelbach when, as a prisoner of war in Russia, I happened to read the report of a war correspondent who was accompanying the advancing Red Army through that area: "Cherries are blossoming along the roads of our advance..."

During my stay in Mistelbach those of us from my native district were promised a furlough by a somewhat thoughtless commander. The German word for furlough is *Urlaub*. As the promised furlough never came, we began to become impatient. Storming imaginary enemy positions during exercises we usually shouted hurrah, hurrah. Instead, now we began to shout *Urlaub! Urlaub!* In wartime a single wrong word or sentence can mean execution, without any of the niceties of legal process or red tape. Apparently, as they say, "our number was not yet up."

I was still in Mistelbach when we learned by radio about the Allied invasion at Normandy which took place on June 6, 1944. I happened to drop into the canteen for a beer, probably during the noon-time break. Whether it was a *Sondermeldung* (special report) or simply part of the regular radio news, all it said was that some enemy units had landed in Normandy and that they were still being chased off the beaches. The exact wording escapes my memory but I remember clearly that many soldiers, most of whom were recuperating from wounds incurred in battle but were well enough to be our trainers, were visibly startled. Sitting at tables, they lifted their heads, turned towards the radio, and listened intently. I don't recall any comments. Everyone was silent. There was almost an air of solemnity.

A few days or weeks later, some small units of the garrison were transferred. Some were sent to the front, but I found myself in Amstetten, a town still in Austria, but farther up the Danube river, nearer Bavaria in Germany.

Life there did not bring anything new. All was *déjà vu,* except that there were apparently no cherry trees, either in blossom or with ripe cherries, anywhere in the area.

Either at Amstetten or near a large *Truppenübungsplatz* (military training area) mentioned later, there was a P.O.W. camp. It was located up a slope just across the road in front of our compound. There were rows of the usual prefabricated buildings, like the ones we had in Litschau, behind a barbed-wire fence, and guard towers here and there along the fence. I believe there were mainly British and American airmen in that camp. Many a time I envied them, or perhaps more correctly, I was tempted to envy their lot. By all appearances they had a much easier life than I. The food was probably comparable. In fact, there were piles of empty cans behind their barracks sent through the Red Cross. And I had really no more freedom than they.

True, they were prisoners, but so was I, in actual fact. Moreover, not only did I consider my captors enemies: I myself was one of them, wearing their very uniform and weapons! It is hard to be a soldier in wartime, suffering for the homeland and hoping for victory. But to march with those who destroyed your own homeland, convinced that their doom was sealed, and at the same time be one of them: how, in God's name, can one describe that?

Indeed, I carried a double burden: it was not only a question of language, homeland, or nationality; it was also a question of faith and morals, with consequences for a believer extending beyond the grave to eternity. For the purpose of our training was not to learn how to plant daisies or tend the sheep...

# THROUGH RAGING STORM

While in Amstetten, we went for a week or two to the large *Truppenübungsplatz* mentioned earlier, for training with live ammunition. We marched from Amstetten for two days to get there. The road led through somewhat unusual land formations: from one quite wide land plateau downhill through forests to the next one, and then to a third and towards a wide river (Danube?). We were to cross it as part of our exercises but for some reason did not.

The area of this large training ground included one or two ghost villages. Grass growing in the middle of streets enhanced the strangeness of the already eerie atmosphere of the seemingly God-forsaken place.

The image of this whole area is not very clear in my memory. This location is not the only one that has been obscured in my mind by the sands of time: nearly 50 years of it. I was in many places as a worker, soldier, or prisoner of war, both during and after the Second World War. Images of places or scenery often crop up in my mind, and sometimes I cannot recall where they were. At times I am not even sure if they are real.

I do know that my sojourn in Austria came to an end in the summer of 1944, when we were loaded on a freight train. Because of the war, our destination was unknown.

We travelled into Bavaria, then through Nürnberg where the grounds for Nazi parades and celebrations, which were very near the railway tracks, could be observed in all their pompous, cold grandiosity. Then the train sped through the lovely Neckar valley with its vineyards, through the cities of Heilbronn and Karlsruhe, and over the Rhine into Alsace.

Our destination turned out to have been a town called Bitsch, with a large military garrison. It was situated in the midst of the massive bunkers of the Maginot Line: one of the most gigantic undertakings since the building of the pyramids and, in my humble opinion, one of the most useless.

Not far from Bitsch are the Vosges mountains or rather hills, covered with bush and forest, dreary and strange. It's odd to see such a melancholy area smack in the middle of Western Europe. In that general area, between France and Germany, some of the most bloody, titanic battles in the history of wars were fought. Names like Marne, Moselle, Verdun, Vimy, and many others, speak volumes.

One memory from that area stands out in my mind. We were somewhere in these drab, bushy hills on exercises when during an air raid alarm, we sought cover in one of the mighty bunkers of the Maginot Line. A couple, evidently husband and wife, were already there when we arrived. In the middle of the monstrous bunker stood a carriage with their baby sleeping in it like an angel.

On the first day of our arrival in Bitsch we were made unmistakably aware that not all was "quiet on the Western front." The invasion was in full swing following the Allied landings in Normandy and the sirens squealed, usually several times every day.

There were three different kinds of signals, each starting and ending on a very low pitch, and lasting perhaps about one minute.

The most dreaded one was the *Fliegeralarm* (fliers alarm): a howl like of a pack of hungry wolves. The sound ascended and descended like waves on a stormy sea. There may have been ten or more such waves in one minute.

Another signal, called *Fliegerwarnung* (fliers warning), consisted of only about three waves, but their crests were prolonged. It meant that the danger of an impending air raid was real but remote. This signal was given relatively rarely, and was followed either by a full-scale alarm or by the *Entwarnung.*

If anyone of the trio could be called nice, it was the *Entwarnung.* I would translate, or better, transliterate, the word as "unwarning." It meant that the danger was over. What a welcome sound it was!

The first two above mentioned siren signals were nerve wrecking, and by night at least twice as bad as by day. To wake from a well-deserved sleep, dress in a nervous hurry, grab the rifle and gas mask, and run either into trenches - rain, shine, snow, or hail - or down into a cellar, is no fun. The heavily-laden planes flying high overhead compound the feeling of utter helplessness and fear of being any moment torn to pieces, buried, or slowly fried alive.

Hundreds of thousands, probably millions, of men and

women of all ages and conditions perished during the Second World War in such grisly ways, in some instances tens of thousands in one single outburst of sheer hell. Such deliberate attacks on residential areas were quite evidently aimed at demoralizing the enemy. Yet, in the case of the British during the *Blitz,* and later in Japan and Germany, the will to resist and fight on seems to have been, if anything, strengthened.

On July 20, 1944, the ill-fated assassination attempt on Hitler took place. I was still in Bitsch at the time and the only perceptible change, as far as the soldiers were concerned, was in the manner of greeting the flag or one's superiors. Although earlier in the State Labour Service we had to greet the flag and our superiors with the well-known Hitler greeting, in the German army the military salute had been identical to the one known in other armies, only somewhat more stiff and brusque - until July 20, 1944. Then it was replaced with the *Hitler Gruss* (Hitler salute). It consisted of the raising of the outstretched right arm with outstretched fingers to about the hight of one's eyes or a little higher. If it took place during a walk, the head had to be turned towards the person being greeted, and the walk turned into the well-known "goose step."

We had been sent all the way from today's Austria to France: certainly in order to regroup, and almost certainly to regroup for deployment on the Western front, established only a few weeks earlier with the Allied invasion of Europe.

It would seem ridiculous to send a contingent of soldiers from Austria all the way to France to regroup, and then back east to far-away Poland instead of to Normandy, not much farther to the west.

However, during our sojourn in Alsace, in July 1944, the Soviet Red Army made a huge breakthrough into southeastern Poland. And so, we headed east again. Of course, at the time of our departure no ordinary soldier knew our destination. Such matters are top secret in wartime. There were rumours that we were on the way to a large troop exercise area near Königsberg in East Prussia, today's Russian city of Kaliningrad, on the Baltic Sea. As it turned out we all too soon found ourselves on the largest *Truppenübungsplatz* in the history of mankind.

The evening before departure was set aside for an *Abschiedsfeier* (farewell celebration). All I remember is that about 10 or 20 of us sat in a rather small room and drank some wine.

Next evening at dusk we took our belongings to a grassy slope in a narrow, eerie valley with a small river and steep, bushy slopes rising on the opposite banks to a hight of perhaps 100 metres. A long train of cattle-cars shunted on the rails on our side of the river, and it was already dark by the time we had it loaded with the usual military necessities, and our own gear. Finally, we boarded the train.

In many places along the route, we could see results of bombardments. One scene reminds me now, if not then, that life is stronger than death.

The train went slowly past a savagely hit area of a small town. I can still see large slabs of broken concrete floors lying in more-or-less inclined positions, in the midst and on top of rubble and over the leftovers of basement windows, doors, and walls. Yet a lively group of happy children found the ghastly site, to all appearances, very fascinating: a new horizon to explore and discover. They were climbing up and down the slabs, full of life, joy and laughter: an image of bubbling life and joy in the midst of death and gloom; a bright ray of hope and love in the darkest night of hatred and despair.

Some of the places through which the train took us and whose names I still recall were Kaiserslautern, Mainz, Frankfurt, Schweinfurt, Bamberg, Dresden, and Hirschberg. The last-mentioned city was already in Schlesien (Silesia), a region that is now the southwestern part of Poland.

Approaching Mainz on the Rhine the train sped through fertile flatland of rich orchards, with vegetables growing between and under the fruit trees and clusters of large bomb craters. In the east far beyond the orchards appeared the hills of Schwarzwald (Black Forest) rising from the eastern banks of the Rhine river.

Halfway up the hill side, in the midst of dark forests of Schwarzwald, a bright patch that looks like a huge meadow or a field of buckwheat in bloom can be seen from far away. It is the famous monument Germania. I do not recall seeing the statue itself because it was too far away. On pictures it resembles the Statue of Liberty, with elaborate grounds surrounding it. This massive structure was built to commemorate the German victory in the Franco-Prussian war of 1870 - 71.

The sun was setting as our train passed over the Rhine: like a reddish-yellow disc about to plunge directly into the waters of this mighty river.

Somewhere farther in Germany there was an air raid alarm, and the train stopped in the middle of a forest. The wise Croatian folk proverb "There is no wind so evil that it would not blow somebody some good" was proven true: we went into the forest to pick some of the most delicious berries.

In Dresden we made a long stop. There I read in the newspaper the names of three or four Polish cities that were *planmässig geräumt* (planfully evacuated): a wartime phrase meaning "lost." Who would have dreamt then what horrible fate awaited that lovely city. It was there, at the station, that huge heaps of charred human remains were piled up to be allegedly doused with gasoline and burned after the horrible fire-bombing of February 1945.

At sundown our train left Dresden; somewhere around the city of Hirschberg the night fell. Before dawn we passed through some forests and heard rifle shots close by; and in the morning the scenery changed. The buildings looked much poorer than in Silesia. Along one embankment a long freight train lay rolled sideways downhill, derailed no doubt by the partisans.

Our train stopped at a small station called Debica. On one side some agricultural machines stood, obviously waiting to be loaded and shipped away. On the other side, among some scattered fruit trees, soldiers were digging fox holes.

We could hear the distant thunder of gun-fire.

Our transport brought from France certainly more than a company of infantry: more likely a whole battalion or more. In successive regroupings, the unit of about 70 or so of my countrymen that arrived in Litschau following our conscription, seemed to have been systematically watered down: diluted, as it were, more or less evenly into larger and larger units. The result was that only a few of us remained in my company, with a few more in the same battalion, and the rest God knows where throughout Europe. Even the majority of my German companions were strangers to me on our arrival in Poland.

No time at all was wasted. Immediately following the disembarkation we all set out, marching, but not all together: companies, or even smaller units, followed their own leaders and destinations. Leaders there were, certainly, but I am not so certain that there were any destinations.

For about two or three days my unit marched almost continuously: sometimes near, sometimes more away from the front; now on paved highway, then through muddy field roads. Most of the time it poured rain. Our knapsacks with their square, brown calf-pelt covers, each with a blanket neatly rolled hard and fastened on both sides and across the top of the knapsack with leather straps, had been put on horse-drawn wagons at the Debica railway station. That was where I last saw mine. But we had to carry all the rest of our military gear.

On our wandering march we witnessed a variety of scenes. During a pouring rain, my platoon dropped into a house near the main road for a short stop. A young husband and wife (I don't recall seeing any children) sat dejected on some wooden boxes in the middle of the room, evidently ready to leave any moment.

On a road through the fields we met another couple on a horse-drawn wagon. They were rather elderly, alone, and also westbound. On the small wagon with iron-clad wheels, there was besides the two lone travellers only some hay with a few bundles and several black pots and pans.

Who can be sure that the flight and plight of one or the other, or both, of these two couples did not end in the infernal fires of Dresden the following February? The city had been spared before and therefore considered safe. At the time of its doom it was packed with refugees from Eastern Europe.

We also passed the remains of a row of houses built along one side of the road at considerable distance from each other and with some fields behind them and then forest higher up a slope. They must have been built almost entirely of wood, for all that was left of them were the fireplaces and the brick chimneys. The rest was ashes. Here and there a little smoke was still rising.

In a small meadow, a man wearing a shield cap lay on his

back, dead: no doubt a Polish resistance fighter.

In an area of fields with some wood-covered small hills beyond, several Tiger tanks seemed to have been waiting for us. Soon they rumbled on, accompanied by our unit forming a line on both sides: men walking a few metres behind each other with arms at the ready. After a while the tanks rolled on while we combed the thick, wet bushes up and down the little hills and through the fields. Once, we came upon a tank that had tried to cross a small bridge on a narrow, winding road up a wooded hill side. It had crushed the wooden bridge and lay in an awkward position in the creek bed, squeezed between the two cement walls at each end of the bridge.

The march went on and on, for two or three days, with little break. No matter how wet the ground: if we stopped, even for a few minutes, everyone just slumped to the ground and fell asleep.

On one occasion I literally slept while marching. It happened at night on a paved highway. The column marched in rows of five and I happened to be on the extreme left edge. Even though the order was not very precise, I noticed that again and again I woke up a few steps to the left of all the rest. When I returned, the same thing happened again, repeatedly. The deviation was always in the same direction: one would have expected bumping now and then into the man on the right. Years after the war the mystery was solved. Most people, I learned, have one leg slightly longer than the other, and I must have been blessed with a longer right one.

Towards the end of this wandering march, we climbed one evening from a fairly deep valley on a steep, winding road through a pine forest up to some meadows. A small farmhouse stood there and a barn with an inviting hay-loft. The owner was very reluctant to accept us, and was really afraid or pretending to be afraid that the loft would not hold the weight of so many soldiers. We slept there on the welcome hay overnight, and nothing happened, except that I lost or forgot there my raincoat: a triangular piece of canvas with a slit to put head through. It was so designed that, from three or more of them, tents could be created. The result of my loss was that from then on - mercifully not very long - I was not only very hungry but also very wet.

During that two or three-day march, I don't think we got any meals.

In the morning, while some open trucks were waiting for us, I had a powerful urge to step behind the building, hide, and wait for the Red Army. What would have happened to me remains pure speculation: the front remained almost stationary for over four months. The final massive push by the Red Army began only the next year in January.

Standing in the trucks, we drove through the village of Jaslo and towards the next one called Krosno where we alighted. Here we got, finally, some good, warm soup and bread. We were also given the chance to sit down on the curb of the road and write a letter. In wartime it is strictly forbidden for a soldier to indicate the place when writing letters. I had heard how in the First World War my mother's brother Frank had written from Bukovina in Rumania. Using his tactics I too wrote some fictitious names of friends, sending their greetings. The first letters of their names, read backwards, spelled Galicija. It was my last letter. After my return I learned that the message arrived and was decoded right off the bat, because my relatives still remembered my uncle's stratagem.

Passing over the bridge in the middle of Krosno I saw a destroyed Russian T34 tank below. It had obviously tried to cross the shallow water but was "liquidated" in the process. A little further on a house had been hit by a shell and another had burned down. Having reached the other fringe of the village, our platoon formed a goose line, walking about 10 steps one behind another, crossed some fields, and passed an abandoned Soviet army cauldron on two wheels standing there. It was uncovered but there was no time to look if there was any *kásha* (stew) left. Further down the fields some 15 or 20 destroyed Soviet tanks as well as some other armoured vehicles lay scattered. Nearby, there was a solitary house with mattresses piled in the middle of the courtyard, and no people in sight. The owners may have hoped that if either the house or the mattresses were destroyed, at least the other would remain to provide some shelter.

After walking for a while in line, everyone turned right to form a row and go up the gentle, ploughed slope towards the top of a hill. It was some time in the middle of the day and the rain had stopped, at least for a while.

Suddenly a swish was heard close overhead, and soon after a mortar shell exploded behind us in the flatland. Then another. And several more. Glued to the good old mother earth I looked back. Small clouds of black smoke hovered over the field. Then suddenly the shells began to fall closer, indeed much too close for comfort. Following the old adage "if you find it too hot in the kitchen get out" I got up and ran uphill, veering to the left. But this devil's kitchen was too big for escape: shells were falling everywhere, with shrapnel whirring past me. There was only one thing to do: lie down in a large furrow between two fields of different crops. It led all the way from the horizon, near the top of the nicely rounded hill, down to near the end of the slope. I expected the "enemy" to appear over the horizon. Instead, when the shelling stopped, two of my "friends" came down the furrow: two unknown German soldiers. They must have sensed there was something out of the ordinary for me to lie there all by myself. One of them beckoned me to follow them and our destination turned out to be my unit commander with a few others crouching behind a hazelnut bush at the base of the slope. The commander looked at me with glaring eyes that were about to pop out of their sockets, while his right hand moved slowly across the stomach and reached for the revolver on the left side of his belt. Perhaps he expected me to jump on him in my desperation, which, in the circumstances, would have been without the slightest doubt the end of my journey.

As he slowly pointed the revolver at my chest, I was much more inclined to think he would pull the trigger than not. On the front a human life counts for little more than that of a bumble-bee. There are no lawyers, juries or inquests. After the war I learned about the tragic end of one of my buddies, a very friendly Viennese. He shot himself - I believe he blew his thumb off - in order to get away from the front. When the truth became known, my friend was dispatched then and there, without any further ado: a friendly teenager, in the prime of life.

As a boy I had heard how soldiers in the First World War would shoot themselves through a loaf of bread to prevent any burns, traces of gun-smoke, or other signs which could betray the real cause of their wound.

Strangely, I could not have cared less at the time if the trigger were pulled or not. Perhaps part of it can be explained by the exhaustion, hunger, and stress, but a very substantial part remains a mystery.

If memory serves, the thought of my mother crying when she would have learned of my death occurred to me. That was hard to take even in my extraordinary situation. In any case, I did the only thing I could think of: I pretended that I was afraid. Deliberately I began to shake slightly.

As far as I can recall, no words were uttered by anyone during this whole encounter. Finally the officer, all the while angrily staring straight in my eyes, slowly put the revolver back into its scabbard and ordered me, with a threat of death, to go to the hill top.

The day was turning slowly to dusk and on the top of the hill some foxholes here and there looked more like shallow graves with breastwork at their end that was nearer the other side of the gently rounded hill top which ran, now higher now lower, in an irregular direction left and right as far as the eye could see. We happened to be on one of its highest elevations. Because of little earth on top of the rocky ground, the holes were only deep enough to lie in. I got into the one farthest to the front, almost slightly down on the other side of the hill, and spent most of the next two nights there, and the day between. There was no need to dig any new holes: we found enough of them for every man of my unit already dug out, complete with a sheaf of wheat in each one for greater "comfort," especially in the rainy weather which predominated at the time.

During all my stay on the hill, we neither ate nor drank, and no permission was given to open our emergency rations, a relatively small can containing something like liver paste, which every front soldier was obliged to carry at all times in his food pouch, but was strictly forbidden to open except on command, in extreme emergency. Now and then a heavy artillery shell would fly high above with its swishy sound, and explode with a thump somewhere far behind us. Here and there in the distance, billowing plumes of thick, black smoke rose high into the sky, apparently from burning oil wells. From time to time, more or less far to our left or right, rifle fire broke out, mixed with short, fast bursts of German machine-guns and the longer, slower rattling of the Russian ones. The latter were water-cooled and not carried but dragged around, mounted on two small wheels. By night tracer-bullets, sparsely mixed with ordinary ones, appeared from time to time both during incoming and outgoing machine-gun fire, for better accuracy. In one outburst of hostilities, there was a lot of commotion on one of the higher areas: silhouettes of men running back and forth on the horizon in evening dusk, amidst much rifle and some machine-gun fire.

Early next morning, just before dawn, an attack was launched against my own unit. Soviet soldiers appeared from behind groups of bushes on the flatland to the east of our positions. They charged uphill in the midst of a pandemonium of rifle and machine-gun fire from both sides, shouting repeatedly *hurráh, hurráh, hurráh la la la laaa...* The shouting was not wild at all but evoked, at least in me, a feeling of pity, almost compassion. It sounded like a pleading for mercy.

My foxhole was so shallow that my shoulders were not much below the top of it. Incoming bullets were striking all around, and many of the outgoing ones also travelled dangerously low overhead, with the majority of the soldiers of my platoon in holes behind mine. I was about to shoot aimlessly into the air above the heads of Russians, but the thought occurred to me that perhaps somebody might be hit by chance somewhere far behind in the lowland. So, I never fired a shot on the front, and no mother ever shed one single tear because of a squeeze of my index finger.

How could I ever thank God for this unspeakable grace?!

I fully expected the Russians to overrun our positions and was planning to pretend I was dead or else to look up from the hole begging by word or gesture not to be finished off by a bayonet.

I don't know exactly how long the whole episode lasted, for I did not even raise my head from the hole, and had no time to think about time.

Our positions were not overrun; once again the wild German machine-guns, manned by soldiers with few equals in the world, prevailed.

The *hurráh, hurráh, hurráh la la la laaa* cries gradually died out, together with the young men (some still teenagers?) uttering them. The shooting stopped gradually, and everything became suspiciously quiet. I have no idea how many attackers died, or how many may have escaped, or what was going on immediately after the battle. All I remember is a short exchange of words between two soldiers in holes behind me. One quipped: "He didn't shoot at all," to which the other replied: "I believe he is a foreigner." That I lived to reminisce is proof that those two were not likely the ones who picked me up in the furrow the day before.

Retaliation for the Russian defeat was not slow in coming.

Some time later in the day a mortar shell was shot from the flatland in front of us; it came down with the fluttering noise of the fins that prevent it from tumbling and losing its proper direction, and exploded dangerously near. Then another. And another. Some were fired from near the bottom of the slope ahead of us. Others came from far away: some from the right, some from the left - from behind trees, hedges, and thicketed farmlands.

Mortars, like other kinds of artillery (I served later in the Yugoslavian artillery from 1947 to 1949) zero in on their target by first trying to overshoot, then undershoot, then halving the distance between the impacts as often as necessary to achieve optimal range. A single gunner can do that for a whole battery. After that, shells can be lobbed on and around the target with relative precision and ease.

At the beginning, one shot at a time was fired by each unit of mortars; then six or seven went off in fast succession. As mortar shells travel relatively slowly, their going-off is heard quite a few seconds before they begin to come down, and one's feelings in between can become very tense. It did not take very long before shells went off far and near, left and right, all over the rolling countryside to the east of our hill range. A cluster of six or seven of them fell just behind, in front, and to the right of me.

Shouts of *Sanitäter! Sanitäter!* (medic! medic!) began to multiply while the air became saturated with the stench of powder.

I was glued to the bottom of my hole with my head

pressed into one corner and my steel helmet shoved as far onto my shoulders as possible. Splinters were whirring all over the place; one or the other hit the inner edge of my foxhole and caused chunks of wet mud to fall in. I was sweating from fear and two things went through my mind as the shells descended: one was the thought of my mother and father crying at the news of my death, the other was the fear that my bowels would be torn out any moment by a shell or shrapnel with terrible pain. The one consoling thought, if it could have been called consoling, was that if thousands of others were able to suffer it somehow, surely I was able to, too.

And do I really need to confide that I was praying? In fact, I even made a vow to say five times the Our Father, the Hail Mary and the Glory Be if spared. It was fulfilled a day or two later.

How long this shelling lasted is hard to guess. It certainly seemed like half an eternity; yet even that came to an end.

The night fell. Rain was pouring. I had no rain canvas to cover the foxhole as I had lost it a few days earlier in that hay loft near Jaslo. Now and then the clouds broke and the full moon shone brightly through.

One or two hours after midnight the night became pitch-dark again and another heavy downpour started. The soldiers were in fox holes covered with their rain canvasses. I knew that the moon would come out again, sooner rather than later.

It was "now or never."

I got out of the hole, leaving my two egg-shaped hand grenades at the edge. Bent down, with my rifle in my hands, I went stealthily towards and then behind a small bush a little to the left and ahead. Had I been caught, I would have said that I heard a rustling there: it would have been no lie, for the heavy rain caused considerable rustle in that small bush.

Immediately beyond it, rows of a potato field stretched all the way downhill, almost to the end of the slope. I knelt down on a knee, rifle in hand, as if reconnoitring the area.

I lay down between two rows and crawled downhill on my stomach as fast as I could. It was still very dark, for the full moon was still behind the clouds from which the rain still poured down. Its noise was welcome music to my ears as it drowned out the noise of rustling potato plants. Although it was merely a potato field, I was still not "out of the woods." There was the possibility of hitting a mine. An even more likely danger could have been a *Vorposten:* a soldier hidden ahead of the main unit, whose job is to observe the movements of the enemy and alert the unit of an impending attack.

At the bottom of the potato field I left my rifle and continued to push ahead on my stomach over the meadow, propelling myself only with my elbows and toes. This was a precaution against being seen, especially on the horizon against the sky. For the rain seemed to have been gradually subsiding, and the night was becoming lighter. I crossed some tracks, probably left by tanks heard rumbling there the day or night before, and reached a patch of trees and bushes in the middle of the field. There I ventured to get up and walk, keeping always considerably to the right, due to the contour of the land. I crossed one or two military telephone wires lying on the ground, and went past a huge bomb crater with large chunks of clay scattered all around it. Not far ahead a few houses stood in an irregular row, with a country road in front of them leading eastwards. Behind the houses and along the road further down, there was a not very high but rather steep slope with orchards. The road appeared to climb further down gradually up the side of the slope, but was soon lost in the scattered thickets and trees.

I stopped at a small well near the first house: the kind with a waist-high, round stone wall around it, two posts with a horizontal crankshaft between them, and a narrow roof above the length of the crankshaft as if made only for it. Water is scooped up by lowering the bucket attached to a rope wound around the crankshaft.

Leaning against the stone wall of the well, I thought about the events of the last few days - and hours - not entirely sure whether they were a dream or reality, nor whether I was awake or dreaming. After all the marching and sleepless nights, with one meal in two or three days, I found myself now wet and cold, muddy and exhausted, at this well in no man's land between two formidable armies and far from home: yet my whole being was suffused with an indescribable happiness.

This well in far away Poland is one of my indelible memories.

Temptation to rest there and daydream for a while was strong, but there was no time to tarry: the front was too close and woe if I got caught.

The accounts of mountaineers in the Julian Alps came to mind. They used to tell us, gathered around the warm oven on some long winter evenings, what happens when thick clouds cover the peaks and mountainsides. One tends to go in circles, always returning to more or less the same spot. At all costs I had to avoid returning back to my own units. So I did what I would never do again in such circumstances, especially in view of later experiences during my escape back through the Iron Curtain in 1950. I knocked on the door of one of the houses.

It seems the people were prepared for any eventuality: even though it was such an ungodly hour, almost immediately a fully dressed man opened the door. God knows what he thought when he saw a German soldier with steel helmet on and in full gear, except for any weapons. I don't recall what I did or said, or even what language was used, except that I asked which way the Russians were. He turned right almost all the way around and made signs with his arm: this way and that. Either straight up the slope behind the houses, or to the left, eastwards along the road. Without much hesitation I chose the second option: the first seemed too parallel to the front.

I took off somewhat to the right of the road, between the fruit trees, over the hill, and down the field on the plateau, coming before very long again back to the same road. All the while I was keeping both hands on my helmet as I had seen Russians doing in war reports shown before every movie. Having come back to the road, I followed it. As the winding road climbed gradually uphill, the bushy slopes on each side became lower and lower until it reached a plateau: an open field stretching far to the left, right, and ahead of me.

Suddenly from the left, in the very early morning silence, a piercing scream resounded: *STOI!* (stop!).

Turning left and lifting my hands high, I stopped as if petrified or nailed to the spot. Across the recently harvested wheat-field, a Russian soldier ran towards me, his arm stretched ahead as if he was chasing it and was about to trip and fall. In his hand, right in front of his face, he held the familiar large, crooked, awkward looking pistol Russian soldiers wore on a chain long enough to remain attached to the belt even while the pistol was being used. Running as fast as he could, he pointed the pistol straight at me all the time.

It did not take very long before he reached me, panting heavily and visibly very nervous. In his place I would have been, too: who knew what was in that gully behind me? He grabbed me and made me walk ahead of him across the field to a gun emplacement, under a canvas tent near the hedge. By then the other members of his crew were up and around. They saw that I was alone and I told them I was "Yugoslav"; both these facts seemed to calm the atmosphere considerably.

My steel helmet was hastily removed, as well as my belt with the bayonet, gas mask, and all the rest that hung about me. I can't recall if I had a watch, the most prized trophy in the eyes of Soviet captors at that time, as my fellow prisoners of war would recount later. Even my handkerchief was taken away. The only two objects left, besides my uniform, were my spoon, and cap which had been tucked behind my belt.

It was early dawn on Friday, August 4, 1944.

A large stretch of my Odyssey had just been completed. A new one had already begun.

I was a prisoner of war: one of the most pathetic modes of existence on the face of the planet Earth.

# Chapter Six

# Under the Red Eastern Skies

There is a popular saying: "From the frying pan into the fire." It describes in a picturesque manner the state of affairs when a very bad situation is succeeded by a worse than the previous one. This chapter could very appropriately be titled: "From fire into the frying pan," or perhaps: "From one frying pan into another."

With all my gear gone, except the spoon and the cap, I was able to "travel light," as the saying goes. A soldier led me down into a shrubby gully at the end of the field and up to a house on top of the other side where a lone soldier kept guard near a tree.

It was still very early and I had to wait for a long time in the courtyard surrounded with trees. After the rains a colder air had moved in and as I was still wet I was shivering. The soldier kept an eye on me until finally the officer and others who slept in the house got up. I was glad to be allowed to go in. It was a very simple house, with a clay floor and beds of simple wooden boxes with straw. I was given some warm soup and food which, no matter how ordinary, tasted heavenly and fit perfectly into my empty stomach. No ambrosia or nectar could have tasted better than the simple, warm broth prepared by the poor Polish lady of the house.

After a brief questioning, I was taken by guard to the headquarters of a larger military unit. A woman officer took me to the edge of a field where we sat and she questioned me in more detail. My mother tongue belongs to the Slavic family of languages, so we were able to communicate well enough for the purposes at hand. She was particularly interested if there were many soldiers in the area, and she seemed very surprised, even worried, when she heard that our transport had just arrived all the way from France.

I was then taken over by a guard on horseback, with a sub-machine-gun hanging around his neck. I walked in front of the horse, on very muddy country roads over a countryside which appeared to me quite strange. It is the area where the Carpathian mountains are gradually turning into the large Polish flatland. Mostly, there are small rolling hills with rich wheat-fields, but this particular district was quite peculiar. It seemed I was walking on ridges while on both sides there were slopes down into not-too-deep, bowl-shaped valleys. I had a distinct feeling of an inverted landscape.

After a fairly long trip we arrived at a barn where there were already about a dozen other prisoners of war. Two were in yellow Hungarian uniforms, and it turned out that they were natives of the area of Yugoslavia occupied by Hungary. They all seemed very downcast and tired. From there we were all taken after one or two days to a military unit camping in a forest. There we were fed some thick *kásha*, which is Russian for just about any kind of porridge or stew, as long as it is fairly thick. At dusk we were taken out of the forest to lie  overnight near its edge, close to one another, with our heads at the roadside and feet pointing away from it. A soldier walked up and down on the road all night to guard us.

As I awakened early the next morning, perhaps just at dawn, I heard a girl singing across the fields. Never before or since have I heard a voice so crystal clear, so heavenly pure. The beautiful song was not in the happy Alpine mood so familiar to me, but a typical melancholy melody of the vast eastern European flatland. But I could never forget the crystalline purity of the voice; its touching beauty is impressed indelibly on my very soul.

The next day we walked from morning to night over meadows, paths, and then mud and gravel roads to a town called Rzeszow. A relatively elderly soldier had to be practically dragged along. He may have been in his forties, but his unshaven, sad, tortured face made him look much older. He reminded me of pictures depicting Christ carrying the cross. He was barefoot and his toes and feet were bleeding. Two of the comrades held him under their arms and coaxed him like a child: "Come on; there is not very long to go. Put up with it just a little longer: we'll soon be there..." It was a long road, but he made it. I can still see his bloody toes on the gravel as we went around a turn, up a winding stretch of the road from a large low flatland through a forest of small trees and bush to a higher level ground.

Everywhere along the road, and here and there through the fields near it, there were traces of war. Especially numerous were destroyed tanks, with the Russian outnumbering the German Tigers by about eight or more to one. The same can be said about the highway on our march to Lwow a week or two later.

During the first minutes after we set out on this march to

Rzeszow, the guards had taken us a little away from the road to a grassy meadow between some bushes, lined us up, ordered us to take off our sleeveless sweaters and pile them up nicely and orderly on the ground. Somebody might have thought we were about to be executed. Fortunately, nobody tried to run away or make some other drastic move: it would have meant certain disaster.

After the all-day march we arrived in Rzeszow late in the evening and were packed into an upstairs room of a house for the night. Next day, we took up quarters in a school near the town, and we stayed there for a week or so. Our ranks swelled, and by the end of our stay in the school we were about 200 men.

Around this time, a Russian soldier offered me half a loaf of bread for my shoes. Just before leaving France we had been issued all new clothing and brand new shoes. His shoes were badly torn and I was sorely tempted, but turned down the offer. Looking back, I was not only wise, but lucky: I could have been left during the coming Russian winter without shoes.

Soon we were "on the road again," as the saying goes. We marched nine days, this time to Lwow. Before the Second World War it was one of the largest cities in Poland, if not the largest after Warsaw; today it is in Ukraine. Its Ukrainian name is Lwiw; in German it used to be called Lemberg.

At the back of the column, two or three local people with horses and small wagons, who had been engaged by the army, followed in case somebody got sick or couldn't walk.

A soldier usually went ahead to find places for staying overnight: in attics, stables, or other kinds of places. Once we stayed in a barn somewhat away from the route, and the next morning one of the men went missing. After an intensive search he was discovered buried in the straw. He had planned to stay and escape, and apparently tried to flee because shots were fired before everything returned to "normal."

We travelled all the way on the main east-west highway in southern Poland.

The highway was like a never-ending river: units of marching soldiers, columns of trucks with soldiers, groups of a dozen or more tanks, canvas-covered trucks, horse-drawn wagons, vehicles with mounted anti-aircraft guns, trucks towing artillery guns. Practically all the traffic, except for our lonely column of approximately 200 men, was moving westwards. Many vehicles had slogans, (in Russian) written on them, such as "Get the beast in its lair!" or "Forward to Berlin!" The most favoured seemed to have been *Vperéd na západ!* (Forward West!).

Most of the trucks were Russian; there were also many American, and quite a few German-made. The latter could be described as passable; most American ones were quite stylish; the majority of the Russian ones looked like moving wrecks. But they moved: and that was what mattered.

The masses of men and material were enormous. The flow was practically never interrupted, day or night.

The advancing soldiers often paid great attention to us: looking curiously at our column as they drove by, waving their hands, or making threatening gestures. Some even threw pieces of bread or apples at us from their trucks, but once we got a fairly long burst of sub-machine-gun fire, followed immediately by two shorter ones. Two or three men near the centre of our column were wounded, but fortunately none seriously. Apparently the aim was to scare, not to kill, but a few bullets flew lower than intended. For otherwise, in my estimation, there would have been at least a dozen or more dead.

We got some especially curious looks from the balconies of an apartment building, which had been turned into a military hospital. Soldiers in all kinds of bandages and some on crutches found us very interesting specimens. Not surprisingly, their predominant reactions appeared rather negative, to put it mildly.

The reactions and attitude towards us by the population along the route also varied enormously. Consideration of the facts of recent history can help greatly, I am convinced, to understand and explain the difference.

Poland had been divided in September 1939 between Nazi Germany and the Soviet Union. In southern Poland, the predominantly Polish area west of the city of Premysl fell under the German influence; the predominantly Ukrainian area to the east of it was occupied by the Soviet Union. Premysl lies in a valley which reaches into the Carpathian mountains and guards the mountain pass to Czechoslovakia. In the First World War bloody battles between the Austrian-Hungarian and Russian armies raged in its vicinity, presumably for the control of the strategically vital pass. Just before we descended the winding road to the city, we could still see remnants of fortifications.

Generally speaking, the attitude of the population towards us before we reached Premysl was quite negative: either indifference or open hostility.

As we were leaving Rzeszow, at a fork in the road, a man stood with his right hand high in the air. He waved it rather slowly, almost solemnly, back and forth. I happened to be at the outer edge of my row and he looked straight at me. His message was unmistakably and ominously clear: just wait, you'll get what you deserve!

Having crossed the provisional bridge over a small river that flows through Premysl which, by the way, was on about the fourth or the fifth day of our nine-day journey, the road rose a little uphill and soon we reached the countryside again. There, the situation changed, suddenly and very radically.

As we passed through village after village, the population flocked towards us: old and young, men, women, and children. They brought round loaves that looked like brown bread but with sauerkraut in them, and other simple poor farmers' food. One woman, very thin and bent with old age, with her face almost hidden in a typical bandanna tied under her chin, came very close with a little pot of milk. She sadly and almost apologetically pointed to it and said *odná koróva* (one cow).

Usually the guards were patient and understanding, but on one occasion they found it necessary to begin shooting in the air, because the people began to press right onto the road. That made the whole crowd run down the embankment like a large herd of sheep only to return, gradually, closer again.

In the last two or three days of the march, a large object appeared on the horizon far in the east. It looked like a bridge with three or four arches. Later we found out that it was the huge hangars, or rather their ruins, at the airport near Lwow, the city which became our "home" for about the next three weeks.

We arrived after nightfall, and were allotted as our quarters a former German camp for the Soviet prisoners of war. Everyone tried to find one of the bunk beds in the darkness, and

I happened to get one at the bottom. Most of its short, removable boards were missing, so I laid down on the floor, but at once something mysterious began to prick my cheeks. It did not take long to solve the mystery: fleas were jumping into my face. With their former hosts gone weeks before, they must have been in a state of starvation. If so - and they seemed to prove it beyond doubt by their behaviour - they soon regained their strength.

We went daily to work on the airfield. The retreating Germans had bombed the runways. We worked frantically filling the craters with earth, then covering the top with ordinary bricks, their width set vertically for greater solidity of the runway. Several times a small solitary plane flew high above. The anti-aircraft batteries would shoot wildly but it always managed to escape, wiggling its way through the exploding shells. Most of the little black clouds appeared at any rate far behind it.

One day, right after breakfast, we had just lined up outside on the camp grounds, and were waiting to march off to work, when suddenly a few planes appeared so low that not only the anti-aircraft artillery but even those of our guards who had rifles rather than just pistols began to shoot at them. We were allowed to take cover inside the barrack. That was the only time I really saw what the inside looked like; we always left our sleeping quarters well before daybreak and returned inside after nightfall.

Later in the morning, as we arrived at the airfield, somebody was giving signs to a twin-bodied plane where to taxi. Several panes of glass on its central area had been smashed but otherwise it seemed okay. We learned that Rumania had just capitulated, and that the planes belonged to the Rumanian air force. It was August 23, 1944.

At that camp there was a regulation in force: soldiers who had been captured without weapons in their hands had a certificate that entitled them to extra food. I never heard before (or after) of the regulation and somebody evidently forgot to give me a certificate. Consequence: no extra food, naturally.

Days at the work sites were filled with boredom or only small incidents. For example: one such incident occurred during the rebuilding of a rather high, destroyed railway bridge not far from the city. One pair of tracks had already been completed when we appeared on the scene. It took us a few days to finish the second pair. Transports were moving frequently but slowly above while most of our crew stood all day in very cold water, shovelling gravel for the placement of wooden pillars. A guard, sitting in the middle of a gravel embankment with a rifle between his knees, yelled almost without any interruption all day long: *Davái, davái, davái, davái; kovyriái, kovyriái, kovyriái*...(give, and pick).

One of the transports passing slowly above evidently carried soldiers to the front. Some were sitting on the steps of box cars and one of them threw a stone down on the neck of one of our crew, which caused him considerable pain. I have no clue where or how he got the stone on a train that was moving, even if slowly.

When later another transport passed above, another missile came down. Everyone tried to dodge it. This time it was a hefty piece of bread.

The one really tragic event was the unsuccessful escape attempt of an inmate. He was shot, I believe dead, on the barbed wire fence.

Rumours began to circulate that we would soon leave the camp and go deeper into the Soviet Union. There was talk about *weisse Bettwäsche* (white bed-linen) waiting for us in the new place: a nice dream, too good to be true. It never materialized, although our days in that camp did come to an end soon.

On September 6 we were loaded on to rather short box cars, 40 men in each one. The entire transport was about one thousand men. There was nothing in the car except its ceiling, floor, and the four sides. The sliding door on one side was opened a little: just enough to install two boards nailed together into a V shape for toilet purposes. However, the door was locked, and the narrow opening above the toilet contraption was covered with a board all the way up. The two small window-like openings near the ceiling on that side had also been boarded. The two on the opposite side were opened, though well covered by barbed wire nailed from the outside. The sliding door opposite the toilet was opened only once a day for *kásha*, (thick cereal meal or stew), and coffee.

For three days we didn't move, except for some shunting. It is interesting how one becomes eager to go after a day or two of waiting. Nobody was in any rush to get anywhere, except maybe to sleep in "white bed linen" and perhaps get more than one meal a day. It was hot, but that did not bother us too much. Yet everybody listened as eagerly for the taps of hammers on the wheels as if we were grooms waiting to be taken to our brides. Even the slightest move brought relief and great expectation. Some explosions now and then during the nights, perhaps bombs dropped by an airplane, didn't cause much alarm. It was the waiting, pure and simple, that became so stressful. Finally, we started moving.

As there were 40 of us in each of the short cars it was so crowded that we could only lie on our sides, one row along each side of the box car, with our feet towards the centre. The nights were particularly hard and seemingly endless. By far the biggest problem was with our feet. There was no other way but to have them either below or on top of those belonging to the men lying on the opposite side. One can stand this for only so long, and that is not long at all. It soon becomes unbearable. We tried to change the position of our feet on a regular basis, but occasional kicking duels took place. During the day we either sat somehow on the floor or tried to get a glimpse through the barbed wire on the small window-like openings.

Whenever the sun appeared we tried to figure out in what direction the train moved. The first two or three days it travelled east or southeast. We figured our destination was somewhere in the Ukraine: the breadbasket of the Soviet Union and not so cold as the vast, frost-bound Siberia. With winter approaching, the question of climate loomed almost as important as food.

Our mood changed drastically when we changed direction to straight north, travelling through seemingly endless forests and swamps, with occasional farmland. The murky skies with almost continual rain or drizzle, coupled with the fall season and our unenviable predicament as prisoners of war, added the final touch to the melancholy.

After five or six days, our one daily meal of *kásha* was replaced by bone-hard, dry bread and coffee, and soon everybody was experiencing a thirst comparable only to that of the ancient mythical Tantalos. The dry bread had a sponge-like effect; it lay in the stomach like some heavy object, drawing with a distinctly felt physical force anything wet around it to itself.

It is said that thirst can be worse than hunger. I had experienced severe thirst many times during the long, exhaustive marches and exercises with full military gear in intense summer heat, yet never like this. I also had experienced hunger later in the P.O.W. camp, near the point of starvation. If I had to choose between a death from hunger or from thirst, I'd opt for the former without hesitation.

One morning we finally reached our destination. It was September 18, exactly 12 days after boarding our transport in Lwow.

As I learned later, it was customary to simply dump loads of coal or wood out of the box cars to the side of the railway tracks at once on the arrival of a shipment. Only later were they delivered to their destination, usually the large nearby factory. This was one of the measures to make better use of the box cars, so urgently needed for the war effort.

Near the tracks all along our transport train there was a long pile of coal. When the order was given to exit, I made a short jump out of the car onto it. But not having made one single step out of the car during the 12 days, the muscles just above my knees seemed to have lost all power. I fell forward and slid head first down the other side of the pile.

When we lined up, the crew from our box car looked like chimney sweeps; it had been used for coal earlier. However, we were much better off than those from the next car. Their clothes, though not as dirty as ours, were hanging in strips, probably from some chemical in their car before. In less serious circumstances their appearance would have been quite comical.

A more or less orderly column was formed and off we went over the bumpy ground along the tracks, through an area that was a combined railway and factory complex. We walked to the right, with the railway embankment on which our transport had arrived on our right and a fairly large crowd accompanying us on our left. The people walked with the same slow speed as we, scattered along the whole length of our column, the closest ones at least some seven or eight steps away from it, with their heads turned towards us. They appeared very solemn, but made no gestures, and no word or sound of any kind could be heard from them. They observed us intensely, for we were obviously the "green people" about whom they must have heard so much, yet whom they never saw really live before.

The only words I remember hearing came from a young German soldier near me. He looked pale and very weak. Two comrades tried to help him walk by taking him under their arms. Visibly annoyed, he shook them away and said with a loud, tearful voice: *Ich will doch meine Freiheit haben* (I want to have my freedom).

We were taken to a factory area where heaps of wrecked airplanes - broken wings, wheels, cogwheels, propellers, pistons, crankshafts, pipes, motors, etc., - were strewn all over the place. Stumbling along the wall and then around the corner of a huge factory building, making headway slowly up and down the piles of wreckage, we finally reached the large entrance at the back.

We had arrived!

Yes, indeed! Approximately one thousand men, but about one-third would never leave.

At the sight of a hydrant on a square pillar inside the building the terribly dehydrated men charged forward, threw the fire hose on the floor, and in no time made a shambles of the red wooden hydrant casing. The stampede, with much shoving and shouting, was a very unlikely scene for a group of people steeped in Prussian discipline. Needless to say the rush not only didn't help but rather delayed considerably the quenching of our tantalizing, enormous thirst. The result was that we spent the night in the midst of the puddles of water that had formed all over the rough concrete floor. I found a plank to sleep on; not everyone was that fortunate.

Weeks or months later I got a real scare near that spot. As I stood there, a woman in coveralls jumped unexpectedly from behind the corner right in front of me. My first thought was that she was hellbent on stabbing me with the bayonet attached to a rifle. It turned out, mercifully, that she was only engaged in a fire-drill exercise: she was carrying a fire-hose with its nozzle.

In view of the state of both the inside of that gigantic factory building and its surrounding area, most of us had no doubt that we would stay there only temporarily, perhaps overnight. I stayed on the grounds for over 16 months, most of the time in that very building. So did the majority of the others who arrived with me. What's more: before Christmas the numbers of inmates almost doubled, and after the end of the war rose to about four thousand.

Our camp, in the beginning only one huge factory building with its surrounding junk-yard, was situated just within the bounds of metropolitan Moscow: in its west-northwestern suburb Tushino. Before our arrival it was part of a very large airplane-motor factory, and was located at the top edge of a steep slope, almost like a cliff, from which one could look far west over the countryside. Somebody once pointed to a rather distant line of electrical poles and remarked that the German armies had come that far.

In spirit, let us transfer ourselves for a while back to the late autumn of 1944 and place ourselves on a guard tower standing along the western fence of our camp, on top of the cliff.

We are turned due west. The P.O.W. camp is behind our back, with the factory further east behind it. On our right and behind us, there is a branch of the Moskva-Volga canal. Its banks are immediately behind the camp's northern fences, and so high that the water level lies several metres higher than the camp-grounds. The canal comes to an abrupt end at the edge of the cliff.

Due west of us are some buildings and fields as far as the eye can see. Close in front, deep down under the cliff, a small tributary of the Moskva river winds its way, flowing left and under the bridge of the *Volokolámski chaussée:* highway to the city of Volokolamsk.

At this point we may recall that *Volokolámski chaussée* had a special ring in the ears of the citizens of the Soviet Union. Even in mine it always evokes almost a feeling of awe. It was somewhere on this highway that about three years earlier, during the first months of the *Velikáia Otéchestvennaia Voiná* (the Great Fatherland's War) members of a group of *Komsomól* (Communist

127

Soviet Youth: the familiar word is composed of first syllables of the three words) threw themselves along with their anti-tank mines under the advancing German tanks.

In front on our left is the aforementioned highway which runs in a generally western direction. Between it and the winding Moskva river further to the west, with the river flowing east towards Moscow, is the historic Tushino military airfield: a large grassy field. At the far west end of the airfield is parked a large number of planes. If we had a pair of good binoculars, we would soon find out that they are made of wood, like huge toys. But we know their purpose.

Across the Moskva river are grassy hills with some oats, barley, and wheat fields. The predominant crop around Moscow, though, is cabbage: at least it was, in 1944.

On the left behind us we may notice some two kilometres away one or two barges going from the general area behind our camp and factory through locks down towards the Moskva river. A boat going over the Volokolamsk highway, with no water but only the grassy canal embankment visible, and the capital Moscow in the background further towards the east-southeast, presents a somewhat strange scene. One is reminded of pictures of the Suez canal where boats seem to sail right through the desert sand.

It is time to return back from our flight of fancy and face reality again, even though we are still dealing with history.

The main, high, barbed wire fence around the Tushino P.O.W. camp was already there when we arrived. Here and there along it were guard towers with searchlights by night. We had to help build another lower fence, about three metres beyond the first; and a third fence, the lowest and simplest of the three, about four metres inside the central one. The outer fence kept outsiders from coming too close to the main fence, while the inner one's purpose was to keep us at a safe distance from the main fence, as we were told in no uncertain terms. The area between the fences had to be, of course, clear and free of any plants or other objects.

The factory building which became our camp appeared to have been constructed very recently. Even so, its vast central hall contained at our arrival nothing but junk and debris here and there: mostly metal, but also some broken boards. Rows of square columns supported a typical factory roof, and there was really no ceiling, except for some beams. Most of the roof area looked like gigantic teeth, or waves with very sharp crests: on one side perpendicular, on the other slantendicular. The only windows in the central hall were on the roof, on these crests, but I do not recall on which of the two sides; possibly on both. I remember very well, though, that practically no light came through, because the windows had been painted as a precaution against air raids. As a consequence, lights had to burn day and night. Only around the end of the war the windows were freed of paint to serve their purpose, but then the roof became even more leaky than before.

The whole building consisted of the vast central hall, as well as a much narrower hall all along its eastern, and a similar one along its western wall. There were smaller rooms adjacent to the north and the south ends of the central hall, whose huge main entrance was at the centre on the north side.

During the first months most of us were lodged in the smaller eastern hall. All its windows had iron bars, and the one and only exit was into the central hall, but at the far corner away from its main entrance. As there were usually several hundred men crowded in that small hall, one shudders at the thought of what could have befallen the inmates in case of a fire. Mercifully, the thought never occurred to me then.

Toilet facilities were very inadequate and totally out of order. So, a huge, deep square hole with a primitive contraption over the top was dug. There was no thought of showers or daily or even weekly washing. Only about once a month we went for what was referred to in German as *Entlausung* (delousing), or in Russian simply as *bánia* (bath). It consisted of putting all one's clothes on an iron ring with a number tag and lowering the bundle through a large, square hole in the wall down into a seemingly bottomless pit. Then everyone got a rather small bowl of water and a piece of soap to have what might be called a quasi-bath, or to use a more modern expression, perhaps mini-bath. Meanwhile the clothes were put into an oven, which was meant to kill the lice. The heat sometimes seemed to have only helped the pests multiply faster.

Ordinarily, the ritual was concluded when the bundles of

clothes were dragged up by a rope at the other end of the building through a hole, identical to the one through which they had gone down. On one occasion, however, a load caught fire in the oven and the incinerated clothes never came up again. It killed the pests, certainly; but it was like curing a toothache with a guillotine.

During the first weeks after our arrival the *Pritschen* (bunk beds) were installed. Constructed of boards and two-by-two beams, they stood in long, double rows with heads together. The two rows were joined together; only a board was installed between the heads. Every row formed one uninterrupted line, with boards dividing every four men from the next four.

There were two main problems with what for want of a more appropriate term must be referred to as "beds." Both were pretty bad; it is hard to judge which of the two was worse. Firstly, thanks to the extreme thriftiness of the designers and carpenters, there was enough space between the narrow boards for one or two fingers. Secondly, the space for each group of four was so narrow that all four could at one and the same time lie only on either their right or left side. As a consequence, all four had to be awakened whenever even one of them could no longer stand the situation and just had to turn around. Needless to say there were no blankets, let alone mattresses. If your hip bone happened to be situated over a space between two boards, it was almost impossible to change its position, because there was practically no room to move it either way on one of them. The result were large brown patches of hardened skin on our hips.

There was a lower and an upper tier of beds. At the end of the war, with thousands of new arrivals, a third "storey" was added. This one was built of stronger boards and stronger beams than the original bunks, and its supporting posts rested directly on the concrete floor.

During all our stay in this camp never having any mattresses, blankets, or pillows, we had to help ourselves as best we could. Shoes or food containers served as pillows, and our green military jackets as blankets. There was nothing left to lie on, for in all my 16 months in that camp I never once slept with my outer clothes off, except for my jacket.

The shoes were taken off only if and when they served as a pillow: they were placed sideways, so that their toes pointed towards each other and the soles towards the bunk's head; their upper parts were placed one on top of the other. For greater comfort, one's cap was usually placed on top of them.

It is incredible how much warmer it is to spread your jacket over your body, than simply to sleep with it on. But it has to be done in the proper manner, "scientifically." If lying on your right side, for instance, the right shoulder of the jacket must cover the left shoulder of your body. The collar runs down over your heart area, and the left shoulder of the jacket rests on or near your left hip: the closer to your knees, the better. The lower part of the jacket has to be spread as far up and down your back as possible. It is advisable to have the right sleeve over your neck and head, and the left one reaching as far down your legs as possible, and resting on them whenever they can be pulled close up to your body. If you happen to lie on your left side, the same rules apply, with proper adjustments.

With these strategies and tactics, the body heat is somehow caught under the jacket. It is truly amazing how much better this works while sleeping than wearing it.

These rules, obviously, are valid only for cold weather. On hot nights they would be counter-productive. They may seem very complicated but, believe me, it would be very worthwhile to keep them in mind for emergencies.

Recalling again the earlier quoted Croatian proverb that "there is no wind so wicked that it wouldn't blow in some good for somebody," let me say that in spite of the bitterly cold Russian winters, and in spite of lousy living quarters, we never suffered freezing while inside.

The only heating device in the whole vast central hall was an empty oil barrel in the middle of it, fuelled by stolen wood brought in from work; the guards usually pretended not to notice it, either on its way into the camp or later. But it was the sardine-can-like sleeping conditions and the overcrowding that kept the temperature quite comfortable, even when the mercury outside fell at times to about -40° (C or F: it is about the same cold).

On such days when the large door opened, a thick,

churning steam appeared at the lower half of the door and rushed in, spreading in all directions, similar to rapids in a flowing river. It was so dense that nothing could be seen through it.

Apart from the rows of massive columns, the bunk beds, and the oil-barrel stove, there was nothing in the large central hall; in the smaller one on the east there was nothing but a row or two of columns, and bunks. There was no room left for tables, chairs, benches or cupboards. The latter would have ben totally useless anyway, for nobody had extra clothing. Moreover, we had no other possessions apart from a spoon, usually worn in the chest jacket-pocket with its handle through the button hole so as not to be lost, and a tin can or some other type of container for food. This most important article was carried at the back of the waist at all times, except during the night. It was held by a string that was tied in the front.

The authorities must have been well aware of the saying "Idle hands are devil's workshop," for the very day after we arrived we were put to work. Never mind that it had all the appearances of work for work's sake. It was work, and apparently that was all that mattered.

As soon as the "outdoor facilities" were dug, we attacked the large piles of airplane leftovers: wings, wheels, motors and their parts, and a variety of pipes and gear. Some of the junk, especially the motors, were quite heavy. At times four men were needed to lift them: one on each end of two iron bars. For other things two men sufficed, and much could be carried by single persons.

We carried everything to one part of the grounds. However, as soon as the work was completed, the whole pile had to be moved to some other area. With such ingenious planning we had enough work until doomsday. Before very long, though, "real" work was found for us outside the camp. My first job was on a housing project not very far from the camp in an until then undeveloped area of Tushino. We built several houses for from four to eight families each. Others went to unload barges on Moskva-Volga canal. Still others worked either on the grounds of the large airplane-motors factory, or in the factory itself, of which our camp was really a part.

While some men had heavier work, at the casting ovens or handling molten metals, one of my main occupations following construction was of a somewhat easier kind: cleaning engine casings.

The motors produced in that factory had, I believe, 12 cylinders, arranged in two rows in a V shape, like most eight-cylinder car motors. There were four main parts to the whole casing, all cast of duraluminium: the two blocks for the cylinders, and two oblong halves to enclose the crankshaft.

Each of the four pieces could be lifted by two people, and was put on two wooden stools to be cleaned after the removal from the mould in which it had been cast.

We used scrapers to remove the crumb-like bits of clay still solidly attached to the inner walls of these blocks. To reach into the various and numerous holes, we used a pneumatic drill-like tool. Instead of an ordinary drill bit it had a rod, not unlike a strong piece of wire, with an oblong, thicker, grooved end to bite away the crumbs of clay. The holes for cylinders were big enough to hang electric light bulbs right into them in order to see. For some unknown reason they were not protected, and it goes without saying that many were smashed by the drills.

On one occasion I was having particularly bad luck with the bulbs, and probably for the proverbial umpteenth time I stood before the forewoman with the leftovers of a smashed bulb. Having stated the obvious - *lámpochka kapút* (the bulb is finished) - I was expecting her to accuse me of sabotage. Indeed, she seemed upset, took the piece, and somewhat angrily threw it away on the floor. I waited for what was about to happen next.

She looked at me with eyes full of pity and compassion and said in an unforgettably loving voice, *Ya vas liubliú, vi molodói.* Her words could be taken with one of two similar meanings: either "I love you, you young one" or "I love you because you are so young"; I was 18 going on 19.

I was pleasantly stunned. I took the new *lámpochka* and returned to work.

The incident is indelibly engraved in my memory. Even after almost 50 years it sometimes returns to moisten my eyes.

With the crumbs of clay scraped away, the cylinder blocks had to be filled about half full with shiny steel balls the size of hazelnuts: some bigger, some smaller. Attached to a machine, they turned for hours around and around in a wobbly manner. The procedure was meant, apparently, to strengthen and make smooth their inner surfaces. No matter what the purpose, three or four such machines - or rather the steel balls in the blocks - produced in a relatively small factory room a deafening noise.

The whole suburb of Tushino was very noisy. From a large, windowless, cube-like building in the middle of the factory complex, a sound similar to a pre-jet airplane motor at its loudest emanated day and night, with hardly any break. If now and then it stopped, it was like taking the water off the mill, to borrow one of my mother's similes. Perhaps the motors were being tested for endurance.

The winter of 1944 - 1945 was a time of great suffering and profound pathos in the P.O.W. camp Tushino.

Days were getting shorter and colder: no other reminder was necessary that winter was near. I still recall the day I first saw the ice in the shape of a heel imprinted in the mud on the camp grounds. It was not a happy sight. The first snow arrived soon after.

From then on and through that unforgettable winter, we watched daily the smoke from the one huge chimney in the factory area. Whenever the wind was blowing from the vast, cold, mysterious land of Siberia (The Land of Slumber), it didn't bode well. The mercury dropped, now and then through the winter, as low as about - 41°, Celsius or Fahrenheit. That is cold, especially with the wind-chill factor added, and more so for us "miserables": prisoners of war with poor clothing, a starvation diet, and hard work, not to mention loneliness, homesickness, the utter uncertainty about the fate of our dear ones, and no end of this misery in sight.

I was fortunate to have at least good shoes, a luxury many others did not have. They had to make their own footwear called, in German, *Lappen:* wooden boards with a strap, and rags tied around the foot. Boards could usually be found at work, while the rest came courtesy of whoever shot down the planes; the rags were made of the canvas that covered the wings. One only had to scrape off the veneer-like layer of paint. The rubber wheels contained layers of good thread inside. With some difficulty thread could be peeled off and woven into strings with which the rags were tied in thick layers around the feet. Another vital use of this string was to tie the tin can or other food containers to our backs, and also to keep our pants on our shrinking bodies, which were gradually turning to skeletons.

While I had a great advantage with my footwear, I had a serious handicap: no shirt. In the very first "delousing" my clothes came back from the oven with the shirt missing. I lived through most of that winter without any shirt.

The houses we worked on outside the camp were built of door-size blocks, about 15 cm thick. Every such block was made of wooden boards and filled with the slack from burnt coal. They were quite heavy, especially when rain-soaked. One bitterly cold day four of us were carrying these blocks on our shoulders. I must have been shivering more than the others, for a lady who happened to come by stopped and looked at me. Wearing a warm sheepskin cap with flaps to pull over the ears, *válenki* (felt boots) and a long sheepskin coat, she enquired *potchemú zamérz?* (Why are you so cold?) Putting two fingers between two buttons of my military jacket, I opened it so she could see the skin of my chest. I said nothing. Neither did she. Throwing her hands into the freezing, windy air and shaking her head, she simply walked away.

One day we were digging all day long a muddy, narrow, shoulder-deep ditch. A Siberian wind drove freezing rain mixed with snow, and every thread of clothing was soaking wet. My upper body was protected by nothing except the rather light green German military jacket. Every move brought about the feeling of being inside an icicle. That night we slept in totally soaked clothing, which dried on us gradually during the night. The next day it was business as usual: back to work, with no colds or any other perceptible results. I say perceptible, for the evil effects would show in some future time.

It is incredible that in spite of frequently bitter cold and poor clothing, starvation diet, and lousy lodgings (literally full of lice) I don't recall ever having a cold while in the P.O.W. camp in Tushino. Human capability of adaptation to adverse conditions is truly amazing! However, now I only have to put my bald head through the door to check the weather on a cold or windy day and I have a plugged nose and headaches for days.

In spite of sub-human conditions regarding work, clothing, and living quarters, it was the food that was our main concern and preoccupation. War or politics were practically never mentioned. Food! The magic word brought about bright images of heavenly delights.

Food!

On the long trip from Poland, for instance, our only conversations were about food. A stranger listening to us would have concluded, quite logically, that everyone in our box car had been the chief chef in a fancy hotel. Interestingly, potatoes in their variety of preparations predominated as the most exotic food, especially among the Germans. *Schmalzkartoffeln, Bratkartoffeln, Salzkartoffeln,* and a great variety of other *Kartoffeln* (potatoes), prepared in the most exquisite ways in Prussia, Saxony, Bavaria, and other parts of Germany and Europe were our daily topics of conversation. Later, in the camp, conversations became more subdued. In the darkest period, we just wasted away on the bunk beds, saying practically nothing and getting up only to eat or look after our most basic needs.

Food, the magic word with images of heavenly delights!

In the worst months of literal starvation I had genuine hallucinations about it. I was never imagining cakes, caviar, or champagne. Not even potatoes! Rather, I saw vividly in front and a little above my eyes large, dark-blue clusters of grapes mixed with large apples with irregular, dark-blue stripes running from the stem to the base and widest, naturally enough, at the apple's equator. Between the blue stripes were areas of bright red and yellow. The whole vision was always tantalizingly close but just beyond my reach.

The majority of the inmates were in their late teens or early twenties. One would have expected other, more "seasonable" topics of conversation in such company. But there is not the slightest doubt in my mind that there has not been a monastery or convent anywhere more chaste than was our P.O.W. camp. I am not saying that no one ever had any untoward thoughts or that no unclean word ever sullied anyone's lips. But I do claim to not having heard any unclean words or seen any unclean deeds, at least not in the winter of 1944 - 1945. The mighty and violent powers of our youthful manhood seemed to have gone into hibernation. By the beginning of next winter, the situation of camp life, or more correctly vegetation, improved substantially. But even from that period I recall only a few occasions of some wanton or lewd remarks by one prisoner or another.

Little by little Christmas 1944 was approaching: the fourth in a row when "by Christmas the war will be over." On one occasion when we were still carrying the junk back and forth on the camp grounds, like a cat carrying her young ones, the Soviet officer in charge suddenly called an assembly. Everyone was excited and some Frenchmen began to shout *la guerre finie, la guerre finie!* (the war is over!) No assembly of cockroaches could have been more thoroughly scolded by a pail of boiling water than were we by the icy reminder: "If you don't work harder you'll get nothing to eat." With that it was back to work...

But how can machines work without fuel? How can living bodies without sufficient food, even though no engine has ever been designed that runs on so little as the human body?

Our daily food rations were meagre from the day of our arrival in Tushino. Moscow's three to four million inhabitants themselves were experiencing a shortage of food. Around the capital there were fields of cabbage, with some rye, barley, wheat and oats. But with so many mouths to feed the bulk of the food had to be brought all the way from Ukraine, and most of the trains were engaged in the war effort.

The problem was aggravated by what could be labelled "attrition." Everybody used any opportunity to pick up things, and our already slight rations were probably very substantially depleted during their transport.

Proof of this could be gleaned from Russian newspapers. I recall reading one of the common "self-criticism" articles. Somebody was reporting that of the 51 cubic metres of wood which left the forest only 22 reached its destination.

Who could blame people for helping themselves in this sort of manner, if everything in a supposedly communist society is supposed to be "ours" anyway?

One day I watched cabbage being hauled to large ground silos. A heavily loaded truck was coming down the *Volokolámski chaussée*. It was expected to turn off the highway and drive towards Tushino, passing near our building site. A group of school children waited behind a corner for the truck, which before long drove slowly around it due to potholes. On top of the truck was a woman with a long stick for chasing away any "attackers." One or two daredevils grasped the side of the truck and tried to climb on it. They were armed with wires made into hooks to thrust into a cabbage head and drag it down. The woman ostensibly tried to chase the kids with her stick; however, it was quite obvious that she swung it to roll some cabbage off the truck, rather than to hit the rascals.

There were guards everywhere: usually women bundled in heavy clothes, with bandannas and rifles that seemed to have been captured from Napoleon's army in 1812. One of them guarded boards at a construction site. A group of children began to shout *Palúndra, Palúndra, drová kradút!* (Palundra, Palundra, they are stealing wood!) And while she rushed to the supposedly endangered area, the kids got away with wood at the other end. I wouldn't be at all surprised that here, too, there was a conspiracy. It was more than met the eye.

The 27th anniversary of "The Great October Revolution" was proclaimed by placards and painted slogans everywhere. It was a day to remember, or more truly put: a day to forget!

It was bitterly cold, and everybody was relieved to be back in the building after the evening counting. However, the gong soon rang again and everybody had to get up from the boards and out: someone appeared to have gone missing. Surely, we thought after the return, that was it. Wrong! For the third time we went through the same cold torture, perhaps the longest of the three.

The mystery was finally solved. A man had sneaked into the cabbage cellar to get a little extra food and before he could get out he was locked in. Nobody had noticed him. He probably wasn't very eager to call for help either. As the cellar was separate from the kitchen, all by itself, nobody had thought to check it - until the third round. I don't know what punishment the man received; probably a scolding accompanied by a few slaps, or maybe half a day in the *Karzer* (the camp jail).

And so we finally made it to bed, but soon it was time to get up again.

That's how we celebrated the great feast. I had the dubious privilege of celebrating the 28th anniversary in the same camp, but under much improved conditions.

Only first names were used in personal relations between prisoners, with very rare exceptions. I wonder if the authorities had any list of names to start with? They never, ever, used our names; everything went by numbers. My number was 323.

For breakfast we got a piece of rye bread, usually very wet, with some grains only broken in half. Usually we had black coffee with it. At noon and again in the evening we received a ladle of soup with another piece of bread. The soup was ordinarily either thin cabbage or pea soup. The latter was usually so thin that often there was not a quarter of spoon of anything else in it: grey coloured water.

As time went on, the ladle was enlarged somewhat and, at one meal, a smaller ladle of *kásha* was added.

As the soup was dished out, one person stirred it with a long stick to bring any peas, cabbage leaves or whatever up from the bottom and achieve a just distribution.

For every group of 100 into which we were divided, three or four men were sent to the kitchen for each meal. One brought slices of bread on a wooden tray; two carried a barrel with one end knocked out. On its sides, two bars were fastened for carrying. If there was a mythical heavenly food, *kásha*, the fourth man easily carried the pail alone: there was not much of it. We might have called it dessert.

If any soup or *kásha* was left over, the next few got a second: it was called *Nachschlag* (literally: after-strike). If at a meal I had been the last man to receive a *Nachschlag*, the lucky ones then were the numbers 324, 325 - as long as the soup or *kásha* lasted. When the whole company had received an "after-strike" the cycle began again. You can imagine the feast if now and then a man got an extra portion of both soup and *kásha*! Unfortunately, there was no such blessing for bread; all the slices were carefully counted.

For a long time I had a preserve can for my food container. Later I provided myself with an oval duraluminium one with a lid, which served as an ideal container for *kásha*. I never washed either the tin can or the "de luxe" container. With my index finger I cleaned it, licking the finger. The tip of the finger and indeed the fingernail could get right into the joint at the bottom for even the slightest bit of food. My mother's perennial motto "What is worth more than a louse on your neck must be turned to use" would have to take second place to this kind of economy!

There were various theories as to how to get the most out of the food: each with its own practices.

The main focus was on the eating of bread. A minority opinion held that one got the most out of any food by gulping it down: more or less the way most people would eat in ordinary circumstances.

Others ate with utmost care, in small bits and slurps, relishing every crumb or spoonful of soup or *kásha*. A branch of this group went to the extent of procuring small rectangular plywood trays slightly bigger than a slice of bread, with a handle and a hole for the carrying string. The tray was added to the only other two pieces of "vital" equipment we possessed and carried everywhere: the food container and the spoon. The big advantage of these trays was that not even the slightest crumb went missing. With a saliva-moistened finger each tiniest bit could easily be picked up and brought to the tongue.

A group within this branch went even a step further in their gourmet excesses. Its partisans thought that breaking small crumbs off the bread with one's fingers was not the summit of the art of eating. So they availed themselves of little knives, made from small iron saws, to cut pieces off the slice of bread. The little knives were manufactured by the gourmets themselves in the factory, or bartered for a piece of bread from fellow inmates. The big disadvantage for this group were the occasional detailed searches by the Soviet guards for just such tools. Every few weeks the knives found their semi-final resting place on a pile in the middle of the large central hall. After every search operation the knives were taken to their final rest - a place that remained unknown. If I be granted the liberty of making an educated guess, the place was the living quarters of the guards, and ultimately their homes.

The meagre food, coupled with heavy work, and winter becoming ever more severe, we all began to turn into skeletons covered by skin. I regret I never thought of weighing myself.

Some men deteriorated faster than others. It may sound strange, but the most robust men went down fastest. Seemingly, just as a bigger car needs more fuel, so a larger body needs more food. And of the various nationalities, the French, generally, weakened first. (They were from the German-occupied parts of France and most of them had been conscripted, like myself, very much against their will). Was it because they were from a warmer climate? Or is there some truth to the view that the French were softened by too luxurious living just before the war? My educated guess is that both these factors, and possibly some others, brought about the undeniable result. Fortunately, they went home during that winter, about Christmas, to join De Gaulle's forces. I can still see their contingent of 30 or so men, marching away with their tricolour carried right in the middle of their column. Through the barbed wire fences we watched them with very mixed feelings disappear down the road behind the factory buildings.

Meanwhile, things in the camp went from bad to worse: indeed from worse to worst.

All the camp inmates had been divided into categories with reclassification about once a month. At every such examination, we had to pass in a single line past a desk where two girls sat. One of them pinched every passer-by and pronounced, the other wrote down, one of four German words: *erste, zwote, dritte,* or *O.K.* This put us into a first, second, third, or O.K. category, the single criterion being the amount of flesh left on our skeletons.

The process was of great significance, for according to categories the *nórma*, meaning the amount of work one was expected to perform, was "scientifically" determined.

Those in the first category were to perform the norm 101 percent; the second category had to do "only" 76 percent, and the third a mere 51 percent. The O.K. stayed in camp doing nothing.

What the characters O and K stood for, I do not know. It probably meant "recuperating company," but it was never referred to in any other way than by its initials. The only lower category, if that's what it could be called, was *lazarét* (lazaret or hospital).

Beyond that was eternity.

Every P.O.W. belonged to one or the other of these five famous - or infamous - groups. As said, about once a month a reclassification was carried out. One could remain in the same category or move up or down. Before the spring of 1945 almost all movement was down. Quite often, perhaps as a rule, the change from one category to another was not a gradual process, at least in the case of downward movement. After remaining on a certain level for a relatively long time, one then dropped suddenly to a lower one.

For the first two or three months I was in the first category. Mostly I worked on construction of wartime housing. However, suddenly I began to lose flesh quickly and experienced a strange weakness above the right knee, so that my right leg began to drag.

During the last few days on construction, two buddies had to help me walk back from work holding me under the elbows. They almost had to drag me up the gentle hill towards the camp. In the army, about the only claim to sickness had been a rise in temperature. Here one had to practically collapse before getting permission to see the doctor.

One day, as columns formed just before going off to work, I stood on the outside of the last row, with my back near the east wall of the camp building. As we began to move down the camp grounds towards the gate I slipped to the back of the O.K. column which happened to be lined up alongside and immediately next to mine. This group moved forwards, then to the left, and back into the camp. I have no clue how they figured out the numbers at the camp gate, since almost without exception every group consisted of 100 men, even if only half that many were needed at a certain work site. The guards probably didn't worry too much if one had been lost inside the camp: they were responsible only for the number received.

Somehow I got the chance to be examined by the Russian

military doctor and an Austrian one. The latter was also a P.O.W. but acted as the Russian's assistant.

I lay on my back on a wooden couch and they tested my reflexes by drawing lines with a scalpel, lengthwise under the arch of my soles. The pressure applied stopped just short of cutting the skin. My left leg reacted with sudden jerks. On the right one, I felt the scalpel clearly but there were no jerks. The doctors concluded that it was an interesting case of partial paralysis caused by Vitamin B deficiency. They gave me a spoonful or two of good-tasting, brown, flour-like medicine.

I don't recall whether the next reclassification happened to fall on the same day or how was I able to remain in camp until the next one; but I do remember that in one month I went from the first category all the way down to O.K. where I stayed for approximately three months.

At that time large numbers joined the O.K., so that we filled the whole of the eastern hall.

We had to take part in all counting, morning and evening. We also had to line up in the morning outside but returned after the others went off to work. Our only other "occupation" was getting up for the three daily meals. The rest of the time was spent lying on the wooden bunk-beds or wandering through the main hall, which was empty, with the other inmates at work.

Just before my reclassification to O.K. I had a close call with destiny.

Nobody dreamt that things could be worse anywhere in the world. So it was with real joy I welcomed, as no doubt everyone in the group did, the prospect of transfer to another camp.

Only members of the first category were the seemingly lucky ones. We were lined up in single file to receive at a kind of wicket some new napkins. They served as a substitute for socks not only in this camp, but also in the German as well as Yugoslavian armies. There was also some other clothing given out, and perhaps even shoes.

As I stood there, the Soviet lieutenant in charge of work arrangements came strolling from behind along the line. I only noticed him as he passed on my left. He went two or three steps past me, then suddenly turned back, stepped towards me, looked straight at me from head to feet, and pulled me gently by the sleeve from the line.

My heart sank; my hopes of better days were dashed. The seemingly lucky chosen ones left, and soon afterwards I was reclassified into the O.K.

When I still went to work I looked at those who stayed in the camp: not with envy but with desire to be among them. However, a few weeks later, I would have preferred to have gone to work just for the sake of going although no worker had any advantages over the ones who stayed in.

By December 1944 the first category had practically ceased to exist, while the ranks of the O.K. swelled. Most camp inmates had swollen legs, some had water in the whole body. Everywhere boards could be seen across the ends of the bunk-beds, for getting the feet higher and water flowing back into the bodies. People began to die of dystrophy: death of starvation, plain and simple. Its victims could be seen wobbling around, usually along the wall for support, for a few days or weeks before: like babies learning to walk.

The image of one dystrophy victim remains clearly in my mind. His surname was Tiedemann. He was a tall, strongly built man who certainly needed more food to keep him going than us smaller ones. He began to drag himself along the wall, slowly, with his hands and elbows held near his head, leaning on the wall in order not to fall as he moved like a child learning to walk.

The cries of "Tiedemann! Tie-ee-de-mann!" still ring in my ears. A fellow inmate was calling him to stop dragging himself along the wall and return to his bed. But Tiedemann paid no attention.

Late on Christmas Eve 1944, a man lying several places away from mine on the top storey of beds, drew some widely spaced, deep breaths. Soon afterwards, two men came with a sheet or blanket and carried away what was left of him.

It was the remains of what used to be the body, and more recently the skeleton, of Tiedemann.

Where did he hail from? Was his family celebrating Christmas, dreaming of a husband and daddy missed in action but hopefully alive and some day returning home? Or had they been buried under the rubble of Berlin, Bremen, or Hamburg? The destruction of Dresden was still to come, in a few weeks.

At Christmas 1944 I was already in the O.K., so I did not go out of the camp at all. Yet even in the camp we had two small Christmas trees: one in the central hall, the other in our very O.K. quarters in the east hall. Our tree, totally bare of any decorations, was fastened at the foot of one of the upper rows of bunk-beds, between two four-men compartments. The tree in the central hall was somewhat taller. It had three electrical bulbs, each of a different colour, and three plywood biscuits in the shape of bells or stars hung on its branches.

The birthday of Christ is among Christians a distinctly family feast. Yet nobody knew anything about the whereabouts of our families. All we knew was that, if they were still alive, they knew nothing about our fate. Reports only read: *für Vaterland gefallen* (fallen for the fatherland) or *vermisst* (missing), which could have meant anything from captivity to death. Nobody was ever reported as captured.

From time to time the truck with bread was delayed. It meant more acute hunger - if that was possible - but then a real feast: three daily rations all at once! That happened to happen the day before Christmas.

On Christmas Eve all inmates were summoned to the central hall. A rather narrow, long area near its centre was free from bunk beds. That is where all who were able to walk were lined up in long rows, several deep, one behind the other. Thick slices of bread - the whole day's ration - were distributed. Then we sang two songs: *Silent Night* and one sung to the tune of the well-known Marian hymn *O, Sanctissima* (O, Most Holy One). In German it is titled *O, du fröhliche* (O, You Joyful); it sings of the happy, blessed Christmas time, and exhorts all Christendom to rejoice in the birth of the Saviour.

I was then 18. There were quite a few my age or a little older, but the bulk were seasoned, hardened soldiers who more than once had seen "the enemy's eyewhites," as German soldiers used to say. They had been through years of war on the great fronts: North Africa, all over Europe, guerilla warfare, and the worst of them all, the immense *Ostfront* (the Eastern Front) with its savage *Massenschlachten* (battles of masses). Many of them had fought under inhuman conditions in howling winter storms of ice and snow, sweltering summer heat, or in the deep mud of autumn and spring.

These seasoned soldiers no less than we young ones sang with incredible emotion. Especially the soft yet powerful melody of *O, du fröhliche* pierced my soul so deeply that whenever I hear it, even today, I am deeply moved. In each stanza the words swelled gradually from piano in a crescendo to a powerful yet mild, heart rending fortissimo, followed by some lower and weaker tones, and then almost whispered ending.

That was our Christmas Eve in the P.O.W. camp Tushino, Moscow, in 1944. I wish I were a Shakespeare, or at least a Solzhenitsyn, to describe the occasion more fittingly.

Around Christmas time 1944 we were united with another large contingent of several hundred P.O.W.s.

The camp population at first was about 1000 men. A few weeks after our arrival this somewhat smaller group came. It was lodged in the west hall, and formed actually a camp within the camp: complete with high wire and absolutely no contact with the rest of us. Although some of them could be seen occasionally through the wire, there was no verbal communication. Finally, the west wall of the central hall was opened and a large door built, so that the two groups were merged.

We learned that this second contingent had arrived from Bessarabia, a district of Rumania. It was composed of much the same nationalities as ours and in much the same proportions, although Rumanians, not Poles were the second largest group after Germans. The men had been kept segregated from us, in quarantine, because of contagious diseases.

Some of their stories were quite unusual, even for our circumstances.

They had been taken prisoners in Bessarabia in the late summer of 1944. In the beginning there were about 40,000 of them, kept and guarded in fields. Frost had already started to appear, and somehow they dug shallow holes in the ground as protection, such as it was, against cold. Their only food was *mamaliga,* a kind of corn porridge. Not surprisingly, sickness soon appeared, followed by death - of thousands - for corn apparently lacks many essential nutrients.

A fellow Slovene told me that he had been a member of a squad whose duty was to pick up the dead and strip them of clothing. I am not sure if the underwear was left on the corpses or not, but the bodies were carried away and thrown over a cliff to be buried, somehow.

I remember two other details clearly. One is that on a single day towards the end of their stay in that field of death, over 700 corpses were disposed of by the squad. He told me the exact number, but I can only recall with absolute certainty that it was in the 700s. The other detail my friend told was of how one corpse had by all appearances still some life in it. As he was removing his jacket or shirt, it (or he?) helped him by gently moving his arm back over his shoulder.

The survivors agreed that if they had stayed there any longer, none would have lived. They were saved just in time by their departure to various destinations, with the few hundred landing in our camp. But the P.O.W. camp Tushino was not exactly a recuperation resort, either. Our ills were not due primarily to predominance of one single insufficiently nourishing kind of food, like *mamaliga,* but rather to scarcity of any kind of it.

The most common, though not worst, complaint was water in the legs. Water in the whole body was usually fatal, but it was rare. Dystrophy, plain starvation, was very bad and quite widespread. Some of its victims died, others survived. But the worst killer of all was dysentery.

At one time the whole east hall was a lazaret and the overwhelming majority of patients there had dysentery. Except for one or two short spells when I thought I had it, I was among the fortunate who never suffered from it during my whole internment.

When the east hall became lazaret the O.K. was moved into a side area of the central hall. Even before the move, a barrel with two hand bars for carrying stood in a corner to serve as toilet for those of us in the O.K. who were too ill to go out. The contents were not unlike a semi-liquid porridge, richly splattered with spots of blood, some black but most of it red. The lazaret was off limits, but looking through the door I did see that there was only one storey of beds with mattresses and blankets, possibly even some sheets.

I was told later by survivors that the greatest torture of the dysentery was an excruciating thirst. However, the difference between the will-power needed to abstain from drinking water and drinking it equalled the difference between life and death. I have no idea where could anyone have found it with no working faucets anywhere in the whole building. Possibly at the fire hose.

The foregoing is to me incontestable proof, if one were needed, that sensual pleasure is not at all a reliable guide to discern what is truly good or bad for human beings. Modern pleasure-at-any-cost mentality too often ignores this piece of ancient wisdom with dire consequences for individuals and society as a whole.

In addition to water in my legs, and partial paralysis mentioned earlier, I suffered for a while another strange affliction. There was a distinct feeling of an invisible pair of tongs pulling my toe nails upward as if about to tear them off. At the same time I felt as if some similar pronged tools were tearing the cushions just behind the toes off the bones, pulling the flesh downwards. It was so painful that I spent long periods of time on my knees at the foot of the bed, rather than sleeping, in order to have the soles of my feet turned upwards. The affliction, mercifully, just faded away after a few weeks.

My three or four months in the O.K. seem to me more like a nightmarish dream: some of its details are not very clear in my mind any more.

Of one thing I am certain: during the worst months we rarely talked. After each meal everyone returned to his bed in silence. One could lie next to someone else for days without uttering a word. It was not real life but a kind of vegetation. This is one image: life at a very low ebb.

The other, quite contrary yet equally certain, is one of unending noise going on day and night. Here I see men sitting on the edge of their beds, with small cubes of steel serving as anvils, and parts of airplane motors shaped like huge nails and used as hammers: they hammered, filed and polished articles they were making, continuously, day and night. I can still hear the deafening silence when the German "camp commander" would come in during the night once in a blue moon and order the noise to cease. For a while it was like taking water off the mill; but soon it was business as usual.

What were the men doing?

They were producing things for our own use, especially spoons and food containers. Mostly, however, production was for "export." Many were, or became under the pressure of circumstances consummate artists, making beautiful things from pieces of duraluminium sheets brought from the airplane motor factory or found on the camp grounds. Various kinds of boxes, mostly tobacco and cigarette containers, were made from these sheets. They were intricately engraved, polished, and taken by the workers out to be sold, usually for a piece of bread or some tobacco, for we never handled any money. Most sought after by the Russians were finger rings. Daily they would ask *u vas koltsó est?* (do you have a ring?).

Airplane wreckage provided a veritable mine of copper and brass pipes just thick enough for making rings. Some of the products were fit to serve as wedding rings for the nobility, if not royalty! No wonder the Russians, both women and men, were fascinated by them.

These two images - one of almost graveyard quiet, the other of a mill-like noise and beehive activity - are intertwined inextricably in my memory. The only way I can explain the apparent contradiction is that they must belong to two different periods of time blended into one in my memory. Just as Charles Dickens in his *Tale of Two Cities* says that "It was both the worst and the best of times" which sounds at first hearing like a contradiction, so does the statement "It was a time (or thing) I could never forget yet I cannot recall."

Some years ago I saw the movie *One Day in the Life of Ivan Denisovich,* produced after Aleksandr Solzhenitsyn's book with the same title. The film may not be material for an Oscar award, but for obvious reasons I found it fascinating. There were striking similarities as well as differences between a day in the life of a Soviet convict in a *Gúlag* camp, and a day in the life of a P.O.W. in camp Tushino.

Let me only describe a day in our camp, and mention here what I think was the greatest difference: the physical appearance of the film characters compared to us (but who'd expect film stars to go on a starvation diet?!).

By way of some preliminary remarks, let me state that the Soviet military guards, and indeed any other Soviet citizens, were only rarely seen anywhere on the camp grounds, excepting the one or two who supervised the everlasting counting of inmates. Others came only at irregular intervals to search the camp and each inmate meticulously for any objects that could be used as weapons: especially knives. All such objects were piled up and taken away each time.

The inner workings of our camp were administered by members of the *Nazional Komitee Freies Deutschland* (National Committee Free Germany). These were P.O.W.s, captured in the earlier stages of the German-Soviet conflict, most of them at Stalingrad. They had been put through political re-education courses, but were still prisoners like the other inmates, except for some marked differences. The most important one was that they were no more starvelings: their physical appearance was quite normal. Also, their living quarters were separate from ours: they made for themselves a few clumsily constructed rooms of somewhat smaller than normal size, next to the main entrance, along the north wall inside the central hall: nothing to brag about, but considerably more comfortable than our quarters. Moreover, they hardly ever left the camp: the commander of every labour group going to work outside the camp was an "ordinary" P.O.W., his principal job being to help the guards with counting of their charges. If they ever did leave the camp, they were guarded like anyone else at all times. The only exception I recall occurred after the war, when I once saw - wonder of wonders! - our "camp commander" walk freely on the road outside the triple barbed-wire fence, coming over the canal bridge behind our camp.

The phrase *ich gehe zum Komitee* (I'll go to the Committee) was occasionally heard as a mild threat in disagreements between us "ordinary" inmates. There was also a rare case when the *Komitee* was expected to intercede on our behalf with the Soviet authorities. But generally speaking, there was very little communication of any kind between the two classes of P.O.W.s.

No prisoner, except perhaps some members of the Komitee, had any kind of timepiece, and so we had to guess what hour it was at any time of the day or night, including the time of rising: probably about 4:00 or 5:00 a.m.

Everybody was awakened by a powerful ringing of an airplane motor cylinder. It hung suspended on wire from the ceiling, near a pillar in the centre of the central hall. A motor cylinder shaft was stuck into it and banged back and forth. It gave off a very loud ringing noise. Usually it was operated by the German "camp commander" or his Polish assistant. The former was a rather fatherly and restrained figure. The latter was of a leaner stature, but a real firebrand; he rang the gong wildly, with a stiff expression of utter determination and even anger on his face.

Rising was sluggish: there was no comparison with the military jumping out of bed and rushing out for callisthenics so familiar to me in both Hitler's and Tito's armies.

It took a lot of shouting on the part of the "rousers" before everyone was up and around. For some time the assistance of a mysterious character was employed. He seemed to have been neither a P.O.W., nor a member of the *Komitee,* nor a Soviet citizen. He reminds me now of king Melchizedek of old, of whom we read that he met Abraham (Gen 14:18), but nothing is known about where he came from, nor where he went after. He would jump onto the top storey of bunk-beds right after the gong went off. Swinging a long stick and progressing near the feet down the row he thrashed the bodies indiscriminately along his war-path, all the while shouting at the top of his voice *anóo daväi podnimäis!* (hey, get up!). Or a combination of the words in that phrase. Some men got halfway up, and as soon as he went on dropped back down for a few more minutes of precious rest.

The rising ritual was followed by the counting ritual.

Everybody had to go outside, regardless of weather, and it took the members of the National Committee Free Germany and the guards quite a while to look under the beds and peer into every proverbial nook and cranny before they were satisfied that no one was hiding anywhere. On bitterly cold days a sigh of relief travelled like an electric current through the columns when we began to move back in. We re-entered through the wide main doors in rows of five, and after every 100 the flow stopped in order to allow the counters on both sides of the column to mark the figure on their writing pads.

It took some time before everything was added up, and more than once the figures evidently did not agree. Then the whole procedure had to be repeated.

Only when the authorities were satisfied that everybody was still around would the breakfast be brought in. It was fetched from the kitchen, situated near the southwest corner of the camp grounds, by three or four men from each "company" of 100.

One hundred was some kind of magic number. We were divided, with most rare exceptions, for everything into groups of 100, headed by one of us as "commander": morning counting, factory work, construction, ditch digging, unloading barges at the canal, etc., and evening counting. Whether or not in certain cases a few dozen men were superfluous, didn't matter one bit. This, of course, was before the computer age: I respectfully surmise that the main purpose behind this policy was a simpler mathematics.

After breakfast came the line-up for work assignment. In the beginning this took place anywhere on the grounds, in any area where 100 men could be lined up between the heaps of airplane wreckage. When things got better organized, an area was cleared along the eastern wall of our living quarters, large enough to hold all the 1000 or more inmates.

We were lined up in hundreds, one such column beside the other, with one of us as "commander" in front of each. Then one company after another proceeded in rows of five towards the camp gate, situated next to the guard quarters at the east fence of the compound. Several members of the National Committee Free Germany, standing on each side, counted the prisoners near the inside of the gate, with a guard or two watching. The same kind of counting was performed, by the guards only, immediately outside the gate. Some of the guards who were to accompany each company to work were among the counters, others were posted at intervals on each side further from the exit, not unlike a guard of honour.

With each unit successfully out of the compound, and the

guards satisfied that they really had got their one hundred, away we went.

I wonder if Stalin himself (some 12-15 kilometres away) was as well protected as we, whether in our living quarters, at work, or on our travels between the two. In front of every unit marched the sentry-in-charge, armed with a pistol; two or three guards marching at either side, and one as the rear-guard, all carried either old-fashioned rifles, or sub-machine-guns; the latter were carried hung around the neck with the barrel across the chest.

At the work site they guarded the exits and kept an eye on us. However, in situations like construction sites they formed a large ring within which we moved freely. Lunch was usually brought from the camp.

At the end of the working day we re-assembled, were counted carefully by both our own "commander" and the sentry-in-charge, as well as one or two of the guards. We returned to the camp the same way as we had come. On one occasion we had to be counted three times before departure: someone was missing. It turned out that the "commander" had forgotten to count himself.

Numbers play an exaggerated importance in situations where materialism holds sway, not only with millionaires counting their dollars. I remember how, back in 1942, when Hitler's armies had pushed all the way to the Caucasus, an officer droned on in a speech for about half an hour the numbers of goats, sheep, etc. etc., that had been gained.

One of our inmates was an innocent Rumanian civilian. He stood in a village, he told us, watching a P.O.W. column go by. As one prisoner had somehow vanished, the guards simply picked him up. As long as they brought the complete "number of the elect" to their destination nobody asked any questions. And no prisoner had the chance to ask any, let alone to give any unsolicited answers, either: such "bourgeois" ideas are pooh-poohed by the captors in "genuine" P.O.W. life.

The counting at the camp gate followed the same routine when "the troops came marching in" as when they went out: in reverse order, of course. The procedure for supper was similar to the one for breakfast. Sometimes, though, especially in the early weeks and months, we had to wait outside on the camp grounds a long time before going into the building. On very cold days each company would huddle into a more or less square formation, with everybody close together and leaning on the back of the one ahead in order to keep warm. As the cold is felt much more on the back, the last row had the least advantage. But where there is goodwill there is always a way to improve any situation. In this case the men in the last row moved after a while to the front. This continued until the doors opened.

But that was not the end of a day yet. The last item on the agenda was counting again - naturally! Who could have imagined, in wildest dreams, the "end of a perfect day" without counting?

The gong would ring, the command would come, and everybody made their way into the outer darkness - or worse: freezing cold, rain, or snow and wind. I don't recall any hail.

Every night before sleeping, especially during the terrible winter of 1944 - 1945, a sigh rose spontaneously from the depths of my being: thank God another day is gone...

But the thought of death, to the best of my knowledge, never occurred to me: at least not of death resulting from the wicked camp conditions. Death of so many others didn't seem to make me realize that I myself could be one of them some day soon. The inmates estimated that of the original 1000 or so arrivals, roughly one third died: the vast majority during the first winter. As far as I know there was only one suicide: a Hungarian who hanged himself in a heap of airplane wrecks.

The bodies, stripped of their clothes, were accumulated in a special freezer morgue: a shack on the grounds near the sentry-barracks. When enough were there for a truck load, they were taken to be buried.

Months rolled by: they dragged on and the winter seemed to have no end. But as always, spring began to arrive slowly. The conditions improved somewhat and the quantity of food notably; not so the quality, but nobody cared much. All that really mattered was to get something with which to fill the stomach. If occasionally in the cabbage soup, by now quite thick, there were multitudes of white worms from the gills of an odd fish head, that was secondary.

Some time after I regained enough strength to be out of the O.K. company, around the spring of 1945, two or three others and I were to go and help with a burial. It may seem strange that P.O.W.s would be allowed to be involved with such a matter. Yet that was the case.

However, the "commander" of my company, an "elderly" Polish man, perhaps in his early forties, for whatever reason did not want me to go. As a pretext he used my age: "You are not yet 20, so you cannot go." Instead, a friend of mine, who was also from Yugoslavia and had been a Hungarian soldier, went. My only regret was the loss of the *Nachschlag,* the extra portion of food, which was customary on such occasions. My friend told me of how they drove to a forest near Moscow, dug large holes, and buried in each hole about 10 bodies with only one marker on top.

At about this time or a little before it, some of the group that had left the camp months earlier - the group I had wanted, so much, to be part of - began to trickle back. Most of them were put either into the O.K. category or the lazaret. They had left in reasonable shape, as members of the first category. Now many could not be recognized. Their bodies were emaciated and they had aged considerably. Some had not returned; others died shortly after their return. A few survived.

These "chosen ones" had been taken to a remote camp somewhere in the direction of Siberia. Daily they had been driven a long way on open trucks, often in bitter cold, to do heavy work in a large forest. The food was scarce and living conditions worse than in Tushino.

I am sure if the good lieutenant had not happened to notice me and my appearance in that line a few months before, I would not be around today to tell the story.

Every prisoner of war has a story: more likely quite a few of them. In fact, he **is** a living story in himself. But the majority of them can be known only by God.

Most of my comrades in Tushino could tell of greater horrors of war than I. Many of them were front-line soldiers when I was still a high school boy. They fought on battlefields from the icy snowfields of Lapland to the burning sands of the Sahara

Desert. And while I was released in 1946, and the Austrians in 1947, the Germans remained at least until 1948. Their starvation was over, but their country in ruins, and many of their families expelled from their homesteads or no more alive.

One sad story is that of Janko.

He was a Slovene: a lively and friendly youth of about 21. He had been drafted soon after his marriage. Deeply in love with his wife, he constantly yearned for her and the child he never saw. Janko had been one of the "chosen ones" in that fateful line. He returned to the camp a physical wreck, a shadow of his former bubbling personality, yet still yearning for his beloved wife and child without knowing whether they were dead or alive.

After his return from the forest camp he was in the lazaret for a while.

In the spring of 1945 he joined one of the truckloads of corpses that were to be buried near that forest, just outside of Moscow.

But even in this dark gloom there were bright spots. There are many anecdotes of basic human goodness, solidarity, and genuine love that knows no restrictions or boundaries of race, religion, or language: incidents that reflect the command of Jesus to "Love your enemies, do good to those who hate you" (Lk 6:27).

The anecdote about the *lámpochka* has already been recounted. Here are some more samples.

In the backyards of the new houses that were being built there were fairly large garden patches with all the cabbage and potatoes already harvested. The ground had been turned again, more than once, by prisoners shovelling frantically during any recess, especially at noon time, to find any small potatoes that had been overlooked. The guards who formed the circle around the site seemed to look the other way. They reacted only if a prisoner came too close.

In one case the circle included some inhabited houses. During the work I saw two teenage girls come slowly to the garden patches, shyly stopping after every few steps and cautiously looking around. They placed a small board on the ground with two potatoes on it and ran back like two young deer.

People going to work in the factory always carried a large piece of bread under their elbows. Apparently their daily rations were weighed, because there was usually another smaller wedge of bread on top. It stuck safely because the bread was always fresh and rather moist. It was either rye or heavy, brown wheat bread, and practically never wrapped.

We would ask any of these workers, men or women, for a piece of bread: *kusóchek chléba u vas est?* (do you have a piece of bread?) and almost always they would give the small wedge if not a part broken off the main piece.

In the evening, too, many people carried home some food, either bought at the *bazár* (free market) or else their daily ration from the ordinary collective store called *magazín.*

Once a woman came by with only a few potatoes in a net-bag. Somebody asked quietly *kartóshki u vas est?* (do you have a potato?). She stopped suddenly, looked around to see that no *milíciya* was near (people had not much affection for gendarmes, referred to as militia), turned the net upside down, and let all the potatoes fall out. She walked on with her empty net, and the potatoes rolled all around and down the slightly inclined ground. We pounced on them. I suspect that the good lady went to bed without any supper worth mentioning.

It may be asked how or where we cooked the potatoes.

The usual and almost the only possible way was to put them in water in our food containers, which were then piled on one another all around the oil-barrel stove in the middle of the central hall. Only a few were fortunate to find a place on the top of the barrel where they cooked much faster.

During our starvation period I happened to work once in a potato cellar. The lady who brought the potatoes with a truck looked down the steps. She saw me eating a raw potato and reminded me that I would die and my mother cry if I carry on eating raw potatoes. A cabbage leaf run over by more than one truck and picked up on the street tastes quite good in extreme hunger; but raw potatoes have no taste even then.

Usually there was no problem in bringing things through the camp gate. Much more difficult was to get anything to take with. On one most rare occasion I had worked somewhere where I had the opportunity to get quite a few potatoes. I stuck them all around, inside my pants and jacket. My greed, however, was soon punished. It must have appeared too obvious that my corpulence was not quite normal: at the gate my whole hoard was confiscated.

Our fuel for the oil-barrel oven, too, was brought through the gate in small pieces: broken boards, sticks, anything burnable. The guards, usually quite lax at the gate, were at times even cooperative.

One of our most beloved benefactors was an old lady, perhaps in her 70s: everybody knew the *bábushka* (granny). She wore a black *bábushka* tied under her chin and lived in a three or four-storey apartment building at the edge of the wartime housing project where I often worked, especially in the early weeks of my sojourn in Tushino. I still treasure the piece of paper with her address in her own simple, clumsy handwriting: Moskva, Tushino, Komsomolskaya Dom 3, Anastasiya Trofimovna Kovaleva. Her apartment building stood just within the circle of guards.

Sometimes she stealthily half-opened the main door of the building and beckoned, smiling, one or the other of us to come and get a piece of bread or even a small bowl of thick soup. Or she would walk slowly around, carrying Yurushka, son of her daughter Valya.

*Bábushka* had a kind, subdued smile that reminded me of my mother's furrowed face when a smile lit it up. In both these remarkable women it was an expression of love, compassion, kindness and pity all blended in one. And there was an unmistakable sign of mellowness in it, the result of suffering borne patiently through many years. Once she showed me her *própusk* (Communist Party membership card) - a small red folder with a postage-stamp-sized photograph inside and little else. I am sure it was no more than a formality: a necessary condition and requirement for her having been a forewoman in the factory, rather than dedication to an atheistic philosophy which, in my view, is utterly foreign to the genuine, beautiful Russian soul. On one occasion she looked at her beloved grandson in her arms with a loving smile and said *Yúrushka, perekrest ís* (little George, make the sign of the cross). Holding his little hand, she encouraged Yurushka to cross himself so that God may keep and save him from being some day in a situation like *diádia* (uncle), turning her head towards me. Then she made the sign of the cross with Yurushka's own hand over his face and chest.

The local people often brought a bundle of firewood home from work on their backs, and held with a rope over the shoulder. It could be bought at the *bazár* (free market). Even the several storeys high apartment buildings, at least in the area of our construction site, were heated by wood stoves. Later people would bring the wood out of their apartments and chop it into smaller pieces right on the cement or cobblestone pavement in front of the building. One could have ridden the axes afterwards, all the way to Red Square. But they did the job, and that's what mattered.

Once a lady, a medical nurse, brought a large armful of wood, dropped it, and sighed, visibly exhausted, *Oi, Bózhe mói* (O, my God). Only then she looked suddenly sideways: she seemed startled at my unexpected presence, and asked me if I believed in God.

"Yes, I do."

She said nothing, nor made any other reaction. She simply took her axe, and went to work splitting the wood. I have no clue what went through her mind but I strongly suspect that she, too, believed in God.

This is only a sampling of anecdotes scattered throughout my stay in Tushino.

As the spring of 1945 approached, the *salyút* (21-gun salute) was heard more and more frequently. I believe it took place on Red Square. Whenever a large city was taken by the Red Army, there was a gun salute that evening. When Berlin fell, the shots seemed even more powerful: the earth itself resounded. At least that was the feeling all around, and especially in my soles.

Finally the end of the nightmare was at hand.

There had been rumours that the end of the war was near.

Very late in the evening of May 8, 1945, the gong rang and the camp was called to silence. We perched on our bunks. The Soviet major, the "real" camp commander, himself walked in accompanied by the P.O.W. camp commander and his assistant, and some Soviet camp guards. The major was wearing his hard military cap with a plastic shield, and was smoking a cigarette. He stopped near the gong, took his cigarette in hand, announced *voiná kapút* (the war is over), threw the cigarette on the floor and joined everyone else in prolonged, wild applause charged with profound emotion. There may have been some shouts but I don't recall that detail.

In no time the whole camp became like an anthill on a hot summer's day. Together with many others, I ran out and a few of us climbed up an iron ladder to the factory roof.

The scene was unforgettable.

I never knew there were so many search lights in and around Moscow: literally hundreds, possibly thousands. They appeared to form a circle all around us, with the highest density at its most distant section: east-southeast, in and around the centre of the capital.

All the searchlights were turning as fast as they could, their beams intersecting one another and producing a magnificent sight. To make the scene even more glorious, high over glowing Moscow hundreds of dandelion-like fireworks of all colours blossomed simultaneously, as well as in fast succession, then fell slowly to disappear into the glow below.

*Moskvá líkuet* (Moscow celebrates) was a phrase often used in papers or by the people when they talked about victories, particularly the captures of important cities during the final titanic Soviet offensives of the war. *Moskvá líkuet,* a phrase always fraught with a powerful charge and a deep emotion that was reflected on the faces of people, would seem almost an understatement for this most special occasion.

During the next day we saw groups of people - some singing, some playing accordions, almost all somewhat wobbly - coming across the canal bridge, presumably from their all-night celebrations.

Even before the end of the war, things in the camp had been improving. The size of the ladle was increased, the soup became thicker, and there was some meat more often either in the *kásha* or even in the soup itself. Many men from the O.K. were able to return to work. There was still hunger, but no more

Parents:   Janez Skumavc and Kristina Lakota.   Wedding photo (1908)

Patron Saint:   St. Francis of Paola.
Native of Southern Italy (+1507 A.D.)

Father:   Austrian - Hungarian soldier,
on furlough from the front in Northern
Italy; with his mother, my mother, Janez
and Rudolf (1915 or 1916)

Who disturbed the boy's nap under a mighty linden? (1927)

Being photographed is a serious matter! With grandma, dad, and Janez (1927)

The whole family (1932 or 1933)

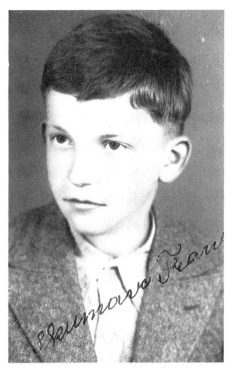

Aged 12 (1938)

Just Confirmed. With Marijan, Tomaž, and godfather (1938)

With Marijan and Tomaž on the Bosnian pony kept in our stable and used only for the Royal family and other V.I.P.s when hunting chamois

With Marijan (holding binoculars) and friends on top of Triglav (September 10, 1947)

Janez with his treasured accordion.

Janez and Angela, widow of Tomaž. (The coloured photo "Springtime in Radovna" is taken from behind the tree just outside the courtyard)

A mini-siesta during a visit from Canada (1965 or 1969)

Dad with his zither, pipe, and thirsty friends

Elementary school in Dovje.  Between it and the traffic sign is a "holy sign"

The College of St. Stanislaus, Št. Vid near Ljubljana.

St. Michael's parish church, Dovje

Grenadier in the German Army (1944)

Junior sergeant of artillery in the Yugoslavian Army (1947 - 1949)

Our battery unit of cadets: Orthodox, Catholics, Muslims, probably one or two Protestants; Lieutenant (Slovene) and sergeant (at his right, Serb) possibly atheists - friends ALL. In second line: second from left, a Bosnian Muslim and one of my best friends; third, a Croat; fourth, a Macedonian; second last, yours truly; last, a Serb (1948)

A priest forever (ordained May 31, 1959)  Dad's last photo (1953)

Last meeting with mother. From left to right: Janez, mother's sister Pavla, three Austrian hosts, and mother (Austria, October 1959)

First Solemn Mass, with Dr. Jakob Kolarič,
C.M., assisting (June 7, 1959)

## Dovje, Mojstrana, and panorama of the Julian Alps.

The Alpine slopes are an ideal training ground for skiing. Most of the Yugoslavian competitors in world ski events hailed from this area.

## Springtime in Radovna.

On the preceding photo, near the left edge, behind the mountain in the foreground, is a glimpse of the remotest area of the mountains seen on this one. (See also black and white photo "Janez and Angela...").

**The Skumavc homestead in winter.**

Let it snow, let it snow, let it snow...

**Early spring in the Krma valley.**

"The fields turn from predominantly purple or pink, to yellow, then blue, then after a week or two some other colour..." (Part I, p.10).

**I will not forget you...**

Mojstrana is on the other side of the "low area in the mountains, a kind of giant saddle" (Part I, p. 2) north of the Skumavc homestead. Are the mysterious forests by night still ghost-infested? Do wild hunts still rage through them?

**Orient Express?**

The main altar in the chapel of St. Stanislaus College.

**"And early in the morning he came walking toward them on the sea...**

So Peter got out of the boat, started walking on the water, and came toward Jesus. But when he noticed the strong wind, he became frightened and beginning to sink, he cried out, 'Lord, save me!' " (Mt 14:25,29-30).

**Hail Mary, full of grace! The Lord is with you;**

blessed are you among women, and blessed is the fruit of your womb, Jesus. Holy Mary, Mother of God, pray for us sinners, now and at the hour of our death. Amen.

A bouquet for you.

starvation like before.

Soon new transports of P.O.W.s began arriving, so that a third storey had to be added to our bunk beds, as recounted earlier. For a period of time I had nowhere else to sleep than on the floor below the bunk-beds. Fortunately I found somewhere a board to lie on; a brick served as pillow. There were only two minor nuisances: the space above me was scarce, and the man above seemed to produce more dirt than expected. It was falling constantly on my face and behind my neck and caused itching.

Some additional buildings also had to be constructed on the campgrounds. The lower half of a large one was dug into the ground, presumably to keep it warmer; it was covered only with a huge canvas. Yet there was still only the one wooden trough with 10 or 12 faucets, mentioned earlier. It served for washing for the whole camp population, which swelled to about 4000 souls. Even so, this was a great improvement over the situation earlier in the winter, when there was no water available. I recall an occasion when I had an urgent need to wash a piece of laundry. The only way to get some water was to break through ice in a thrown-away sink in the piles of junk on the yard, where it gathered from snow and rain.

The trough stood in the courtyard. If I happened to wake up in time, I usually went at three or four o'clock in the morning to wash. Later it was hardly possible to even get near the trough. One morning, when it was still dark and I was about to wash, I took the religious medal that I always wore, off my neck. It was a special medal, known among Catholics as the Miraculous Medal. However, it fell into the mud, which was naturally all around the trough as to my knowledge there was no drain. I never found it again, to my deep regret, for I had cherished it very much. As it happened, the one and only object I brought into the Soviet Union and back - apart from my own body and soul - is the *Erkennungsmarke* (identity-tag). It is a pewter pendant, oval and fairly large; it had to be worn by soldiers on a string around the neck at all times. Lengthwise it has a line with three perforations at its centre. Both parts have the identical inscription: the unit number and blood type. In case of death, one half was sent to the unit, the other was buried with the corpse. In the P.O.W. camp it was totally ignored; few if any of us still had it, and I wonder how come it was not taken away from me in one of the searches.

Some time between the end of the war in Europe and August 1945 one of my countrymen, a fellow Slovene, came with the news that something was in the offing. He was one of the "eager beavers" and somehow usually got the news first. A curious company was being set up. It was to consist of one hundred men (what else? the magic number again!) taken more or less proportionally from the various nationalities: most would be Germans, then Austrians, Poles, and so on down the line. Accordingly, there would be also a few Yugoslavians.

The rumours turned out to be true, even in regard to national representation. In the next few days a new company was set up hurriedly and given the name *Vospomogátelnaya Kománda* (Auxiliary Commando). It was a real curiosity, more so because the war in Europe was ended.

True, we saw some large transports of soldiers moving eastwards, presumably towards the Japanese front, soon after the European shooting stopped. But one would have expected more soldiers released for guard duty. Yet it was now that the V.K. was set up.

Its members were P.O.W.s; they were kept behind the triple barbed-wire fence and guarded anywhere outside the camp like every other prisoner. They, too, had to have on the left arm of the jacket a square piece of cloth cut out and another piece with the letters V.P. (*voennoplénnyi:* prisoner of war) sewn in its place, like every other inmate. In addition they wore, also on the left arm, a band with the letters V.K. Both inscriptions were in the Cyrillic alphabet, of course. They were also counted like everyone else, yet they were to guard other prisoners.

At the time I was glad to accept the offer to join. We had no weapons of any kind, and all we did was to stand in the plant or any other working place where we were posted by the guards and see that no fellow prisoner passed by.

We lived at first in a separate tent. Later on we moved to the west hall (where I also celebrated Christmas 1945). There is no comparison between this outfit and the situation that was supposed to have existed in Nazi concentration camps. No one considered us traitors, informers, or collaborators, yet the memory of it leaves a somewhat bad taste in the depths in my soul.

I stayed with the V.K. to the end of my prisonership of war.

The war was over, time went on, but nobody knew how long we were to remain in captivity. Most Russians used to say to us *skóro domói* (soon you'll go home). However, some opined to the contrary: "You'll stay here at least 10 more years: until you restore all that you destroyed." I had a feeling, ingrained into my whole being, that it was impossible to ever be free again. I often imagined myself standing on the slope behind my home, looking over the house and the field towards a group of hazelnut bushes and the scattered small pines further on. I saw myself going freely from the house over the field towards the bushes. More correctly: I imagined how would it feel, for at the same time I had a strange feeling that it could never be again. It seemed utterly impossible that I would ever again be free to go anywhere without being guarded by armed soldiers.

Once I had a very disquieting dream. I was suddenly on a mountain side, northwest of my home, close to the top on one of the tower-like rocks. The area is actually called The Steeples. Looking down the steep slopes I saw my home deep in the valley. Then as if by a magic zoom camera, it came closer and closer. In each of the several moves the image of the buildings became more distinct and their pathetic condition became more scary. Finally, I knew that my home was nothing more than a burnt-out hulk with blackened holes in the place of windows, and no life of any kind anywhere near it.

As I woke up, I wondered whether that was the actual fact or just a bad dream. Even though I like to think that I am not superstitious, the curiosity and anxiety about the fate of my family and home became more acute and frequent from then on.

In the camp there was a so called "wall newspaper": a sheet of thin whitewashed plywood. One day in August it carried the news of the attack on Hiroshima, and the force of the bomb dropped on the unfortunate city. A German soldier who read it, exclaimed: "Atomic bomb!", even though there was no mention that it was atomic. I find it curious that I never heard the word before, or even thought about it, in connection with any weapons, although there was much talk, in the Army, about "new weapons," especially regarding the series of the so called V weapons (V stands for *Vergeltungswaffe:* Revenge Weapon. They were the weapons to revenge the enormous destruction wrought by Allied bombing).

The one outstanding event in the late summer of 1945 was to have been the first post-war *Den Vozduhoplóvstva* (Day of Aviation). It was to take place on the historical military airfield of Tushino. The papers said that several hundred thousand people were expected to attend, including Stalin himself. A special viewing balcony was prepared for him and presumably for his entourage on a building overlooking the whole airfield.

Prisoners of war helped in the preparation of the grounds. The most feverish activity, though, was in the air. A large group with beautifully checkered, double parachutes dropped from some planes. We could hear them shout to one another just before they touched down; then they tumbled and folded their chutes. In a breathtaking stunt four parachutists dropped from great height at the same time and very close to one another. After a very long fall they let their parachutes open almost at the same time, with loud cracks. After a few fast twists back and forth like worms they slowly came to the ground.

There were women fliers, too, according to the announcer. They piloted about 15 planes flying next to each other, then made sharp left turns one after another so that they flew in single file just above the place where Stalin was to have been.

There were also at least one or two tragedies. One was a parachutist who dropped from a single small plane but his chute did not open. There was no chance he survived because he was too close to the ground when he disappeared from sight beyond the low hill on the other side of the Moskva river. Hopefully it was only a dummy. The other one occurred in the same general area, but that one was certainly real. A pilot did all kinds of acrobatics, especially large loops. One of them took him too low. As soon as he disappeared behind the hill, a cloud of black smoke appeared.

On the great day we prisoners had to stay in camp. Before

the activities even started, the weather turned bad and there was a deluge-like downpour. Not long afterwards thousands of would-be spectators passed by on the road east of our camp, up and over the canal bridge, soaking wet.

Thus ended the first post-war Air Force Day in Moscow. The following year things were better, both for the Moscowites and myself: I saw pictures of the event in a review at home.

Time dragged on and on. Another winter came. And another Christmas. And we still languished in captivity. Now and then a prisoner would still die, but there was no comparison with the numbers of the previous winter. During our stay in the V.K. tent we were lucky: we escaped "the last plague": bed bugs. Their German name is *die Wanzen.*

They are, in some ways, worse than lice or fleas. Some become like little round bladders of blood; and unlike lice, they crawl all over the walls. A bloody war raged between the pests and the prisoners, and the walls and pillars in the central hall turned red with the blood of the bugs, or more correctly, of the prisoners. The bug war went on and no side surrendered.

Rumours began to circulate that the Poles in some Soviet P.O.W. camps were sent home. Then, quite unexpectedly, in the last days of January 1946, the incredible happened: the Yugoslavians and Czechoslovaks were summoned to go home, on the spur of a moment.

As we came on a freight train, so we left. But this time the weather was colder and there was an oil barrel in the middle of each car, for heating, and towards each end of it a two-storey wooden platform. We were able to lie with our heads or feet towards the centre of the box car: this time there was lots of room to stretch one's legs.

Our favoured pastime was catching lice and dropping them on top of the hot barrel. We watched as the air in their bodies suddenly expanded and then the lice exploded. It made a small popping noise and was strong enough to blow away the dust in the area of a thumb nail.

We were still under guard. However, whenever the train stopped, we were allowed to get out and buy sunflower seeds. They were sold by local farmers who brought them to the railway stations and sold them on the free market, using drinking glasses as a measure. Russians are real artists in eating these seeds. They carry them in their pockets, bringing them out in handfuls and popping them, one by one, into their mouths like machines. Each has to be brought between the teeth, cracked, husk spit out, and then the contents consumed. We, however, needed much more time. And that was the advantage to us, in the circumstances. Boredom was almost as great a reason for the habit as the good taste of the *sémenchki* (the seeds).

Loaves of brown or rye bread were also available on the stations along the route, and *mochórka* (tobacco) was also sold by the drinking glass. It was of two basic kinds: brown and green, and looked almost like oats. To make a cigarette one made a long, very narrow, paper tube from a piece of newspaper. At the mouth, it was just thick enough to get the smoke through after a piece of it was first pinched off. At the other end it was considerably thicker; the paper had to be folded so that the contents did not run out.

The money we had was earned - hard earned! We are all familiar with shrewd legal devices such as "skill testing questions" (e.g. how much is 2 + 3) or buying a car for one dollar, in order to make what is really a forbidden game of chance a legal transaction. Apparently the international laws regarding prisoners of war require some compensation for their work. So, just before going home we were paid. I received 21 roubles: enough to buy two or three loaves of bread. I bought some bread, some sunflower seeds, and took the change home as a souvenir.

Fuel for the oil barrel oven had to be "organized." A stop on some sidetracks was usually quite opportune, especially if it was night and a car of boards or anything flammable parked nearby. On one occasion, somewhere in Rumania, the gate to a house ended up in our oven. We were still under guard, but seemingly nobody worried very much that anyone would escape. Consequently, we were able to buy things at railway stations, as well as provide the fuel.

After many days, the Carpathian mountains began to appear in the distance. Our passage from the Soviet Union into Rumania, over the famous Mytla pass, was by night, so we saw nothing of its natural beauty. In Rumania we stayed one week in a camp in the town called Muramares, in Rumanian, or Marmaros Sighet, in Hungarian. All I recall from that camp is mud. Here those from Czechoslovakia and Yugoslavia were separated, each to go their own way.

The closer we got to the Yugoslavian border the more curious we became. What does the new money look like? Or the new military uniform? Somebody had the crazy idea that we would be received with a music band.

Human imagination, indeed, seems to have no limitations for both intelligence and stupidity.

We arrived to the border town of Velika Kikinda at dawn: not to a music band but to a band of ragged armed men, members of the Yugoslavian People's Army. They awaited us with unmistakable displeasure. We were led under tight guard to a bombed-out kitchen or bakery: there was a row of large built-in kettles along a wall, and the whole building seemed to have been only one room. A few times I carried heavy bags of grain somewhere in the town: always under armed guard.

The straw on our floor was wet. I remember sitting one night on the brink of one of the kettles with my legs in it and watching , through a broken window, the large moon, hoping it would move a little faster. But it seemed to have got stuck in the sky. I sat there rather than lie in the wet straw. When I think of the scene I am always reminded of the picture of St. Vitus as depicted in old almanacs. He is supposed to have been martyred by being boiled in oil. So he is pictured standing in a huge cauldron, just like the one I sat in that long night.

After about a week we were again locked in cattle cars. The only view was through some cracks at the sliding door. In Zagreb, the capital of Croatia, we got some food, and a very angry looking officer appeared. Like a hawk he moved along the line, looking fiercely from close range at one after another of us. He pulled a few out of the line and sent them away. I have no idea of what it was all about, or what happened to the literally hand-picked ones.

After a short stop in Zagreb we continued on our journey, and arrived in Ljubljana, the capital of my native Slovenia, just before the dawn.

The city was still. A small detachment of armed soldiers was lined up as our car opened, and we were ordered to jump out. They arranged us into rows of five and told us to hold one another around the neck. With a final reminder that one single word means "you're dead" we went down the deserted streets and under a bridge to the Collecting Base for Repatriates and Prisoners of War. Ironically, it was the confiscated, brand new diocesan seminary, not quite finished at the time the war broke out in 1941. It is there that I would have studied for the priesthood, barring any unforeseen circumstances.

We stayed there about one week, well protected by sub-machine-gun carrying guards walking the corridors. A young guard from Dovje recognized me and, as I learned upon my arrival home, notified my relatives about my whereabouts. Until then they only knew that I was missing in action. My German commander had written a very cordial letter to that effect to my father from a military hospital.

On March 7, 1946, we were summoned to the counter at the end of our corridor. I only remember two of us being there at the time. Each of us was given a small slip and the other man asked, "What do I do with this slip?"

"You can go wherever you want."

I suddenly felt a mysterious force in the front of my shoulders pull upwards, which made me almost duck instinctively, for I had the feeling that I would hit the ceiling.

We were instructed that all we have to do is to report the next day to the nearest secret police station. Then I went with one or two others in a state of stupor or euphoria to the railway station. I have no clue what we talked about on the way: it all seemed like a beautiful dream.

As it was already dark and I had to be the next day in Jesenice, I decided to get off the train in a suburb of that city and stay overnight there. With great anticipation I knocked on the door of the apartment where my brother, Rudolph, used to live.

"Is Rudolf Skumavc living here?"

"No!" answered a strange woman's voice. My heart dropped, but soon I was reassured: he and his family were alive and well somewhere in the other end of Slovenia, and his wife's parents were still where they used to be, about 10 minutes walk, in a factory apartment house.

I thanked the lady - she never opened the door - and went to try my luck with Rudolph's parents-in-law. They lived on the second floor; the entrance was at the top of iron stairs, outside.

I knocked, hoping somebody would still be up.

"Who is there?" came the voice of Mrs. Vidic. As I identified myself she exclaimed "Oh God, I hope not," apparently thinking instinctively that it was my ghost.

After a long pause the door opened and there she stood, somewhat bewildered, with a good shot of whisky in her hand.

There were no telephones, and the news of my return did not yet reach her. She told me that my parents and brothers were all alive (the guard in Ljubljana couldn't communicate much with the prisoners), how my brother, John, was mobilized in February 1945 by Tito's partisans as he was milking cows one evening, and given one hour to get ready. And in the last days of war, Rudolph was also mobilized, on his way home, by the advancing partisans. By now both were released. We had a lot to talk about.

I asked her if I could stay overnight there, but I was full of lice and didn't want to sleep in bed, so I just lay down on the kitchen floor with my head under the table.

It was late in the morning when I woke up. I was told later that when Mr. Vidic came home from his shift, very early in the morning, he thought at first sight that his wife was lying there dead. His first reaction can well be imagined.

After breakfast I left by foot: a half-hour's walk to Jesenice. Having gone through two or three rooms - and past as many guards - I reached the "holy of holies" of the secret police headquarters in Jesenice. I did not feel very comfortable as the officer sitting behind the desk asked sternly: "Did you not know where we were?"

Of course I knew! I explained that I would have joined the partisans rather than answer the draft summons, had I not been seriously sick and under the doctor's care, and convinced that the Germans would let me go. He seemed reluctantly satisfied. I was free to leave. The walk home would take me about three hours.

On the road I met a farmer from Dovje who recognized

me. We talked for a while. Having come close to Mojstrana, I was too nervous and embarrassed to go through it in my P.O.W. outfit. Rather, I turned left before reaching the village, went uphill over patches of deep snow and muddy fields, and returned back to the road to Radovna.

Coming downhill through the forest, I peeped from behind the corner down to the entrance of the house. I was not aware that they already knew I was still alive and on my way home. My memory of stories about people who dropped dead from excessive and sudden joy kept me from making a too-sudden appearance.

My oldest brother came outside with a washbowl.

"Janez," I called him softly.

He turned, recognized me, smiled, exclaimed something quietly, and started to go back into the house.

My parents must have been in the vestibule, for he simply said, from the threshold, "I brought you a Russian."

In no time my dad and mum appeared and looked up at me. They could still see nothing but my head with a typical Russian cap. Only then I went down.

It was my 20th birthday: March 8, 1946, around noon.

My father seemed happy, surprised, and looked at me as if doubting that it was really me. My mother had the kind of peaceful smile that only people who have suffered much can have. I shook hands with my father and with John. My mother embraced me and planted on my cheek a warm kiss seasoned with the heavenly aroma of snuff tobacco.

We went into the kitchen, father fetching on the way his zither from "the house." He hadn't touched it since I had gone missing. Now he played it again, gesturing with his breathing and bushy mustaches, as well as his head covered with a hat all decorated with various pins and especially a bouquet of chamois hairs, which swayed on the hat with the tune.

Then we sat down to lunch. It just happened to be one of my favourite meals: cottage cheese and grit mixed, seasoned with fried onions, and wrapped in buckwheat dough, cooked, then cut into large chunks and generously enriched with lard and bacon crumbs. A most welcome meal indeed! I must have eaten at least three servings.

Mrs. Carole Birss, the good lady who typed my manuscript, wrote on the page a remark at this point: "I'd like you to expand more on the delight of being home. Reader needs a few roses after all those thorns and before any more thorns also."

Well, if I were William Shakespeare, I might write a play about it; if one of the great modern film geniuses, I'd like to make a beautiful movie. Being who I am, all I can say is that it was an ecstatic, unforgettable event, and I invite the reader to take in spirit my place for the occasion. In a nutshell: it was indeed "loverly," almost heavenly!

We had a lot of news to share: I told them of my adventures, and they told me about the family and the friends I knew, and the dangers they lived through, yet most survived.

Among other items they showed me an interesting letter.

The division to which I belonged on the front happened to be a so-called *Sperrdivision.* The German word *Sperre* means bar, barrier, or barricade. What it really meant was that the division was to perish rather than retreat, if so required. One of my countrymen who happened to be in my unit and survived the war told me later that perhaps 10 to 15 of its more than 200 men survived.

The commander of my company was evidently wounded, and this is the letter, in my English translation, which he wrote to my father who gave it to me on the occasion of my return (O.F. before the date in all likelihood means *Ost Front:* East front):

O.F. Nov. 25, 1944.

Hugo Bauer, Oberleutnant
Unit 34808C
at present Military Lazaret
Military Mail #34661B

Very honourable Mr. Skumavc!

The task fell upon me that I must send you today a painful news.

Since the beginning of August I stood in the foreland of

Carpathians in heavy defensive fight against the Russians. As the company gathered on August 4, 1944 after a successful counterattack it was established that your son was not present. He counts therefore as missing. About his whereabouts I have been unable so far to establish anything so certain that I could send you as official news. You can be assured that I find it especially hard that at this time I can not yet say anything definite about the fate of your son. As soon as that should become possible, I will at once inform you. In upright sympathy for the cares and pain which these lines must cause you, I am greeting you with

Hail Hitler.

This letter and its circumstances are to me a clear example of the superb German organization, which did not break down even in most terrible situations until the very end. I am grateful to this gallant soldier for his deed of kindness and I admire his sense of duty even while languishing in a military hospital.

Thank you, Hugo, and God bless you: wherever you are, dead or still alive!

I arrived home in reasonable condition, as far as weight and appearance were concerned, but for the next few weeks I had a voracious appetite. Soon I became overweight, and the local people thought I must have had a great time in the Soviet Union.

Meanwhile I worked at home on our small farm, until October 1947 when I was once again drafted: this time into the Yugoslavian People's Army.

For over two years I served in the artillery, in various parts of Croatia and Slovenia. Our unit was divided into two equal halves: one motorized and the other with horses. Each gun was drawn either by a truck or a three-pair team of horses: two light ones in the front, followed by two middleweight, and then two heavy ones; there were three mounted drivers and a five-men team to each gun, as well as a mounted commander of the unit. Four guns formed a battery.

It goes almost without saying that I fell into the half with the horses, which meant being kicked now and then, bitten, and thrown. Some were angels and some were devils, with most in between.

It also meant that I had no opportunity for mechanical training, and last but not least, a daily loss of one hour's sleep, compared with the soldiers in the motorized part. Every morning for an hour we groomed, fed, and watered the horses and cleaned their stables. Besides that, they had to be guarded day and night by several soldiers, the same way as the whole camp. The duty, of course, was performed inside the stables, and included the keeping of cleanliness. The only "weapons" were fork, rake, and shovel. As guards we had two hours sleep, followed by two hours of readiness, and two hours of duty, around the clock, for about a week. Then we returned to regular routine for a few weeks before the next round of stable duty. Our garrison had more than 200 horses, quartered in several separate stables.

After a few months our battery became, initially without our knowledge, a training unit for junior sergeants. That meant more severe training, two stripes on the epaulettes in due time, and responsibility for one gun with its team and equipment, including the horses and their drivers.

Except for manoeuvres or long marches, our daily routine was divided into two parts: political and ideological indoctrination (let's call it simply brainwashing) in the forenoon; military training in the afternoon.

Since childhood, my soul was already firmly committed to Christ, to his Church, and to the priesthood. If anything, the brainwashing only strengthened my commitment. Nazis did some, Soviets did some, but by far the most intense brainwashing took place in the Yugoslavian army, both before and after Tito's break with Stalin.

The military training included hours of left turns, right turns, etc. After thorough mastery of such basics some four or five years earlier, this seemed like being sent from grade five back to kindergarten: it was utterly silly.

A battery in the artillery is equivalent to a company in the infantry. Every unit the size of a battery or larger had two commanders: the military one and the *politkomisar* (political commissioner). The latter always had a rank at least equal to that of the military commander's, and usually one level higher. Moreover, while soldiers could be released for chores around the camp during military training, everyone had to be present for indoctrination. The reason given was that it was more important to know why to shoot than how.

Soon after my draft in 1947, tensions around the vital Adriatic port city of Trieste began to increase. During the struggle in the U.N. between Italy and the Western Allies on the one side and Yugoslavia with her Eastern ones on the other, a point was reached where war could have erupted any minute. Our unit moved from Croatia into Slovenia, closer to the trouble-spot. Gradually tensions diminished.

In 1948 Yugoslavia got into hot water with its Eastern Allies. Things went from bad to worse until a war was imminent along the Bulgarian, Rumanian, and Hungarian borders. So our unit moved back to Croatia, near Hungary. Our training also intensified, especially night alarms, which were designed to shorten the time during which the whole garrison could be ready to march. Everything had to be done in darkness, including the harnessing of horses, and we achieved a high degree of efficiency in a short time.

In every larger room, including every dormitory, the inseparable trinity used to be present: pictures of Lenin, Stalin, and Tito in a triangular formation, with Lenin at the top. One morning Stalin was missing. The unthinkable and unimaginable began to happen. The political commissioners' sky-high exaltation of the Soviet Union and Stalin turned more and more to criticism and complaints about the calumnies committed against Yugoslavia and against its Communist Party by the Soviet Union and the *Kominformbureau* (the mighty Soviet empire in Eastern Europe), the forerunner of the now also defunct Warsaw Pact. Yugoslavia was a member before its expulsion after the break with Stalin.

Some large projects had been built soon after the war, including two railway lines in central parts of Yugoslavia, and a large, show-case type of suburb of the capital, called Novi Beograd (New Belgrade). Due to its improper location at the confluence of Danube and Sava rivers the suburb, which was to include some huge government buildings, allegedly began to crumble before it was completed.

Now a new large project was started, the highway

between the two largest cities in Yugoslavia: Belgrade, the capital of the state as well as of the province of Serbia, and Zagreb, the capital of the province of Croatia. Serbs and Croats are the two largest nations of Yugoslavia, and their relationship has a troubled history. It was natural, then, that the project was named *Autoput Bratstvo-Jedinstvo* (Highway Brotherhood-Unity). However, because of the feverish activity involved in its construction and the current political tensions, I strongly suspect it was primarily a military project: something like the German *Autobahns* 10 or 15 years earlier.

Part of our unit was sent to help with its construction.

There were thousands upon thousands along the route: youth brigades, prisoners, soldiers, and others. The next section to that of our unit was a group of about 3,000 women prisoners. A ring of women guards, some with sub-machine-guns, some kneeling at machine-guns resting on bipods, was around their section. The women, like anyone else, worked with wheelbarrows from morning to evening. Next to them farther east from us was allegedly a contingent of about 5,000 male prisoners.

The whole area looked like an immense anthill bustling with feverish activity on a hot summer's day, but nobody had to work as hard as the soldiers.

We were building escarpments so the highway could pass over a railway line. Daily, every group of either three or five was given a section to fill with earth: a strip of a certain width and height across the whole highway. The earth was dry and hard; it had to be dug with spades and brought up the escarpment by wheelbarrows. Only the pressing of the earth was done by machinery: tractors with large rollers full of big spikes.

I am very well acquainted with many kinds of manual work, but never in my life have I worked as hard as here.

The wheelbarrows were very clumsy, built of heavy wooden boards and squeaky, iron-reinforced wooden wheels. We were told to run with them, back down the wooden plank paths, as a way of relaxing between the trips uphill, when they were filled to overflowing. For the first few days my wrists felt after the shift as if they were on fire, so that I had a hard time sleeping in spite of exhaustion.

We worked with our shirts off, even in the fall and on

night shift when it was quite chilly. In the early morning, steam could be seen rising from our backs and shoulders. The main reason for taking our shirts off even in chilly temperatures was that otherwise they became soaking wet from sweat, and quite uncomfortable and cold until dry again.

In addition to full working shifts, we also kept up our military exercises. Not for nothing were all in our unit honoured at the end of our three or four months' work with the official title of *Udarnik* (hero worker), receiving a kind of medal or pin and certificate.

Of the 25 or 30 members of the elite battery slated to make junior sergeants, I got the highest marks in the final exams, along with the title "First according to Rank." I also received two book awards: the novel *Young Guard* by a Soviet author translated into Slovenian, and a complete edition, in Serbian, of Karl Marx's *Das Kapital.*

From a visit home I brought the *Young Guard* with me to Canada as a souvenir. *Das Kapital* had a more tragic fate. In the seminary, in the 1950s, we learned that the Church law in force at the time called for severe sanctions for possession of books like *Das Kapital.* So I asked my mother to throw the accursed object into the stove. In her next letter she simply stated: "Your wish regarding the book has been fulfilled." Now I almost regret it.

Incidentally, let credit be given where credit is due. No soldier in the Yugoslavian army was allowed to be discriminated against in any way, in deed or word, on account of his war history. And that included service in foreign armies as well as in the various anti-communist domestic forces.

Consequently, my success in final exams made me a candidate for "higher things." Together with another junior sergeant from my class, I was slated to be sent to Belgrade for studies as a reserve finance officer, with prospects of a military career, with a good salary. As reservists we didn't even earn enough for cigarettes: from time to time we had to write home for money if we wanted to go to town on weekends and have a beer.

A most fateful event turned out to be my enrolment as candidate for the Communist Party of Yugoslavia. In any Marxist system, membership in the Communist Party was at the time practically a must for any position above an ordinary labourer, let alone an army officer. I was called into the office of the youth leader, a young officer, and somehow or other I became a candidate, very much against my desire. After a period of from six to 18 months, I would have become a full-fledged member. I attended meetings of the party cell of our military unit, but had to leave for certain points on the agenda, and could not vote.

God only knows how the universe would have unfolded for me had it not been for a monkey wrench thrown into its gears by Pope Pius XII.

The newspaper *Borba* (Fight, or Struggle), the official organ of the Communist Party of Yugoslavia, reported that the Pope decreed automatic excommunication for all members of Communist parties. For me the whole ball game suddenly changed. My reluctance became an outright crisis of conscience, and I began to look frantically for a way out of the mess. Before long an opportunity seemed to appear on the dark horizon.

Unlike active members of the armed forces, those in the reserve, including sergeants, had to have their hair cut short: no longer than one centimetre. That, of course, was much too short - even before the age of hippies - for the delicate taste of young ladies; however, the measure was designed not to keep away the ladies, but lice.

To the pleasure of us young sergeants, the regulation had not been applied to us. My head boasted a beautiful growth. (My present baldness may be the punishment for my pride).

The birthday of our Supreme Commander, Marshall Josip Broz-Tito, was May 25. In honour of that occasion, every military unit was expected to do something special. So, as his birthday in 1949 approached, my battery commander, pressed for some bright idea, came upon the unhappy notion of having his junior sergeants' hair cut short for the occasion; and what's more: keeping the letter of the law from then on, which was even a greater calamity, if a greater one can be imagined.

So I refused to obey: not for the sake of the hair, but in secret hope to get kicked out of the Party candidacy.

The details of the drama are too many to recount here, but the trick worked. However, there was a price to pay.

The commander had a great regard for me, but I remained

stubborn in the face of his entreaties. Soon I found myself in jail for five days, by order of the garrison commander.

Other adverse things came my way: evils as well as blessings in disguise.

With the rapid growth of the Yugoslavian army and the increasing prospect of war, there was a great need for leaders of junior ranks. Thus, with my demobilization due after two years of service, in October 1949, heavy pressure was put on us to sign up for three years' active service, with good pay. But there was little response.

A friend of mine, a Muslim from Bosnia, married and father of one or two children, a simple working man, had knuckled down under pressure and signed. Almost immediately he realized his mistake, but it was too late. More than once I saw him writhe on his bed, repeating constantly: "My God, what have I done? What have I done!" He confided to me that one of the officers asked if I had given him any advice and what had I said. Fortunately I had foreseen that possibility and had been careful not to say anything controversial.

A so-called "box for unclear questions" had been set up in one of the corridors. A note was allegedly found in it to the effect that the cutting of junior sergeants' hair proved how little the Yugoslavian People's Army appreciated them. I did not write it but I was accused of it.

One day I was questioned non-stop from after breakfast until supper time by two secret police officers in our garrison. They wanted to know every detail of my life from babyhood on.

At one point a friend of mine from the same unit was brought in for his testimony. The officer suddenly opened a drawer and threw on the desk a device consisting of a chain with two T-shaped irons, one on each end. The two irons were made to overlap and fit into one another, for better grip. The contraption could be put around the wrist of a victim and turned until it crushed the bones.

The young soldier winced and instinctively took a step backwards. The device was not applied on that occasion.

The chief questioner was continually falling asleep sitting behind his desk and often, in his drowsiness, wandering into saying silly things and asking irrelevant questions. Towards the end of the ordeal he stood before me with his piercing eyes, grabbed my ears with his palms, and turned them upwards and backwards to make an almost complete circle. Then he shoved his thumbs into my eye sockets, and the ritual ended with a hefty slap on my left cheek, accompanied by the remark "you rotten type" in a cutting voice.

As he carried on the interrogation, the officer typed everything in sixplicate on onion skin paper. At the end, I had to sign each sheet. By that time I was in such a shape that I could not recognize my own signature: it was just a scramble.

Their objective was to make me admit that I wrote the accursed note.

"Did you write the slip or not?"

"I did not."

"Then sign that you did not and you will be free. But know that if it can be proven by scientific or any other means that you did, you shall be shot, your family taken to camp, and your family farm confiscated."

"I did not write it but I cannot sign that statement."

"Then that proves that you wrote the slip."

"I did not."

And so on.

Of course I couldn't sign!

The government seemed to have an insatiable hunger for confiscation. Not only monasteries, Church schools and other properties were taken, but also many forests and the better lands of individual farmers. Not the poor ones, though: they were not profitable! For centuries our people had tilled the lands and shed their blood to defend them against the invading Turks and other attackers. Now they were taken away by a stroke of the pen of "liberators." There were also rumours about certain people vanishing. To even ask about the whereabouts of such persons was risky.

Like in the Soviet Union after the Bolshevik Revolution, the Yugoslavian Communist government wanted to industrialize the country in a hurry, chiefly for military purposes. It also wanted to do away with private farms, at least in the fertile areas, turning them into either state-owned enterprises or cooperative communes. Yet in spite of state robbery in the form of confiscations, and exorbitant taxation, the economy went from bad to worse.

These thoughts shot through my mind when I was asked to sign the crucial statement. I feared that they would say they proved I wrote the slip, get rid of me, expel my family, and take possession of our ancestral land, especially the forests, well preserved due to my parents' diligence and wise economy.

The whole circus ended without my signing the statement.

I was never called to go to the reserve finance officers' school in Belgrade. Meanwhile, the political turmoil between Tito and Stalin intensified to the point when war seemed almost inevitable.

By October 17, 1949, it had been two years since my draft, and the term of service was two years. So I awaited demobilization with indescribable yearning.

At the time I was working on the Belgrade-Zagreb highway. One day the order came to line up for a special announcement. Surely it would be the news to write home for civilian clothes!

The disappointment couldn't have been more devastating, except if it had been an announcement of war.

We stood at attention like statues and the commander read the order from the Supreme Commander of the Yugoslavian armed forces, Marshall Josip Broz-Tito, that due to the need arisen, and according to paragraph such-and-such of the Constitution, all those who should be demobilized in October 1949 remain in the army indefinitely, until further notice.

Let me not try to describe my reaction.

We asked our officers later, "How long?" and were told that as long as there was a need; one or two years were mentioned as educated guesses. Insult was added to injury: that it served right the junior sergeants who refused to sign for three years of active service. Now they would have to serve anyway, but with fewer privileges and without salary.

Thank God, things turned out better than expected. In

November our group went back from the work on the highway to rejoin the bulk of our unit in the Bjelovar garrison in Croatia. It was the town in which I had begun the service with the Yugoslavian artillery, and three weeks before Christmas 1949 I was home.

As we were leaving, we were told how to explain our rather unexpected demobilization to any inquirers: we were to say that because Yugoslavia had just been chosen as one of the two non-permanent members of the Security Council of the United Nations, the danger of war with the Soviet Union had receded. I'd say it was about the time, too. I had more than enough of that nonsense.

Nobody ever told me what happened to my candidacy for the membership in the Communist Party. However, at the time of my demobilization I was given a sealed envelope to give to the Party cell leader in my municipality. Rather than carrying out the directive, I opened it. I expected to be called any day to give account of its whereabouts.

From then on I sought to escape the country at the earliest possible date. I say date rather than opportunity, because at that time there were practically no opportunities to realize such unorthodox ideas. The borders were closely guarded. The results of escape attempts were comparable to escapes over the Berlin Wall: some made it, some didn't.

I still keep the contents of that envelope as a souvenir. Until a few years ago I didn't mention my candidacy to any soul under the sun except my pastor in Toronto. I told him simply because I was worried that Yugoslavian authorities might denounce me to my superiors in order to "liquidate" me as a priest, to use a word in the Marxist jargon. I doubt that any faithful bishop would be very happy with a genuine candidate of the Communist Party in the ranks of his priests.

Had I told my mother she would have probably fainted. During the war she had been a dedicated supporter of the partisans, putting her life many times in jeopardy. For protection they even gave her a *nom de guerre:* Olga. My father, who had been an Austrian-Hungarian soldier and military gendarme in the First World War, was a game warden with many friends among the local German soldiers. Some of them were passionate hunters and often dropped in at our home on their patrols. So, it is understandable that he was less unfavourably disposed towards the Germans. Yet he, too, had friends among the partisans and supported them, although more reluctantly than my mother.

My mother told me after the war that on one occasion she had been summoned to the military headquarters for questioning about a heifer that she had allegedly given to the partisans. A local woman-informer, who was executed later in a most grizzly fashion by the partisans, was suspected to have been the cause of the denunciation. My mother said her calm in front of the most formidable questioners was a miracle, for she was "guilty" and nothing was more certain than a firing squad if her deed was admitted or proven. Yet, towards the evening, she was back home; only then her knees began to tremble.

Only she knew how much bread and milk she gave to the partisans, especially during the last winter of the war when they often came by in groups, hungry and cold. After the war, she said she felt the bread multiplied miraculously as she cut wedge after wedge of heavy, sour rye bread off large round loaves. And I encouraged her to support the partisans when she visited me while I was serving in the German State Labour Service. Her disillusionment after the war was virtually unlimited. The rulers of the "New Class" wanted to destroy the farmer, and they persecuted the Church by confiscations, atheist indoctrination of children, and utterly unjust imprisonment of priests. Most of them spent up to five or more years in jails, with heavy labour, for no crime whatsoever.

Before they assumed power, the Communists cleverly used a handful of Catholic priests in their ranks as decoys, to conceal their true intentions. Now they showed their claws.

As pointed out earlier: had I told my mother that I was a candidate for the Communist party, she would have fainted.

Neither did I indicate in any way to my mother, or any other living soul, my intention to escape. I knew the methods of interrogation in vogue at the time. I knew that if my parents were aware of my intentions, the authorities would extort the truth from them. And I was sure that for not denouncing me they would be severely punished: probably sent to a camp and their farm confiscated.

I heard many years later that the Yugoslavian regime was at its worst from 1948 to 1952. Subsequent events confirmed the validity of my fears and correctness of my policy.

Chapter Seven

# Across the Blue Western Sea

My sun was setting in the red eastern skies, heavily overcast with churning storm-clouds.

A new dawn was about to break over the clearer western horizons.

After my demobilization I dreamed of many possible and a few impossible ways to escape: including the crazy idea of making a bat-like contraption to glide from a high mountain in the Julian Alps over the lower Karavanke into Austria. I had chronic headaches and nightmares due to constant thinking, planning, and plotting without being able to come to any decision. Many nights I dreamt of exhausting and dangerous, but successful crossing of the Austrian border, in deep snow over wooded mountains, only to wake up in utter disappointment.

While going to Christmas 1949 midnight Mass, I thought of escaping after the Mass over the mountains, but I caught my foot in a rut while riding on the sleigh. The hurt did not prevent me from walking, but I had to cancel the plan to escape.

One of the more exotic ideas was to jump on a train and ride through the almost nine kilometres long Karavanke tunnel. The trouble was that there were several border guards on the Yugoslavian side of the tunnel, and patrols along the railway escarpment between the tunnel and the border station in Jesenice, some 3 kilometres to the east down in the Sava valley.

One branch of the famous Orient Express runs through Austria and through that tunnel. The other branch runs through northern Italy; they meet in Slovenia.

Very early one morning I went to observe the situation from some bushes a short distance from the railway escarpment. At the scheduled time, two strong lights from the locomotive of the Orient Express emerged from the many lights of Jesenice and the train began its run up the slope which is unusually steep for a railway: west along the Sava valley railway and gradually further and further leftwards from it, then north over its short tunnel underneath, then again west along the Sava valley railway but higher up the mountain, then turning right just before the hamlet Hrušica towards the Karavanke tunnel, hidden from my sight by some orchards. Although the climb is unusually steep for a railway, the train cruised at such speed that there would be virtually no chance to hitch a ride on it.

March 11, 1950, turned out to be one of the most profoundly decisive days in my life.

In the morning I went on my knees and scrubbed the tamarack floors as I often had done on other Saturdays, in preparation for Sunday. In the afternoon I was to go by train to pick up spools of wool that had to be sent to a small factory in order to be spun into really fine threads.

During lunch the spoon fell from my hand into a bowl of soup. My father, who sat at the end of the table to my right, stopped eating, took a long, steady look at me, shook his head saying nothing, then continued to eat.

That was the last time I saw him.

Before leaving for the train on that fateful Saturday, I went upstairs. In the large bedroom there were two well-known pictures: *Ecce Homo* (Behold the Man) and *Mater Dolorosa* (Sorrowful Mother). One depicts Jesus with the crown of thorns; the other shows Mary with a tear running down her cheek.

I knelt on the floor between the two pictures, burst into tears, raised my hands, and prayed with my whole being, rather than using any definite words: "What should I do?"

Then, as it were in a timeless instant, something mysterious happened. I felt as if the weight of a very heavy stone had suddenly vanished from inside my breast. I knew, without any thinking: "Do it!"

I do not wish to speculate on the precise nature of the extraordinary experience. Was it self-delusion? Some kind of psychological phenomenon? A special grace of God? Or what? It is quite possible that in spite of it I could have still been caught or killed in my attempt to escape. But I do know that the experience was very real and that it happened exactly as I described it, to the best of my ability.

I was going to "do it" that very evening on my way back

186

from the wool-spinning shop, under the cover of darkness. But first I wanted to take another look at the area during the daylight.

The first station on the Sava river valley railway west of Jesenice was Hrušica, the second Dovje-Mojstrana. (The tracks west of Jesenice have since then been removed). I boarded the train in Dovje-Mojstrana and descended at Hrušica. I went, rucksack on my back, up a narrow, slowly ascending road and soon under a bridge or through a small tunnel of the railway to Austria. As I came through this underpass, the Karavanke tunnel was only about 100 metres to my left. I turned right and walked on the narrow path along the tracks. No patrol was in sight, but it didn't really matter: the path was obviously there for public use.

As they come through the tunnel from Austria, the railway tracks run in the shape of a large S down towards Jesenice: south, east, south (then again east, coming near the station parallel with the Sava valley railway). Under the first curve is the little tunnel I just came through, under the second one is the tunnel for the Sava valley railway.

All of a sudden I noticed in the distance, over the horizon, a plume of thick smoke shooting straight into the air. Soon a chimney appeared, and then the locomotive.

A locomotive working at full capacity, with wheels turning from time to time as if on ice, was not an unfamiliar sight to me. Before the war I had seen, more than once, both trains racing simultaneously westwards from Jesenice: the proud, sleek Orient Express racing left along ours gradually uphill, and our humble passenger train puttering along. It happened that the Express would run over our train by the time ours was in the short tunnel underneath it, then again on our right but rather higher. By the time we would reach the Hrušica station, the Express would have veered northwards and into the tunnel, just beyond the view.

This time it was a very long freight train. The locomotive passed me and was gradually turning right, along the first curve, to disappear among the orchards towards the Karavanke tunnel. The locomotive that pushes the train to the middle of the tunnel and then returns was just completing the curve over the Sava valley railway tunnel: I suspected that a border guard or two may have been on board, and I already saw the mechanism which turns its wheels.

At this moment I happened to be between the two curves forming the S figure, but already closer to the end of the train. On my right was the train; on my left, an escarpment just high enough to hide me from being seen from the fields beyond it. The time was about two o'clock in the afternoon.

Like lightning the thought blitzed through my mind: "Now or never!"

I jumped to my right, grabbed a rail, pulled myself up and ran up the steps to the little room for the brakeman, opened the door, and closed it behind me.

My heart raced, my breathing was at least double its usual rate. I fell on my knees to thank God, and wondered if I was dreaming.

My car happened to be designed for coal; so were the ones next to it. I stood up, looked through the little window and over the cars towards the end of the train, but then ducked as fast as possible. Along the railway tracks appeared suddenly a small observation tower which I had not noticed before; on top, a soldier in a long mantle, bent over the guard rail. He looked very attentively down on the coal cars, sub-machine-gun at the ready and aiming.

Indeed, I was still not "out of the woods." What if the train was stopped for inspection? There were enough border guards around the tunnel's entrance to search every car.

Suddenly darkness enveloped everything, and the noise became louder.

What if the train stops for inspection in the centre of the tunnel, at the actual Austrian-Yugoslavian border? The tunnel was made for two sets of tracks, although one had been taken out: there was ample room for guards to be stationed there, and travel back and forth.

Thank God, it did not stop: the brakes began to squeal, and the brook that emanates in the middle of the tunnel and flows northwards began to be heard in spite of reverberation of the train's rumbling.

After 15 or 20 minutes of total darkness the daylight suddenly appeared again: hopefully truly a new day - a new, more tranquil future in my stormy life.

Just as the southern half of the Karavanke tunnel is sloped southwards, so the northern half is sloped northwards. No doubt it must have been full of smoke. It never occurred to me, at the time, that if I had not been inside the little brakeman's booth I could have probably suffocated. In spite of the brakes, the train was moving fast after the middle of the tunnel.

Just as there are Austrian authorities in Jesenice, so also are Yugoslavian ones in Rosenbach, the border station on the Austrian side of the tunnel. As I was afraid the latter would have the authority to apprehend and return me, I decided to jump off before the train stops. My best opportunity came when it wound its way around a steep, brick wall escarpment, when neither the front nor the back cars could be seen.

I opened the cabin door and gripped the handrail on the escarpment side. I descended the steps, this time opposite the side on which I came up. Looking to the ground below, all I could see was gravel left after the second set of tracks had been removed, with weeds growing through it. In fact, the train was moving so fast that all one could see were illusory lines produced by the gravel and weeds.

Leaning sharply backwards, and pushing myself away from the steps, I left the handrail go.

The speed was too great and my legs too weak: as soon as they touched the ground I was thrown forward and in the next moment stood practically on my face, with my feet high up in the air. The only thought that shot through my mind was: "O God, let me not fall unconscious!" The bottle of machine oil, requested by the shop as part payment for spinning the wool, slipped from a pocket of my rucksack and broke. Pieces of glass and oil splashed all around my head.

The train rumbled away and as far as I know no one had noticed me. When I got up, I saw that I had bleeding bruises over my whole right side: face, hand, elbow, and knee. But nothing very serious. I walked over the tracks and downhill to a small apartment building. I knocked on the ground floor and explained my predicament to the astonished lady. While I washed my wounds and she was getting ready to put some medicine on them, her husband returned from work.

My intention was to exchange my Yugoslavian Dinars and catch a train for Amstetten in northern Austria. Perhaps there was just enough money for the trip. Southern Austria was in the British occupation zone; Amstetten was in the north, in the American zone. That caused me some concern, but I hoped the crossing might be accomplished without too much difficulty.

Amstetten was the home of one of a fellow P.O.W. His parents owned both a butcher shop and a restaurant, and when I was leaving the Tushino camp, he gave me their address with the request to let them know that he was alive. I had written them in the spring of 1946, and was delighted to have received a reply: a nice letter, opened and approved for delivery by the American authorities. The parents were overjoyed to learn that their only son was alive and well. They had had no word of his whereabouts for two years (and Austrians were released only in 1947).

Meanwhile, the husband at the apartment said he knew a place where the money could be exchanged and "kindly" offered to go with me. At one place he asked me to wait while he went up a lane between some houses and fences. After a while he returned.

"No luck. Let's try at the railway station."

On the platform a man in distinctly Austrian civilian attire (short leather pants with beautiful, Edelweiss-decorated H-shaped suspenders) casually joined us, and we exchanged a few words about the weather or some such "timely" topic. The man who had brought me somehow vanished, and soon the trend of the conversation changed. I couldn't quote his exact words but he bluntly informed me that if I had come to sit along a highway and write down numbers of military vehicles, I was in the wrong place.

Nobody needs to be a genius to see the nature of this scenario. If any proof was needed that I had been betrayed and stupid enough to walk into a trap, it was provided by the arrival of two Austrian gendarmes. They took me to their quarters to search and question me, after which a jeep came to take me away. My new escorts were from the F.S.S., a British military outfit, apparently a kind of secret service, which had its quarters in a village a few kilometres farther down the road.

It was there that I heard English spoken for the first time

in my life. I had never heard it even on the radio: England was too far away for the simple battery-run radio my brother Rudolph operated. It seemed as if they were speaking with potatoes in their mouths and I doubted that I could ever learn such a mumble. Today I think English is a very beautiful language: just one more proof that something, or someone, cannot be loved until known.

Also, it was at the F.S.S. quarters that I first saw someone putting milk into the tea which, in my native land, would have been considered utterly ridiculous. Today, a cup of good tea with milk is one of my favourite drinks.

By nightfall of the event-filled day, I found myself in the district jail in Rosegg, a town some 10 or 15 km north of the Austrian end of the Karavanke tunnel. I was sentenced to three weeks in jail, "for illegal entry." The authorities were generally lenient in cases of this kind: the law asked for three months.

The official interpreter at the jail recognized me at once: he had been a military gendarme in Radovna during the war, and well acquainted with us, especially with my father. Through him I got the work as farm-hand in Rosegg, but first he wrote to one of my aunts in Dovje on my behalf (as I was in jail) about my whereabouts. It took about a week for the message to arrive.

I never heard what was my mother's reaction as I simply vanished: unexpectedly, without a trace. At that time someone or other was said to have disappeared never to be seen or heard from again. And nobody dared to ask any questions.

My father was devastated. He was in his 72nd year and still dreamed of handing the little farm over to me and to enjoy a little rest. The dream was now shattered.

He used to drop in at our friends in Jesenice for a cup of coffee after his visits to the doctor. They told me later how he sat on the box for firewood near the stove and could not be consoled.

Even today it still hurts me to have caused him such pain. Yet I saw no other reasonable way out: had I given the slightest hint of my intention to escape, the ruthless authorities would have found out the truth due to the kind of questioning methods then in vogue, and my family probably dispossessed for not reporting me to them in time.

One of my cousins, who had been a leading guerilla

fighter, happened to be at the time an important Communist Party functionary in Mojstrana. He was very honest, sincere and well-meaning, and utterly disillusioned when he saw his wartime dreams of justice and honesty turned to nightmares after the war. Later he hanged himself. He told my parents confidentially with what great difficulty he convinced the authorities that my parents had really no idea of my intentions, and thus saved them from grave consequences.

Years later I heard that when the hard-working people in the neighbourhood were crushed by exorbitant taxes and requisitions of produce and livestock, they would say: "We'll have to go for the wool."

Having served my jail sentence, I was sent for three weeks to a so-called quarantine camp not far away.

Finally, towards the end of April 1950, I got work on a large farm in Rosegg. For legal protection I registered with the I.R.O. (International Refugee Organization), a now disbanded agency of the United Nations.

I had wanted to emigrate overseas at the earliest opportunity: not only because the Austrians thought they had already too many foreigners left there after the war, but to continue somewhere, sometime soon, somehow, my studies for the priesthood so suddenly interrupted on March 31, 1941.

In 1950 all emigration from Austria was apparently at a halt. The Austrians would have been glad to bid farewell to the thousands of former *Ostarbeiter* (workers from the East), who refused to return to their Communist-dominated homelands, as well as newly arrived refugees. But no one was willing to take them. Rumours had it that overseas lands would soon open their hearts and ports again to refugees: especially Australia, Argentina, Venezuela, Canada, and to a lesser degree the U.S.A. I decided to go wherever the first opportunity offered itself.

In the late fall of 1950, I received the news from the I.R.O. that a Canadian commission was coming to Salzburg to interview refugees interested in working in Canada. Everyone would have to sign a contract with representatives of the Canadian Ministry of Labour to work at least one year wherever the Ministry decided, but under the same working conditions as

Canadians. At first this work was said to be in mines, but as the time for the signing arrived, it became work in the bush.

A telegram later summoned me to Salzburg, and although I was worried about my "tainted" past, I told the whole truth and was accepted. In December another telegram from the I.R.O. called me again to Salzburg. A day or two later I was on my way to Bremerhaven, Germany, to board the *General Harry Taylor,* an American Navy ship for troop transportation. There were many families travelling to the U.S.A., but about 20 young bachelors, like myself, were heading for Canada. It turned out that all of us had been placed in the same bush camp.

The voyage was rough. The small ship, about 12,000 tons, coupled with December storms on the North Atlantic, made things worse. Children were the most immune to the sea sickness. We others had a veritable Neptune of a time. However, the last two days at sea were more quiet and we celebrated Christmas with a party, complete with a tree and the good things that go with celebration - minus any religious aspects. On December 26, 1950, land appeared on the horizon, and at noon a few of us disembarked in Halifax and after the usual formalities boarded a train. The rest travelled on to New York.

A couple of representatives of the C.I.P., (Canadian International Paper Company), now took care of our group. My travels in Europe as well as the boat fare had been paid for by the I.R.O. The rail trip from Halifax was paid by the C.I.P. but it had to be refunded at the end of our work for the Company: $28.00 in all. It included my delicious first dinner in Canada, in a hotel across from the railway station in Quebec City. The evening and the city with its lights, Christmas decorations, and snow had the air of a dreamland.

All I possessed were the clothes I wore, including a long, warm overcoat given to me in the refugee camp in Salzburg, a pair of torn shoes, a pair of torn rubber boots, and two or three ragged pieces of clothing. What I wasn't wearing could easily be carried in my rucksack and a rather small hard cardboard handcase. Of a wallet there was no need: all the money I possessed (one American dollar) could easily fit into any pocket. At the time it was probably worth less than its proud Canuck cousin.

Our loggers camp was located somewhere between Trois Rivières and James Bay but so far north that the waters flowed into the Bay. The pulpwood we cut had to be hauled a few kilometres to the south, piled on frozen lakes and rivers, and in the spring floated southwards to the paper mills on the shores of the St. Lawrence River.

Most loggers were French-speaking Canadians. The group of us were lodged separately in a log cabin. A former Czech student, the only one who spoke some English, was kind enough to lend me an English-German dictionary with about 3,000 most important words. All my spare time, evenings and weekends, I spent learning the language. I transcribed all the words in the dictionary on to sheets of paper, together with the indication of their pronunciation, and simply tried to memorize every one by constant repetition. The book *This is Canada,* an illustrated basic history and geography of Canada, which had the appearance of a *Life* magazine, served as a guide. I read it sentence by sentence and jotted down every new word and its pronunciation. Soon I was a long way from the day in Salzburg when I was tempted to become envious when I heard a man say something like "senk you fairy madge" and did not know what it meant.

Time passed. The bitter cold gradually changed to spring-like weather, the deep snow melted, producing floods, and eventually the mosquitoes and blackflies appeared. By June no one could stand it. Clouds of the nasty little creatures flew right into the eyes and ears. I recall the man jotting down the numbers called by his companion who measured the logs, sitting with his jacket over his head for protection against the blackflies, with his sleeves dangling on both sides. The camp had to close. Although we came on a one year contract, we had to look for the next job ourselves.

Someone, somehow, found out that the gold-mine in Bourlamaque near Val d'Or would hire us, and I worked there until January 10, 1952. Some of the immigrants with whom I had arrived in Halifax came to the Bourlamaque mine. Of most of the others, I lost track.

Somehow I learned of an American Slovenian newspaper,

*The American Home,* with some articles in English and some in Slovenian, and subscribed to it.

In one of the issues I read a report about a Slovenian church picnic in Toronto. My old grade three teacher, living in exile in Austria, had informed me before my departure that most immigrants to Canada settled in an area called Ontario. I don't think I had ever heard of Toronto.

I read that there was a Slovenian priest in Toronto, which was big news for me. Before long I wrote to the reporter, whose name and address were fortunately given at the end of his article, and asked him to send me the priest's address. He was kind enough to do so in a short time, and so I wrote to the priest.

I have never composed any letter with more care. I started with the Slovenian proverb: "They say that a word is not a horse..." - meaning that it doesn't cost to talk about things - and ended with the request for information regarding the possibilities of continuing my studies for the priesthood. I held it through the narrow slot on the top of a mail box for a long time, with the letter dangling inside, before my fingers let it drop.

This was another turning point in my life.

We exchanged two or three letters. The priest advised me to come to Toronto in September, at the beginning of the school year, but I decided to complete my contract with the Ministry of Labour. I left my job in the Bourlamaque gold-mine on January 10, 1952, and at once travelled to Toronto. I stayed at first at the Immaculate Heart of Mary church rectory in Scarborough, where the Slovenian priest, Dr. Jakob Kolarič, lived as guest of his Vincentian confreres. He found a boarding house for me in Toronto. There, the landlord and the housekeeper, as well as a young man and a young woman who lived in the house, were from my native land.

I owe much gratitude to all, especially the landlord, Mr. Ivan Kavčič, and the landlady, Mrs. Cecilia Šehović. The latter had arrived a year or two earlier in Canada as a refugee and widow with three pre-school-aged children. The former was a typical Slovenian farmer who had come to Canada as a refugee, worked like a slave, lived like a saint, and later established his own successful construction company. He was deeply in love with his wife, who was still waiting in Yugoslavia (seven years after the war!) for permission to rejoin her husband. After he fled, she spent a long time in jail while their five children were taken care of by their relatives. We discovered later that she had been one of the 3000 or so jailed women who had been working in 1949 on the highway "Brotherhood-Unity" next to my unit. In the mid-1950s she and the five children arrived, and the couple had four more born here in Canada.

The people from my native Slovenia suffered persecution and exile for their loyalty to God and the Church. In spite of their relatively small numbers in the great cosmopolitan city of Toronto (about 18,000, in late 1980s), in spite of the fact that they arrived with practically no money or material possessions, and even though the vast majority of them were farmers and labourers with no formal education beyond elementary school, they now have their own businesses, companies, credit unions, homes, a senior citizens home, and two thriving parish church complexes, which were all built and paid for entirely by their own contributions in work and money. But they had not formed a ghetto. Their children are integrated into the fabric of Canada, making it richer by their distinct ancestral culture and traditions.

However, it must never be forgotten that it was not only the diligence and faith of the newcomers, but also the kindness and welcome they found here that made their success possible.

Finding work in the middle of January, with the winter slow-down and my poor knowledge of English, was not easy. In the house where I lived, the landlord and the young man had work, but the young lady and I used to buy *The Toronto Star,* which at the time cost 3 cents, to search the ads in the "Help Wanted" column. Every day for two weeks I walked the streets of Toronto in vain. These were the only two weeks in my life during which I was unemployed and looking for work.

Finally, a job in St. Augustine's Seminary laundry became vacant. I was to spend the next seven years there as a student, starting that fall. The Seminary is located in Scarborough, at the time a borough (suburb) of Toronto. Its rector, Msgr. John H. Ingoldsby, was a humble, kind, truly wonderful man, loved by all who knew him.

Before starting to work and moving into the basement where the maintenance staff had its quarters, the Monsignor put me into the visitors bedroom on the main floor. He assigned a senior seminarian, also a refugee and the only countryman of mine among the some 200 students, to help me settle in. The seminarian wondered who had allowed me into the guest room: he had a hard time believing it was the rector himself. But that was only one of the good Monsignor's acts of kindness towards me. Every Thursday from January to the end of the school year in May or June 1952, he allowed me to walk after supper with the Slovenian seminarian in order to learn English. In those days, communication between students and maintenance staff was forbidden.

The seminarian is at the time of this writing the Most Rev. Dr. Aloysius M. Ambrozic, Archbishop of Toronto. I am grateful to him for the many hours of his recreation time sacrificed for my benefit.

In the Seminary laundry the Sisters of St. Martha were my kind bosses and benefactors. My pay was lousy but the two Sisters who were in charge of the laundry were my true mentors. Sr. Cornelia was unusually tall, and Sr. Paula very short. It was amusing to see them walk through the corridors with their blinker-like head gear and bags full of rags and brushes. Sr. Paula almost ran to keep up with her tall companion. But the difference in their size was a shining example of complementarity. Sr. Cornelia needed no ladder to clean the upper part of the rooms in professors' suites - and they were high in the old building - while Sr. Paula hardly needed to bend to reach the floor. When I finished my work in the laundry I also helped them with theirs.

Some wealthier (or less poor) students left clothing and shoes for the more needy ones with the Sisters, especially at the end of the school year. The good Sisters mended the underwear, the pants and jackets, but above all the socks. With that management I needed to buy no clothing throughout my seven years of study. The Sisters' loving help was most welcome, for my only source of income were my summer jobs, and none paid very much. The Sisters, and the faithful of Toronto Archdiocese, who paid half of my tuition fees and never asked for a refund, enabled me to make ends meet, as well as to pay the other half of the fees.

As soon as I started working in the Seminary laundry, I began to take night courses in French and Latin at Meisterschaft College, one evening a week in each language. I finished the courses in June 1952 with flying colours, even though I began them only at the beginning of February.

My success with the two courses may have been one of the decisive reasons for my acceptance to the Seminary in September, 1952. It was a total surprise. In Slovenia I had been only in the second of eight years of high school when the war brought an abrupt end to it all. Having lost 11 of my best years (15 to 26), I was ecstatic to get at least some back, as it were. Thus I entered the Seminary with less than eight years of formal education. Again, I owe it to the saintly Msgr. John H. Ingoldsby.

Every year I placed among the top three or four students in a class of about 30. I was endowed with good intelligence and memory (although lately I am becoming quite forgetful), but I also worked hard at my studies.

The seven years in the Seminary seemed an awfully long time when I started. Looking back now, I wonder where the time vanished.

Chapter Eight

# Reaching the Destination

The great day of ordination was fast approaching, but first there were the final exams to pass. The big one was the jurisdiction examination, covering matters from the whole four-year theology course, especially the subjects of Moral theology and Church law.

Just as a medical doctor must pass hard examinations before the practice of medicine, so also the Church wants to ensure that no quacks be allowed to heal the spiritual disease of sin. Only God can forgive sin, but the ordinary way of his forgiveness, established by Christ, is through the ministry of the Church. In the Sacrament of Penance and Reconciliation, referred to also as Confession, the priest acts as God's instrument. The main source of this Church teaching is found in the 20th chapter of the Gospel according to St. John (Jn 20:19-23).

The jurisdiction examination ensures that a priest knows his job, generally, and in particular that the faithful can trust him in Confession. For in this Sacrament a sinner doesn't simply rattle off sins and receive forgiveness, but also gets salutary advice how to avoid sin in the future. Who would trust an unqualified doctor in a heart operation or prescription of drugs? Who would trust an unqualified person in the celebration of the Sacrament of Penance and Reconciliation?

There were other matters to look after: special invitations, pictures, souvenir cards - much like making preparations for a wedding - and I had no relatives in Canada to help, not even a distant cousin.

To justify the invitation of bishop Rožman who had confirmed me some 21 years earlier, I invited him to preach at my First Solemn Mass. Although he lived as a refugee in Cleveland, U.S.A., he graciously accepted. It was his last visit to Toronto; he died of cancer a few months later.

Like any other newly ordained priest, I yearned to celebrate my first Mass in my home parish church, with my mother, relatives and friends. But I could not yet go home. It was only in the early 1960s that Yugoslavia gave amnesty to those who escaped after the war, if they had no other charges pending.

My ordination took place in St. Michael's cathedral in Toronto on May 31, 1959. The First Solemn Mass at my parish church, Our Lady Help of Christians (Slovenian) in Toronto was the following Sunday, June 7.

My mother was almost 72 and was unable to come. Her main gift was a silver and gold, custom-made chalice. Many relatives contributed wedding rings and watches that were melted and cast into that chalice. It is beautiful in its simplicity. Instead of a customary cross in front at the base there is a red crystal-like piece about the size and shape of a large drop of blood which it symbolizes. It looks like a genuine ruby, but it is only glass.

Difficulties arose when the chalice was ready to be shipped to Canada. The main reason alleged was that it came under the law for protection of cultural monuments and as such it was forbidden to be sent abroad. Piles of paper went back and forth to the provincial and even federal authorities, and many telephone calls were made by a local friend of mine both to Ljubljana and Belgrade, all to no avail. The chalice had to be smuggled, weeks after my first Mass, to Austria by an American tourist, who hid it in the bottom of her luggage.

Similar problems arose with the wooden crucifix whose corpus was carved from linden wood. It was also my mother's gift for my First Solemn Mass. A family friend took it to the authorities, who ridiculed her and asked, laughing, what it was. However, as she was leaving one of the officials called her back and accepted the crucifix for shipment, but it also arrived too late.

One of the most touching Slovenian customs on the occasion of a priest's first Mass concerns a crucifix.

On top of the steps in front of the church a small girl, dressed in white, with a white veil held on her head by a garland of flowers, waits for the procession. She hands the crucifix surrounded by a wreath of white flowers to the priest as he comes by. He carries the image of the crucified Saviour down the isle: not unlike a bridegroom and bride approaching the altar of God to promise love and loyalty till death.

# REACHING THE DESTINATION

"God writes straight with crooked lines," the saying goes. In his infinite goodness he can draw good even out of evil caused by sinful human beings. Because my crucifix didn't arrive on time, I had to buy one for the occasion of my first Mass: a smaller one of brown wood with a white ivory corpus. Later I kept my mother's crucifix, but gave her mine. I was told that she kept it near her bed, on a shelf. In her last illness her greatest consolation was to keep looking at it for long periods of time.

Besides the chalice and the crucifix, her letter for the occasion was also memorable. She was sure my father would smile in heaven to see his "mischievous little Franc" (my common epithet in my pre-teens) celebrating his first Mass. And at the very time of Mass she would pray at home the Magnificat, the song of praise of the Virgin Mary: "My soul magnifies the Lord..." (Lk 1:46-55).

It was a heartbreak that none of my relatives was able to be present at my ordination to the priesthood and first Mass. But my mother wrote: "I am too old to travel over the ocean. However, I could try to meet you in Austria."

Now I found myself on the horns of a dilemma.

One often reads that there are many genuine priestly and religious vocations in Third World countries. These fine young people could do so much good not only for the Church but for their countries as well, yet for lack of money they never reach their goal. I had about $1,600.00 in donations on the occasion of my First Solemn Mass, but I worried about spending this on travel when it could help many others reach the goal I have just reached. And dollars can buy so much more in the poor countries of the world than in North America.

On the other hand, the case of Judas Iscariot came to my mind. As Mary anointed the feet of Jesus at Bethany with "a pound of costly ointment," he protested: " Why was this ointment not sold for three hundred denarii and given to the poor?" Jesus rebuked him: "Let her alone, let her keep it for the day of my burial. The poor you always have with you, but you do not always have me" (Jn 12:3-8). So I wrote to bishop Rožman, explaining my thoughts and asking his advice.

"You make your own decision," he replied; "For myself,

I am certain that there would be no greater joy for a mother like yours than to be present at least at a few Masses celebrated by her son. She may be able to do so for a short time only; the need for support of others will be there for a long time to come."

By the time I finished reading his lines my decision was made.

In 1959 it was still very difficult in Yugoslavia to obtain permission to travel abroad. To give my visit as reason for a request would have meant certain refusal. My mother had a cousin in Southern Austria; she applied to visit her. The request was granted, but she had to wait a long time for her papers. Meanwhile, I had to wait in Austria.

To use the three weeks allotted more economically, I visited Rome while waiting for my mother's arrival in Austria. I wondered if I would have another chance to visit the Eternal Holy City - which is neither eternal nor, allegedly, very holy. It has, however, a glorious history and invaluable cultural and artistic treasures. In four days I saw the highlights and not much more: the four major Basilicas, the Catacombs, the Coliseum, the Forum, as well as some other tourist attractions.

One of the two most impressive sights was a short stretch of the road over which marched the victorious Roman legions just before entering the Forum Romanum and parading past the emperor. Its silent, worn cobblestones spoke to me volumes. The other was the magnificence of St. Peter's basilica and a public audience in it, in the company of thousands of tourists and pilgrims, with Pope John XXIII.

Soon after my return to Austria, my mother arrived. She came, to my surprise, accompanied by her sister Paula and my brother John. Like on my return from the Soviet Union some 13 years earlier, I was treated again to the aromatic snuff tobacco reception.

My visitors were able to attend several Masses I celebrated in the local parish church. All, but none more than my mother, were overjoyed about it.

Days passed quickly and soon it was time to say goodbye, this time forever as far as this world is concerned.

I can still see my mother waving from the coach window

as the train struggled up towards the spot where nine years earlier I had jumped off one coming down. Her train continued farther uphill, around a bend, and towards the Karavanke tunnel. It was late October in 1959.

She died in 1965, a peaceful and holy death, similar to my father's in 1954. Both died of dropsy, both at home, and both fortified by the Sacraments of the Church shortly before their death.

I am forever grateful to bishop Rožman for his wise counsel, and glad that I listened to him. I am also glad that I followed another advice of this great man whose wisdom had been made more profound in the sufferings of war and revolution, persecution, calumnies, and exile.

As mentioned earlier, he preached at my First Solemn Mass in Toronto. His theme was the Mystical Body of Christ: basically the teaching of St. Paul in his first letter to the Corinthians, chapters 12 and 13.

He was also the main after-dinner speaker at the banquet later in the afternoon. He was very hilarious, even joking and laughing.

In a less mirthful, yet joyous and happy vein he assured me that I will learn in my priestly life and service, even in the midst of trials and tribulations, how good is God. And he reminded me that while at the age of 33 Jesus completed his work on this earth, I was at that age only beginning my sharing in his Eternal Priesthood.

His most touching remarks, though, were about my mother and especially her Magnificat.

Priests pray the Magnificat daily at the Evening Prayer. Before a hushed banquet hall he urged me that I, prompted by the example of my mother, should pray a second Magnificat every year on the anniversary of my ordination: in thanksgiving to God for the unspeakable gift of priesthood, and in memory of my mother:

"My soul magnifies the Lord,
and my spirit rejoices in God my Saviour,
for he has regarded the low estate of his handmaiden.
For behold, henceforth all generations will call me

blessed;

      for he who is mighty has done great things for me,
      and holy is his Name..." (Lk 1:46-55).

So far I have prayed a second Magnificat, this beautiful hymn of praise and thanksgiving, with joy and gratitude well over 30 times on anniversaries of my ordination to the priesthood.

How many or how few more times are still left for me to pray it here below, I leave in the hands of him who is Almighty, all-true, all-loving, all-merciful, and holy is his Name.

And beyond my last Magnificat here below, "O Lord, my God, forever will I give you thanks" (Ps 30:13).

# PART II

## A BOUQUET FOR YOU

*I expect to pass*
*through this world but once;*
*and any good thing, therefore,*
*that I can do*
*or any kindness*
*that I can show*
*to any fellow creature,*
*let me do it now;*
*let me not defer or neglect it,*
*for I shall not pass this way again.*

Author Unknown

Chapter One

# One-Way Path

No human being has or ever had a lasting abode on this planet. St. Paul very picturesquely compares our human existence to living in a tent: "For we know that if the earthly tent we live in is destroyed, we have a building from God, a house not made with hands, eternal in the heavens" (2 Cor 5:1).

In all truth we are all nomads: people without a permanent home.

We are all people on the move. The Church itself is referred to in the documents of the Second Vatican Council as The Pilgrim People of God, to give but one example.

And every individual human person as well as nations and the whole of humanity is progressing along a one-way path.

O yes, you or I may find ourselves again in the very same situation: sitting in the same old chair, doing the very same thing. But is it really the same? By no means! It only seems so, for no passing second of time will ever return, while in space we shall be millions and billions of kilometres away. We should bear in mind that with fantastic speeds we are incessantly being shot through the immensity of space by our Earth, the Sun, and our native Milky Way galaxy.

Lately I stayed a few days in my friend's cottage. Browsing through the books, I came upon Pierre Berton's *The Klondike Quest.* Somebody, for some reason, glued on the first page a slip like a holy card with that thought beautifully expressed: "I expect to pass through this world but once; and any good thing, therefore, that I can do or any kindness that I can show to any fellow creature, let me do it now; let me not defer or neglect it, for I shall not pass this way again." (The author's name was not on it: I believe it is unknown).

Everyone's path through life is in some aspects the same, but in others entirely different. In actual reality, it is absolutely unique. No two lives are identical, never were and never will be.

Those who die very young have really never "hit the

road." They were taken along for a short stretch by their parents: asleep on their hands, so to speak.

The length of the road - the length of one's life - is not an accurate measure of its difficulty or ease, eventfulness or placidity. Some live long, yet their path is relatively smooth; others die young after a stormy life full of ups and downs.

The Sacred Scripture itself recognizes this fact. Speaking about the early death of a just person, it states: "Being perfected in a short time, he fulfilled long years" (Wis 4:13).

Lives of most of my contemporaries have been all but placid. My own life to this point in time, described in terms of the allegory of one-way path, has not unexpectedly been also quite eventful. I am proposing to sum it up at this point allegorically, but with literal truth from time to time eclipsing the allegory. And not in perfect chronological order, nor thoroughly, but in a broad, general outline.

After a peaceful start at the first streaks of dawn, my path soon led into and through all kinds of weather, scenery, and other conditions: good and bad; kind and inclement, rough and smooth; ups and downs of longer or short duration; some recurring, now and then with certain variations, others never repeating themselves.

There were periods of pitch-dark night, sunny days, early morning dawns awakened with the chirping of happy birds' choirs, last breaths of dusk, and any kind of day in between.

Seasons succeeded one another in their everlasting cycles: winters with blinding snowstorms, purest Alpine air and deep virginal snows; sweltering summers; balmy springs with meadows abloom; and melancholy autumns.

Longer or shorter stretches I traversed had the nature of anything from a goat trail in the high Alps or barely recognizable footprints through a grassy meadow to multi-lane super-highways through the outskirts of a sprawling North American megalopolis.

The path varied from narrow to broad; dusty, icy, muddy, stony, paved, soft, hard; straight or winding; level or with ups and downs over lowlands and proud mountain ranges.

Yes, it is even lost in the mighty, seemingly endless and bottomless waters of the Atlantic ocean which it spans four times from east to west and three times from west to east. And it soars once in both directions through the dizzy heights way up over the Atlantic.

The weather along my path of life can perhaps best be described as variable: hot and shivering cold; times of peaceful, soothing breezes followed violent storms; cloudy skies; drizzling mist; freezing rain; snow, sleet and hail. There were storms in darkest night, split repeatedly by peals of thunder and lightning, with glorious rainbows appearing next day in the skies.

After every winter there came spring; after every night dawn; and after every violent storm peaceful calm, with air cleansed and invigoratingly freshened.

Everyone travels through life on a one-way path. We never return to where we have already been before. Every second passes into eternity from which it can never again return. No scene will ever be the same again, even though it may appear to be the same.

In a sense, our life's path is utterly solitary, because it is unique and unrepeatable by any other person in the past, present, or future. From another point of view, one can travel alone, with a spouse, in a family, or as member of a group or society.

Enemies may put obstacles at our feet to make us stumble; they may even shoot at us from ambushes. But we are blessed if in all our trials we have faith in God and support of our relatives and friends. This contributes greatly to making our trip endurable and even filled with joy.

It is good to take now and then a look ahead, and occasionally back. But most of the time our attention should be directed to the present scene. Jesus of Nazareth himself, in his Sermon on the Mount, advises against worrying about the future: "Therefore do not be anxious about tomorrow...Let the day's own trouble be sufficient for the day" (Mt 6:34).

Most worries about the future never materialize. The past is passed, gone forever. Leave the past to God's mercy, the future to his loving care, and pay attention to the present!

This, of course, does not mean to ignore the past or the future entirely. There should be some plans for the future, as well as some attention to the past. It has rightly been said: "Those who ignore the lessons of history will have to suffer the same mistakes in the future."

May I repeat here my mother's so wise saying: "Listen to experienced people; they know more than the learned."

Allow me to share with you some of my experiences of life. They are lessons from my past as I understand them. I myself cannot doubt the truth of what I saw, touched, or otherwise experienced. Also, I do not doubt the truth of my ideas and of conclusions from these lessons, unless explicitly stated in the text that I consider one or the other doubtful.

It is my purpose and fervent hope that at least some may be of some benefit to you, dear reader. If you are also pleased, or entertained, or amused with them, so much the better, although that is not my primary goal. It can be imagined that some people will be anything but pleased with certain passages. A patient may not be very pleased with the diagnosis, or the medicine, or the diet. But the very love and concern for the good of the patient will urge the doctor to speak the truth, no matter how reluctantly.

I like to imagine the thoughts and ideas presented here to be flowers plucked along my path of life. Every chapter is a flower. They are gathered into "A Bouquet For You": just for you, not for an impersonal, amorphous humanity ("O how I love humanity, but I hate the noisy neighbours down the street"), but for you personally. You may want to look at the whole bouquet, or at least one or the other of its flowers. Perhaps you will examine them, savour and enjoy their colour, shape, or aroma. Hopefully you will get some benefit from them.

There are flowers with thorns. The most exquisite roses have them: very prickly, too. Others have odious, repulsive odours, but these may be precisely the most medicinal ones.

The bouquet is yours: do with it as you see fit.

This is meant to be a bouquet of flowers, not a bale of hay. What I mean to say is that there are other experiences, observations, lessons and ideas which I could share with you. I would like to, but there are too many of them to fit between the covers of this book. These few have been chosen more or less at random from among the many gathered along the one-way path of my life's journey. One or the other valuable idea may be waiting hidden to be plucked from the pages of the first part of this book, others are gathered in this humble bouquet and offered to you, with love.

As explained in the chapter "The Why and the How," the bouquet became even humbler, with fewer flowers (chapters and ideas) left in it, after the preceding paragraphs had been written. Still, it is offered to you, with love.

Chapter Two

# The Why and the How

Why should someone like myself who has achieved nothing great in the eyes of the world, presume to write a book that could be classified as an autobiography?

Why, indeed!?

Is it not presumptuous? For there are millions of refugees, expellees, emigrants, immigrants, and others who used to be categorized after the Second World War as "DPs" (displaced persons), many of whom could tell more interesting stories than I. There are soldiers, for instance, who spent many years in the uniform, and who lived through much greater horrors of war than I did. Multitudes of them were front-line soldiers when I was still a high school boy.

Is it not also a waste of time? True, I am not spending much time allotted for my duties as parish priest for this work. But could not my free time be spent more prudently?

Good and valid questions! Such and similar thoughts occurred to me from the outset, and frequently.

On the other hand, there seemed at least as many or more good reasons for going ahead with the writing.

It wasn't the challenge: I am not the type to attack dragons or try to climb Mt. Everest. It wasn't fame or money, although I hope to make some of the latter for charitable purposes, ultimately. My life taught me some useful lessons about the real, very low, value of these for one's personal benefit, except for what is necessary for normal life.

My life story is not intended as an end in itself. It is meant to be merely a framework and vehicle to give thanks to God and at least some of my benefactors and convey truths and insights that will hopefully benefit the reader: to enlighten, edify, ennoble, console, encourage, promote reconciliation and peace in hearts, families, nations, the world; to foster faith, hope, and love of God and neighbour.

I pray that these chapters may contribute, even if just a

little, to make their readers more sensitive, generous and ready to alleviate any and all human suffering; more compassionate, understanding and forgiving, so that at least the presently immense amount of man-made, mutually self-inflicted suffering may thus be more and more banished from this world and replaced by the joy of God's children.

In regard to any "preaching" or lecturing, I tried to avoid the extremes of too much and nothing at all. Even so, some will no doubt find too much of it, and others not enough. It is hoped that only a minimum of lessons is being served "on a platter." Let them rather be extracted like honey by a diligent bee from flowers, savoured, enjoyed, and stored for later use.

I don't mind very much if some or most of my ideas be altogether rejected. Nature produces seeds in superabundance. There are thousands of acorns on an oak. Only one may produce another oak: but what a mighty tree!

I am certain that nobody will suffer or be worse in any way on account of reading this book. If one single person should benefit, thank God: the work and effort were not in vain.

Actually, I have discarded dozens of pages of material prepared for Part II of this book. It was here that most of the aforementioned lessons and ideas were to have been found. St. Augustine writes about the roses of martyrs, the ivy of wedded couples, the violets of widows, and the lilies of the virgins (Cf PL 38, Sermo 304). Similarly, I had in mind to dedicate individual chapters - "flowers" in the Bouquet - to the married, the old, and especially to the young. For it is the latter to whom the future belongs and who will shape the first century of the third millennium.

Perhaps the longest and most elaborate chapter in Part II was to have been titled: "Peacemakers Of All Lands, Unite!" However, a friend suggested: "You don't have to spell out your zeal for peace: your life story is a clear enough lesson."

War and weapons of mass destruction should be banned, period! However, too many people fear that if the millions of soldiers throughout the world would be demobilized, and factories stop producing weapons, there would be widespread, unbearable unemployment, overpopulation and degeneration. These are real, enormous problems. I do not presume to know their solutions, but wanted to offer at least some "starters" for more powerful minds (perhaps occupied now with designing of ever more sophisticated weapons for killing) to develop.

There is the vast desert of Sahara (still spreading) and other deserts: couldn't the joint force of millions of soldiers, hundreds of billions of dollars now spent annually on military purposes, modern technology, and abundant solar energy in the deserts turn them into mighty forests, blooming meadows and fertile fields?

A pipe dream? Yes, but so was flying to the moon: and not so very long ago; besides, deserts are closer to us than the moon!

As for degeneration: surely war and useless military exercises must not be the only means of preventing the rot of softness, especially in our youth! Sport, callisthenics, and more manual labour (to provide meaningful employment and exercise, as well as help preserve non-renewable natural resources and reduce pollution of environment) should take care of this danger in a world at peace.

The danger of real overpopulation in a world at peace is likewise by no means unavoidable. And I wish to emphasize that there is no need whatsoever of abortion, contraception, sterilization, euthanasia, or any other immoral means to avoid it. For the married, the Natural Family Planning (N.F.P.) is the answer. Those who practice it properly, testify that it helps rather than hinders love and good marital relationship. With both spouses having to practice periodic continence and showing love to one another in other ways during such periods, both know that none is a mere object of the other's selfishness. Also, too much of anything, even honey, usually brings about total aversion to it. Couples practising the N.F.P. enjoy a "mini-honeymoon" every month. Moreover, the N.F.P. is so simple that Mother Theresa of Calcutta had outstanding success teaching it even to illiterate couples. Let the world set aside a few billion dollars annually from military budgets and spend the money for N.F.P. programs!

For the single, the only proper answer is total abstinence. Mass media, generally, despise chastity and simultaneously campaign for fewer births. What could be more utterly self-contradictory?

If both the married and the single would strive earnestly, with God's help, for these lofty ideals, there would be no danger of overpopulation, yet children would be treasured as gifts from God, the giver of life. There would be fewer broken marriages, more true love, less AIDS, and virginity valued for what it really is: heroism and one of the most beautiful virtues.

This does not mean any devaluation of sex and its use as planned by the Creator. One of my seminary professors used to say: "Sex is God-given, lust is devil-driven."

In this connection, I would like to at least mention what to my mind is a fascinating phenomenon: the Madonna House Apostolate (I had in mind to dedicate a whole chapter to it!). There are several Madonna Houses throughout the world; I stayed in the Motherhouse, in Combermere, Ontario, six weeks, as mentioned later in this chapter. Several dozens of men and women, many, perhaps most of them, only in their 20s or 30s, live there a well ordered community life. Men and women have separate living quarters, but they all take part in one daily Mass, have one common dining room, and work together. They live on a farm and are not only self-supporting, but involved in much charitable work. What is significant is their life of total celibacy for the sake of God's Kingdom and the love of neighbour. What many would deem even more significant is that one couldn't find anywhere a greater abundance of genuine love, joy and peace.

My original plan was to develop these and some other ideas in much greater detail. However, gradually the need for some substantial trimming dawned on me.

That is a long shot from the original intention of going so far as to add a Part III. There were two or three reasons for that "temptation."

First, the example of Our Lord himself. After the multiplication of loaves and fishes he told his disciples: "Gather up the fragments  left over,  that nothing may be lost" (Jn 6:12).

Also, recently I read Blaise Pascal's famous *Pensées.* The book is mostly made up of little bits and pieces, neatly grouped and numbered. Apparently he had them gathered with the intention of writing a book, but ran out of time.

# THE WHY AND THE HOW

I had, as said earlier, dozens of pages of such bits and pieces, gathered for *A Bouquet For You,* but turned into "leftovers" for a third part of the book.

However, much of the material would have caused copyright problems, and when I read the material a second time, I felt much less enthused about it, to put it very mildly. Not only did I abandon the idea of a third part: I seriously considered discarding not only a few chapters of the second part, which I did, but the whole of it - or even the whole book!

The hope of some truly beautiful illustrations was one of the reasons for going ahead with the publication.

I met Mrs. Marta Brestovansky providentially, or by a curious coincidence. While printing our Sunday bulletin, the photocopier broke down. I called several places before finding a machine to do the job. My friend, Father Garnet Sauve, the Pastor of St. Columbkille's church in Uptergrove, some 30 kilometres north of Beaverton, had one. In his rectory some very beautiful original paintings caught my attention. I learned that the artist was Mrs. Marta Brestovansky, an acquaintance of Father Sauve, who lived only a few kilometres further north, in Orillia. (Of Slovak background, she insists that there is no "h" in her name). To make a long story short: we called her, arranged a visit at her home, and she graciously agreed to illustrate the book.

Also, I found some encouragement recalling St. Thomas Aquinas. He is arguably the greatest of theologians. His voluminous writings are so sublime that one of my professors at the seminary considered them, as he put it, quasi-inspired. Yet, it is said that at the end of his life he considered all that he wrote as so much straw. If that is how he felt about his monumental works, small wonder I felt dissatisfied about my humble effort.

However, aiming unwisely for the best impossible to achieve, one could well fail to achieve the good. In other words, let the best not become enemy of the good.

Taking into account the view of Fyodor Dostoevsky, the mere biographical matter as such should serve some useful purpose. In *The Brothers Karamazov* he writes that there is nothing more noble, powerful, wholesome and helpful in our life than some good remembrance. This is especially true for memories that go back to our childhood: to the days of our life at home. Perhaps there is no better thing in our maturing than some beautiful, sacred memory from our childhood. Many such memories can save us for the rest of our life; and even one can be the instrument of our salvation. (Cf Epilogue: Alyosha's talk to the boys on the occasion of the funeral of their friend Ilyusha).

This insight of the great 19th century Russian genius is well worth keeping in our mind and heart. Mary also "kept all these things in her heart" (Lk 2:51), having lost her boy Jesus and finding him after three days in the temple in Jerusalem. And the famous writer C.S. Lewis writes in the preface to his book *Surprised by Joy* that he never read an autobiography in which the parts dealing with the earlier years were not by far the most interesting. Perhaps there is a connection here with Jesus' tender love for children: "Let the children come to me, do not hinder them; for to such belongs the kingdom of God" (Mk 10:14).

Of itself, **keeping** in mind good memories doesn't seem sufficient reason for **writing** about them: much less about bad ones, surely. Mary herself never wrote about things she kept in her heart, as far as we know.

However, I would go even one or two steps further than Dostoevsky and say that one's memories shared can benefit also other people. And that we can profit also from bad and painful experiences, if only we want to learn from them.

Whether or not you consider my earlier years "by far the most interesting," I don't know. I hope at least some things will be found interesting enough to read about. Above all, I hope and pray that you may be enriched in one way or another by reading this book.

It has been said: "The good is the enemy of the best."

It has also been said: "The best is the enemy of the good."

What is the truth? Are they mutual enemies?

Not at all! We are here face to face not with a real, but only an apparent contradiction. We find a number of them in the very Gospels where, from a genuine Christian point of view, there can be no real ones.

To mention but two: "Peace I leave with you; my peace I give to you" (Jn 14:27) and "Do not think that I have come to bring peace on earth; I have not come to bring peace, but a sword" (Mt 10:34). Or: "Let your light so shine before men, that they may see your good works and give glory to your Father who is in heaven" (Mt 5:16) and "But when you give alms, do not let your left hand know what your right hand is doing, so that your alms may be in secret " (Mt 6:3-4).

It's the context that makes all the difference! Christ indeed brought us peace, but not at the price of preferring anybody to God. We must indeed give good example to others, but not in order to show off and pamper our pride.

If I would be satisfied with a sloppy, half-baked work, it would amount to the good being the enemy of the best. On the other hand, realizing that I am not an artistic genius and therefore shirking the writing, would be a case of the best being the enemy of the good.

So, I tried to do my best in the humble awareness that it may not amount to anything worth bragging about. But if it brings some good to somebody, it is worth the effort - and thank God!

Alcoholics Anonymous is a well known organization or fellowship spread throughout the world. It is amazingly successful in helping alcoholics.

An essential feature of every A.A. meeting is "witness": a vivid sharing by a member of his or her past experiences with the whole group. It is not hard to guess that some accounts are quite grim; yet invariably they end on a note of hope and gratitude.

In Oshawa, where an A.A. group used to meet in our church hall, I attended several meetings by invitation. At first I was annoyed with their stories. I thought they amounted to navel-gazing, ego-trips, at best a waste of time. Soon, however, I learned that they were not only quite interesting, but also beneficial. Invariably something came up in which I saw as in a mirror my own self or my own experiences, and learned a lesson for myself or my work as a priest. The wisdom of one of my mother's many favourite sayings proved time and again to be true and genuine: "Listen to experienced people; they know more than the learned."

Everyone has a life story to tell that is worth hearing. Usually it contains powerful and valuable lessons: either things to imitate or to avoid. And no two lives are identical, because every person is absolutely unique: there never was and never will be another you or I. It is a picturesque way of saying it but it is true: when God made you he threw the mould away. The same he did with mine, and everyone else's. And that is one of the reasons everyone is so very special. Everyone is irreplaceable. Everyone has a purpose, even if it may be just like a pause in one of Beethoven's symphonies: not amounting to very much in itself, yet truly indispensable and necessary for the perfection and beauty of the whole. And everyone has a work to do that nobody else can ever do: even if just being an object for others to love and serve. For if everyone were completely self-sufficient, there would be no need of spouses, parents, doctors, bricklayers - nor any other of the hundreds of vocations and professions. Everyone would be completely useless.

It is hard for the ones on the receiving end to acquiesce in this state of affairs. But this is the reality and it should be a strong, magnificent consolation for all the crippled, bedridden, unemployed in spite of their best efforts, aged, or for any other good reason in need of help and loving care.

Another reason for our nearly infinite value is inherent in human nature itself. St.Paul speaks of it as "spirit, soul, and body" (1 Thes 5:23), while we usually say that we are of body and soul, substantially united. I don't see any opposition between the two statements, but I think this is all we should say here on that point.

At least in so far as man is a material body, he is next to nothing: "When I look at thy heavens, the work of thy fingers, the moon and the stars which thou hast established; what is man that thou art mindful of him, and the son of man that thou dost care for him?" (Ps 8:3-4). (Incidentally, I heard that a copy of Ps 8 was sent by the late Pope Paul VI with the first astronauts to the moon where it rests with certain other objects in a capsule).

When we hear scientists speak of billions of stars - our own Sun nothing more than a middle-sized one of them - in our Milky Way galaxy alone, and about billions of galaxies, and billions of light years of known space, and billions of years of time since its beginning: what, indeed, is man? Nothing but next to nothing!

Take into account also this stunning fact: if the atoms in

an adult human body were crushed so as to do away with the empty space between their particles, all that would be left would be a dot visible only with a microscope - and we are left with an almost perfect nothingness, materially speaking.

However, the very next two verses of the same psalm are: "Yet thou hast made him little less than God, and dost crown him with glory and honour. Thou hast given him dominion over the works of thy hands; thou hast put all things under his feet" (Ps 8:5-6).

Human dignity and value, then, is not due primarily to our material quantity, but rather to our quality which derives from the spiritual dimension of our essence and existence: the immortal soul with its powers of intellect and will.

It is not too hard to grasp that, placed on the scales of values, each and every human person outweighs the whole material universe. For all the matter in the universe can neither think, know, will, choose, feel...nor say "I love you" and mean it. You and I can.

Every human person is in a real sense the very centre of the universe. For you from your point of view, and for me from my point of view, everything else is outside of us: north, south, east, west, up, down, left, right, before, behind...Even God, in whom there is no past or future but an eternal present, who "dwells in unapproachable light, whom no man has ever seen or can see" (1 Tim 6:16) and is totally distinct from and infinitely above his creation, yet present all the time everywhere, chose to be "another" for you and me, respecting our identity and freedom: "Behold, I stand at the door and knock; if any one hears my voice and opens the door, I will come in to him..." (Rev 3:20).

In virtue of the spiritual element of human nature, we have fathomed the depths of the universe, measured distances and mind-boggling speeds of stars, their individual sizes, weight, luminosity, and even discovered what stuff they are made of. No less breathtaking are our insights into the world at the other extreme of the scale: the atom and its wonders.

Having considered these wonderful truths, there is one very deflating number in the equation: the shortness of each individual human life: "...from everlasting to everlasting thou art

God. The years of our life are threescore and ten, or even by reason of strength fourscore..." (Ps 90:2 and 10). What is the longest human life compared to the age of the universe?!

For the ones who believe in God, other infinite vistas open up: the belief in a spiritual, immortal soul which will survive the duration of the material universe and live forever. For a believer, death is not the end but only the beginning.

Finally, Christians believe that the human race has been lifted up from the abyss of sin (the original sin of Adam as well as the personal sins of every individual sinner) by the Incarnation, Death and Resurrection of the only Son of God himself. What is the value, then, of each and every human being, created "in the image of God" (Gen 1:27) and redeemed, not with "the blood of goats and calves" (Heb 9:12), but with the blood of his only Son, through whom "all things were made" (Jn 1:3)?

I have no adequate answer to that question. But there is no shadow of doubt in my mind that, in the light of the preceding considerations, the value of every human being is literally inestimable. Therefore, everyone - including you and me - is worthy to be known, loved, and heard.

It has been said that history is the best of teachers; the trouble is that most of us are bad pupils: refusing to learn its lessons and thus repeating the same old mistakes. The only thing most of us seem to have learned is that we have learned nothing.

Not only nations have their history: every human life is a history in miniature. It would seem logical, then, that we could learn useful lessons from every human life: its joys and sorrows, ups and downs, successes as well as mistakes.

That should answer the **Why** of this book. It is by far the more important of the two questions, yet hopefully one or another may find the **How** also worth reading.

One of the biblical stories from the life of the mighty prophet Elijah is a good illustration of this book's genesis.

The evil king Ahab turned to false gods and committed other abominations: so much so that he "did more to provoke the Lord, the God of Israel, to anger than all the kings of Israel who were before him" (1 Kings 16:33). So Elijah went to him and said: "As the Lord the God of Israel lives, before whom I stand, there shall be neither dew nor rain these years, except by my word" (1 Kings 17:1).

It is not hard to guess that Elijah had to scram very fast to save his skin from the rage of Ahab and his equally evil queen Jezebel.

When finally time came for the drought to end, Elijah went to Mount Carmel, a beautiful green hill on a peninsula, with a view far and wide over the fertile plain of Jezreel to the east and the Mediterranean sea to the west. He sent his servant repeatedly to the top to look towards the sea, but the servant saw nothing. Only when he went up the seventh time, he saw "a little cloud like a man's hand rising out of the sea." It did not take very long before "the heavens grew black with clouds and wind, and there was a great rain" (1 Kings 18:44-45).

Only God knows how great or small a "rain" this book will turn out to be, but at any rate its coming into being reminds me of the slow growth of that little cloud.

More than once after the Second World War conversation would just naturally turn to my personal experiences in it, and in my prisonership of war. And more than once I was advised or even urged to write a book about them. That's what sparked the idea.

My first attempt had been made some time between 1962 and 1966, during my first service as associate pastor at St. Bernard's church in Toronto. A good beginning is very important for the success of any venture or work. I wanted to begin in the best possible way. So, late some evening I went to the church. Kneeling at the marble Communion rail, half-way between the tabernacle and a statue of Mary, I laid the paper pad on the rail and began to write. I have no clue what I wrote late that evening. With my pastor in poor health and much work, that was the end of the first try.

The second attempt at writing occurred in the late 1960s or early 1970s. It was during a short stay of about five days in St.Michael's hospital in Toronto. I was there only for some check-ups and felt quite well. But again my pastoral duties prevented me from going beyond a dozen or so pages.

No scrap of paper or trace of my first two starts can be found anywhere among my belongings.

# A BOUQUET FOR YOU

Elijah's servant went seven times to the top of Mount Carmel to look for the rain cloud before it appeared over the sea. The circumstances of my third attempt were such that I said: "This is it! No turning back this time! If God wants me to finish this work, nobody and nothing can stop me. If not: his will be done."

On October 31, 1984, I was relieved of my pastorate of St. Philip's church in Oshawa, Ontario. For the following six weeks I had the fortune of staying at Madonna House in Combermere on the Madawaska River, by Canadian standards not very far from Ottawa.

The founder of Madonna House, Catherine de Hueck Doherty, was an extraordinary woman. Born into a Russian baronial family in the mid-1890s, she became a refugee from the Bolshevik revolution. After her wanderings through several countries of Europe and North Africa she emigrated to North America where she married a rich and famous journalist, Eddy Doherty. Even though of noble background, she dedicated her whole life to the poor, establishing Friendship Houses to serve them in Toronto, then in the slums of Harlem in New York, and finally the Madonna House in Combermere, where both Eddy and she are now buried. Her whole life and work is perhaps best summed up in the title of one of her books: *The Gospel Without Compromise.*

I met Catherine in 1966 in Toronto when she addressed a large assembly of priests. We were very impressed by her powerful, enthusiastically delivered message: Give Us God!

Although I read later some of her books, I never saw her again. My strong desire to meet her during my stay at Madonna House was thwarted because of her illness. A few days after my arrival she did return from a Toronto hospital, but she was not well and her log cabin was out of bounds.

My daily routine called for three hours of manual labour in the bush, the stable, the kitchen, or one of the workshops. It also included about five kilometres of walk, apart from the daily Mass and prayers. As there were no other duties, the idea of writing surfaced again in my mind.

My spiritual guide and confessor, Father Cullinane, was

a holy and friendly priest, in his late 70s. He had been associated for many years with the Madonna House Apostolate, and had a manly, tender devotion to the Blessed Virgin Mary.

"Father," I said during a session, "for many years I had been playing with the idea of writing a book. Several people urged me to write it, and I truly hope that it would be for the good of at least some of its readers. I was a soldier in the Second World War, a prisoner of war in the Soviet Union, and now a refugee. I would like to share some of my experiences; no doubt the readers would come to appreciate peace, food, and some other goods better, and be more grateful for them. Maybe one or the other would even get the idea to become a priest."

He listened and looked at me very attentively.

"Dear Father," he replied gravely after a few moments of deliberation, "I have been appointed by lawful Church authorities your spiritual director and confessor. Therefore, I can rely on the support of the Holy Spirit in giving you advice and guidance." After some more deliberation he continued: "I advise you against the idea of writing" and added, as an afterthought: "Let us wait for a sign from the Blessed Virgin."

I do not recall whether or not he gave me any reasons for his advice. I was disappointed, but accepted it, reluctantly, because I took it as God's will. To be honest, I had not much hope of any signs from the Blessed Virgin.

One evening a week or so later, I hung around in the dining room after supper, browsing through the books which fill shelves on all four walls from the floor to the ceiling, except for the doors and the windows.

"How is B?" I asked casually a middle-aged lady cleaning the tables after the meal. We usually referred to Catherine by her nickname which she had picked up somewhere in the United States. "I wished so much to talk to her. I met her only once, back in the mid-sixties, in Toronto. I am sorry that she is not well enough to have visitors."

"She is not very well," came the reply, "but now and then she has some better moments. Day and night there are two women looking after her. Tonight is my turn; right after this cleaning I am going to her cabin. If she is in one of her better spells I'll ask her if she'd see you. Wait here: if she agrees, I'll call you right away to come over to the island."

Do I need to say how happy I was that there was still a chance to talk to the charismatic baroness?

Within the next half hour the telephone rang in the kitchen. A girl stepped into the dining room: "Father, you are wanted on the telephone."

My heart jumped.

"B is willing to see you," said the voice at the other end of the line, "come over right away."

I knew what great love Catherine had for priests. It was due to a great extent to the fact that she saw a priest actually nailed to a door during the Bolshevik revolution. This is not hear-say: I heard herself speak about it on an audio tape. But I was in my working clothes and my barrack was too far away to think about changing them fast.

"Don't worry about clothes," the caller advised, "just come while B is able to see you."

I sped over the narrow wooden bridge across the swampy stretch which separates the so-called island at the shore of the Madawaska River from the rest of the main grounds of Madonna House. I had heard that Catherine loved to hear in her old age her mother tongue. But my Russian is not very good. So I prayed all the way that things would turn out well.

Catherine's bed stood in the middle of the log cabin: head to the wall, feet to the centre. She lay on her left side tucked under blankets and looked towards me as I was coming from the door. She seemed surprised: as if wondering what I was doing there.

As I greeted her and said a few more words in Russian, her face brightened noticeably and she seemed more alert. The Holy Spirit must have been with me, or her, or both of us, for she understood most of what I said.

Having introduced myself, I believe I told her about my meeting her once before in Toronto; and how the priests appreciated her powerful message; and how I was glad to see her again: "I also read some of your books and liked them very much. I understand you lived before the revolution in St. Petersburg, today called Leningrad. I was a soldier in the last World War and from 1944 to 1946 prisoner of war in Moscow. Sometimes I wondered if it would be good to write a book about it." In this last sentence I used the word *horoshó* (good, or well).

Suddenly Catherine's face lit up. She tried to raise her head. As I bent a little so that she could hear and see me better, she put her right arm around my neck and pulled me down to her cheek. Relaxing gradually her grip, she almost exclaimed *tchudésno!* (wonderful!), with a big smile. Then she became drowsy again. I knew it was time to say goodbye.

That was our second and last meeting. The following year she was buried, several weeks before I learned that she had died.

The next day I told the story to Father Cullinane. He listened very attentively. Then, after a short deliberation, he said: "We shall take that as the sign from the Blessed Virgin. You may go ahead with your writing."

It was the feast of St.Nicholas, December 6, 1984. I wrote the first few lines on that very day which evokes so many fond memories of my childhood. We children used to set up on the eve of it little baskets, and woke up next morning to find them full of nuts, apples, hazelnuts and other gifts to our heart's delight. But the sign from the Blessed Virgin was more welcome than any material goodies.

Yes, this is the third start, and this time there is no turning back. No turning back, God willing: for I am well aware of the wisdom of the late Father Sean O'Sullivan's statement in his book *Both My Houses* to the effect that there are times when our plans for God may be thwarted by God's plans for us.

A week before Christmas 1984, I was appointed associate pastor at St.Anne's parish in Brampton, a sprawling suburban city northwest of Metropolitan Toronto. And since April 30, 1985, I have been pastor at St.Joseph's in Beaverton, a predominantly rural parish on the shores of Lake Simcoe, about one and a half hours by car north of Toronto. Life's tempo here is slower than in the cities, yet even so there have been periods of several months and one over a year when not a sentence had been written.

There are two points which I want to emphasize.

First, that I have not been asked by anyone of my superiors to write. Therefore, I am writing merely as a free citizen of Canada: in no way whatsoever do I intend to commit the Church whom I am serving as priest.

Secondly, my writing has been done mainly in my free time: on holidays and days off duty, as a hobby.

In regard to the form, I am trying to make my style as good, pleasant, simple and readable as possible. But please remember kindly that I am not a literary genius, and that English is not my mother tongue.

What I consider more important, though, is the contents, the matter, the ideas. In that regard everyone is very much a child of his or her time and environment. Everyone is affected to a notable extent by a number of external factors: geography and climate, war or peace, health, social and family conditions, education, ideology, religion or lack of it...and yes, even pre-natal factors with their beneficial effects or traumas.

Sir Winston Churchill is supposed to have said that democracy was the worst form of government, except for all the other forms. Debates in a genuinely democratic parliament could serve as an illustration of what I mean. On just about every subject heated, radical disagreements develop. Honest people, top experts in their respective fields, hold sincerely and tenaciously widely differing and often opposite views on problems and their solutions. What one lauds as a panacea, another condemns as deadly poison.

My mother used to say : "No human work is perfect." Imperfection is at the very root of the human condition. Nobody can please everybody all the time. Trying to do so is the surest recipe for pleasing nobody. To put it in more picturesque words: I have no intention to enlarge a grey wall, but rather to add a small but unique and beautiful pebble to the splendour of the magnificent mosaic of world literature.

Chapter Three

# My Croatian Connection

It was in the beginning of June, 1966.

"Father, the Archbishop called while you were out. He wants you to return his call as soon as you return." I believe it was the good old Mrs. O'Heir or her daughter Ann who gave me the news. Both lived in St.Bernard's rectory in Toronto, where I was assistant priest of Fr. Austin Marshman, the founding pastor of the parish. Ann worked in an office and in her spare time looked after the parish accounts, while her mother kept the house and cooked. She suffered from Parkinson's disease, and when something serious happened to be happening, her hands shook even more than usually.

Archbishops don't call just to wish you a good day. So both of us were excited (although I wasn't shaken enough to shake). Instinctively the thought flashed through my mind: "What have I done?"

That day the schedule called for my monthly visit to one of the two Catholic schools in the parish. The principal kindly offered me his office to call the chancery. After a short wait which seemed notably longer than it really was, I heard His Grace pick up the telephone.

"I am Father Frank from St.Bernard's. I understand you called me earlier, and."

"Good morning, Father," the Archbishop interrupted the sentence. "Thank you for returning my call. Do you know Father Kamber of Our Lady Queen of Croatia parish is not well?"

I didn't.

As a matter of fact, I had met Father Charles Kamber; but only once, as far as I can remember. The occasion was a get-together of a dozen or so Slovenian priests from Southern Ontario for some very special occasion. As almost all of them attended school before the Second World War in Yugoslavia, everyone had to study in grade three and up regularly two hours the so-called "Serbo-Croatian" language every week, and thus had a fairly good command of Croatian.

I sat next to Father Kamber, the pastor of the then only Croatian ethnic parish in the whole Archdiocese of Toronto. He appeared very vigorous, jolly and talkative: the centre of attention and undisputed leader of the very lively conversation. Later I learned that he was a close friend of Father Andrej Prebil, the pastor of the Slovenian parish in Toronto. I suspect that this meeting reminded him of me when he needed somebody to replace him temporarily later on.

"You must certainly be aware that the Croatian parish is very big?" continued the voice at the other end of the line. "During the Council in Rome I already asked the Archbishop of Zagreb to send us a priest. He agreed, but there is much red tape, and it takes time. Right now I have nobody who could speak the language. I understand you speak some Croatian? I'd like you to go and help out temporarily. How old are you?"

"I'm forty."

A fairly long pause followed, so that a kind of embarrassment made me think not necessarily to say something, but at least just something to say.

"On the occasion of my ordination I promised obedience to Cardinal McGuigan and his successors," I blurted out to break the oppressive silence. "I'll go wherever you send me. I can stay at the Croatian church for a while after the other priest comes, or go to some other parish. I have been here four and a half years, and became well acquainted with the area between Keele and Jane Streets along Lawrence Avenue West; if you so wish, I'll gladly return back."

"Oh, no: You'll not go back to St. Bernard's!" was his swift reply.

Who could have believed then that my "temporary" sojourn at the Croatian church in Toronto would last six years and three months - and that the same Archbishop would after it send me right back to St. Bernard's for another four years! He probably forgot what he had said over six years earlier, and I was careful not to remind him about it. I would have loved to stay at Our Lady Queen of Croatia church. But as I had to leave, I was quite happy to return to St. Bernard's.

# MY CROATIAN CONNECTION

I called Father Kamber and arranged a get-acquainted lunch with him at his rectory. There I also met Ludvik and Rosa Rajtek. They were of Slovak background, but hailed from the fertile district of northeastern Croatia, near the Hungarian border. They were getting on in years, but were still doing a splendid job: Ludvik as caretaker of the church and its large hall, his wife Rosa as housekeeper and cook. They were one of the most lovable couples I ever knew. Rosa reminded me of my mother. The main difference between them was that my mother was a lousy cook, while Rosa made the most exquisite pancakes and buns this side of heaven. In preparing stews and other meat meals she was quite an ordinary cook, but her flour meals were out of this world. Fridays were for me not "meatless days of penance." Quite on the contrary: I always looked forward to them for Rosa's delicacies.

The pastor, Father Charles Kamber, whose associate pastor (assistant priest) I remained until his death at the age of 67 on June 30, 1969, had a very strong, masculine personality. Endowed with that enviable character in which strength and kindness are admirably fused and balanced, he was a true father and friend to me. In spite of his macho appearance and behaviour, he had a heart of gold. I have nothing but fond memories of him.

He was born on December 9, 1901 in Ruda, Dalmatia, a strip along the Adriatic Sea coast with mild Mediterranean climate. It is the homeland of such notables as St.Jerome and the Roman Emperor Diocletian. Not surprisingly, its people generally seem to have a softer character, too (although that could hardly be said of Diocletian!). It is very evident from their music and melodies, which are reminiscent of Italian folk songs.

Similarly as the father of the good "smiling pope," John Paul I (Albino Luciani), the father of Charles Kamber also had strong Socialist sympathies. So much so that he had to leave his home town.

When Charles was about four, the family settled in Bugojno, Bosnia, which is to the north of Dalmatia. It is very different from its southern neighbour: mountainous, with colder Continental climate, and very rugged. Bosnia and Herzegovina were occupied over 400 years by the Turks. In post-Second World War Yugoslavia, the two districts were joined into one of its six provinces: Bosna-Hercegovina. All during the long time of

Turkish occupation the people struggled to preserve their national identity and Christian faith. While in Bosnia there is a large percentage of Muslim and Serbian population (besides Croats), Herzegovina is predominantly Croatian, and its people very patriotic as well as very devoutly Catholic, generally speaking. Franciscans remained with their people to celebrate Mass and administer the Sacraments: secretly, for they had to stay underground until Austria-Hungary occupied Bosnia-Herzegovina after a short war in 1878. Even nowadays a Franciscan priest would often be called *ujak,* which means mother's brother, (father's brother is *stric*). The custom originated during the Turkish occupation. It was to make sure a child would not unwittingly betray a visiting priest to the authorities, which could have cost him his life.

Although born in the sunny Dalmatia, Father Kamber considered himself a full-blooded Bosnian: sturdy, rugged, rough - like *Bosna Ponosna* (Bosnia the Proud).

During the 1960s four Croatian seminarians formed a musical group: not unlike The Beatles or one of the many similar bands that mushroomed after them. They called themselves *Žeteoci* (The Harvesters). Known all over Yugoslavia, they became so popular that more copies of their record were sold than required for the award of a Golden Record. It was denied them only because they were Catholic seminarians: students for the priesthood.

A few months before Father Kamber's death they arrived for a very successful tour of Croatian centres in North America. In Toronto, they played and sang before a packed Croatian church hall. Among the folk-song numbers of their repertoire the mellow, soft Dalmatian melodies seemed to predominate. Even though the audience was very enthused with the lively performance, the good Father wasn't quite satisfied. Supported by his crutches, he wobbled near the stage and got hold of a microphone. With a forceful upward thrust of his hand he exclaimed: "Come on, strike me a Bosnian one!"

And they did!

I have so many fond memories of Father Dragutin Kamber, and no bad ones. Dragutin is Croatian for Charles, and as a rule he was referred to by his people as his mother used to call him: Dragutin, which means darling. The root meaning of the name Charles is "dear one," *carus* being Latin for dear.

He told me so many interesting things about his Croatian people, and especially the Bosnians!

The parish had a so called Funeral Society. We had agreement with a nearby funeral home for special rates for deceased members of the Society. If a member died, every other member paid two dollars which covered the funeral expenses. However, the casket had to be the cheapest kind: a simple box, covered with grey, felt-like material. Now and then somebody would complain that it was too cheap, but Father Dragutin always had a standard answer ready: "King Tomislav himself wasn't buried in such a casket!"

He told me many stories about the ancient Croatian king Tomislav who reigned over his then free nation a thousand or so years ago, and about many other historical personalities and heroes, from kings to beggars.

Croats suffered perhaps more than any other nation from the Turkish assault on Europe. As said earlier, Bosnia was for over 400 years under Turkish occupation. Around it, through the very heart of Croatian lands, ran a militarized defence belt, called *Vojna Krajina* (Military District); while most of Western Europe flourished in every sphere of human endeavour, the people of these areas were perishing for the survival of Christianity in Europe. So much so that Pope Leo X in 1513 honoured Croatia with the title *Antemurale Christianitatis* (The Forewall of Christendom). Even so, the Turkish hordes would repeatedly break through to strike in the direction of the very heart of Europe.

One of the most heroic episodes of this era is the Battle at Siget in 1566. Huge multitudes of Turks, led by the Turkish Sultan Sulejman II himself, set out on a campaign against Vienna and Middle Europe. On their way they laid siege to the fortress Siget. Its Croatian defenders, led by their captain Nikola Zrinski and aware that they could not hold out much longer for lack of supplies, decided on sally. They perished to the last man, but not before inflicting very heavy losses on the besiegers. Most importantly, the Sultan himself was killed. In sorrow, his whole huge army returned back where it came from.

Even today, there are great numbers of Muslims in Bosnia. Its capital, Sarajevo, with its many mosques and their minarets has the appearance of a Turkish rather than European city.

Father Kamber had a doctorate in Islamic studies. He was well acquainted with the *Koran,* the Muslim holy book, as well as with Croatian, and especially Bosnian, history and literature.

At his pleasant discourses, usually during and after our meals, he would remind me that the patron saint of Bosnia, very appropriately, was the mighty prophet Elijah. As additional proofs of Bosnian manliness (probably not realizing I was well aware of it already), he recited to me from memory passages of powerful epics: very loudly and accompanied by forceful gestures of hand and yes, even crutches once upon a time. I wish I could translate the beauty of the mighty verses, all beautifully rhymed! Let me mention here at least two samples of such epic poetry.

One sings of the mighty deeds of heroes who destroyed a Turkish fortress: "And they applied the living fire to the powder. The Turks flew to the heavens. Third day they were falling from the skies." The second recalls the fire which destroyed a small city called Travnik. The heroine here is a Muslim girl: "What is this? What's happening to Travnik? Are the Turks taking it by storm, or is it attacked by a violent murderous plague? No! Neither are the Turks taking it by storm, nor is it attacked by a violent murderous plague: a girl looked at it through her face-veil with her black eyes!"

Some powder! Some eyes! Some look! Geniuses like Dante or Shakespeare himself would envy such imagination.

This noble son of *Bosna Ponosna* (Bosnia the Proud), Father Dragutin, had quite a bit of the spirit of this land in his heart. He had little use or ability for little details or modern gadgets. Rather, he reminded me of an eagle soaring high over the Bosnian mountains: not noticing every detail, but seeing the whole vast landscape to the farthest horizons. Noticing that I often called by telephone people in invalid marriages, or in one way or other not practising the Catholic faith, in order to arrange visits or meetings with them, he once said to me: "Father, you look for work and problems as if you didn't already have more than enough of them. A priest must be like a general leading his army in battle against the enemy. Certainly, there will be casualties here and there, but he must go forwards!" He practically shouted the last word, emphasizing it further by an accompanying powerful thrust of his hand forward and up. "If he would pay attention to every single wounded or dead soldier, he would lose the battle before it began."

One could, of course, debate the morality of the last sentence. If by attention is meant personal involvement of the general himself, I think such conduct could hardly be condemned as immoral. If taken as it stands, I am not so sure.

In any case, the talk about a general was not very far fetched. At the beginning of the war, Father Kamber was pastor in a Bosnian town called Doboj. Once, when for a period of time all the local government collapsed, he took personal charge of civil authority until order was restored.

*Nezavisna Država Hrvatska,* often referred to simply by its acronym NDH (Independent State Croatia), came into existence as a consequence of the break-up of Yugoslavia in April 1941. It could exist as such, at least for the time being, only as a satellite of the Axis powers or not at all. It is not quite just, then, to say the least, to blame Croatia for its alliance with the Axis powers, which frequently happens. With the defeat of the Axis powers in 1945 the NDH also ceased to exist as such, of course. It became a province of the new post-war Yugoslavia.

The Archbishop of the NDH capital Zagreb, Dr. Aloysius Stepinac, who later became a world renown cardinal, was during the war the official chaplain of all the armed forces of the NDH. As he was obliged to reside in Zagreb, the state capital and his archiepiscopal see, Father Dragutin Kamber was appointed his personal representative in the field. For all practical purposes he became the supreme army chaplain. In that capacity he got acquainted with many government and other authorities and leaders.

In the spring of 1945 the bulk of the NDH government, army, and masses of ordinary civilians tried to escape to Austria. Many made it, but dozens of thousands, captured by the victorious Marshall Tito's forces or returned back to them by the British, were simply executed without any legal process and any further ado.

Father Kamber, as acting chaplain of the NDH armed forces, joined the exodus. Travelling with members of the government, he learned at least one lesson which proved advantageous for his peace of mind many years later. As mentioned, he had no talent for details. Neither were the finer points of parish financial administration his cup of tea. But he was not overly concerned about it.

"On the way into exile I had a conversation with the NDH minister of finances," he reminisced with me over a meal. "He was a very fine and capable man: you couldn't be finance minister of a state if you were a dummy! I told him that I cannot understand the workings of economy and finances; they seem so terribly complicated."

"Yes, they are, indeed," the minister replied, "neither can I."

"Well," Father Kamber concluded, "if a finance minister of a state cannot understand the workings of economy and finances, how could a simple priest be expected to understand them!"

I myself, once upon a time, found consolation in this anecdote: in all likelihood I am not alone?

There is another anecdote, concerning also 'an NDH government minister. While about the finance minister I remember the portfolio but not the name, in this case it is the other way around.

The minister's name was Andrija Artuković. He lived in exile in the USA, but the Yugoslavian government and certain American lawyers tried repeatedly and stubbornly over many years to have him extradited for alleged war crimes. Father Kamber, a good friend of Andrija, was utterly convinced about his innocence. As a very knowledgeable witness of the minister's wartime attitudes and actions, he wrote letters and testified many times on his behalf, more than once before very high American authorities. Father Kamber was convinced it was mainly because of his efforts that Andrija was not extradited. It was only years after Father Kamber's death, I believe, that he was finally sent to

Yugoslavia: a very old man, seriously ill and almost blind. Perhaps things changed by then so much that he would not have been executed after all; in any case, he died a natural death.

Having heard about Croatian nationalism, I was at first reluctant to go and serve as a priest among them. "This is a Croatian ethnic parish," I imagined them saying, "Why saddle us with a Slovene?" The ordinary people couldn't have been expected to realize that there was just no Croatian priest available at the time, while their only one had to go to the hospital. When on top of that I saw at once the Bosnian character of the pastor, my apprehension doubled. Moreover, I never distinguished between the Serbian and the Croatian language. In school, as well as later in the Army, we always spoke about the Serbo-Croatian. Although the writing is very different (Serbian uses the Cyrillic alphabet, Croatian the Latin), differences in spoken language are not very great, though real. I would compare them to the differences between English in England and in Canada: mainly different dialects, but also some different words. Above all, I couldn't afford using the Serbian accent, let alone Serbian words. The well known feelings between the two peoples are, generally speaking, just too sensitive for those kinds of mistakes. That is why at first I used to write all my sermons and had them checked with my pastor. As far as the dialects go, I soon learned a few important general rules of pronunciation, which pretty well solved that problem, too.

The Croatian pastor in Toronto was expected to be, and was, not only a priest, but also a community leader, and to a certain extent even a political one. There were several political groups in the Croatian community and church congregation. Most of them were at the throats of each other: partly due to clash of personalities, partly to difference of ideologies. Their goal was basically identical: an independent Croatia. They differed in regard to the means to achieve that objective. A great tragedy befell their beloved homeland during and after the Second World War. The result was an exodus of multitudes of their compatriots to the four corners of the world, while the Serbs moved in large numbers in, so as to turn large formerly Croatian areas into ethnic

Serbian territory. The emigrant leaders seemed at a loss as to what to do about this and other problems. Actually, there was precious little or nothing they could have done. For example, Father Kamber, himself an exile, refused to sign the papers for one of his close relatives to emigrate to North America, because he did not consider him a genuine refugee. "I am not going to help the emptying of Croatia!" was his unwavering reaction. On the other hand, he did all he could for so many other refugees from his homeland.

On top of it all, there is no doubt that the strong Yugoslavian consulate in Toronto, together with the Croatian and other sympathizers of the post-war regime in Yugoslavia, fanned the fires already burning strongly.

Right at the beginning I told my new pastor that my understanding of the Croatian socio-political situation in the homeland as well as in Canada was very scanty, to say the least. I'd not be able to be much help in that area, but would of necessity have to limit my activity to the religious sphere, leaving the more specifically "Croatian" matters to him. He was quite amenable to the arrangement which, in retrospect, appears to have been the best one possible. As a matter of fact, little did I dream then how packed would my appointment calendar and days be with essentially religious and spiritual work alone.

Almost immediately after my arrival the pastor left for check-ups in the famous Mayo Clinic in U.S.A. He returned one or two months later. During the next three years he spent about half of the time in hospitals or recuperating away from the rectory. About half of his stay at the rectory he spent in bed, often in excruciating pain, while the rest of the time he appeared in excellent health and full of energy. About one week before his death he underwent an operation. Only then cancer was diagnosed. Doctors justified their unbelievably late discovery with the explanation that it had been hidden behind the spine.

My parish work at the Queen of Croatia church was overwhelming, both before and after Father Kamber's death. People would come from all over the Archdiocese of Toronto for baptisms and weddings, even if they attended Mass elsewhere (or nowhere). Every year there were hundreds of baptisms, and three years in a row over 100 marriages: 130, 110, and 105. For every baptism a simple visit to the baby's home sufficed: to make sure the parents were aware of their responsibilities as Christian parents, to arrange for the amendment of any defects in their marriage situation or marital relationships, to get the necessary information for the baptism register, and to line up the ceremony. In the actual ceremony in the church, there was hardly any difference in the amount of work for one child or for a dozen of them. Also, the current Archdiocesan rules allowed the option: either to visit the child's parents or arrange an individual visit with them, or have any number of them come to the church together for one or two sessions. The choice was up to the pastor, but one or the other option was mandatory. We always chose the home visit, and I still do. It gives the priest the opportunity for a truly pastoral visit: personal and intimate. Such meetings can be very beneficial, for not infrequently urgent matters come up which would otherwise never be brought to the attention of the priest until it becomes too late for any remedial action.

Marriages were quite a different matter. There were Saturdays when I had to officiate at five weddings. Usually I would take them in two groups: two and three together. The couples were very understanding that it was impossible to take them separately (especially as almost all wanted a Wedding Mass), and the ceremonies as such were a relatively minor chore. The bulk of work went into the long preparation: filling out a fairly detailed pre-marriage questionnaire with each of the two parties "separately and not in the presence of each other" and gathering of documents, including those from overseas, (with some churches destroyed during the last war), for all the requirements of both the civil and the Church law must be faithfully fulfilled. Above all, there were always the regular pre-marriage lessons: marriage as Sacrament, as covenant, as contract; communication and dealing with disagreements; why marriages fail; duties of parents towards their children; morality in marriage; the ceremony...If one was not Catholic, there was an additional lesson, intended to prevent any future problems resulting from the difference in religion. On top of it all, the language of communication was Croatian, which for me was more difficult than English, for I never studied theology in Croatian.

Here the question may understandably be asked: "There must have been quite a few marriages when one party was not Croatian; surely in such cases the communication had to be in English?" The correct answer to such a question would be: "True, there were quite a few such couples; but that was of little help, for in such cases, as a rule, both languages had to be used."

Besides the regular parish work, I had to act often as interpreter for the parishioners, mostly at the Immigration and Employment offices. It was nerve-wrecking to wait for hours while there was so much work waiting to be done. I would take with me a book, writing pad, and breviary (prayer book) to save at least some time.

When finally, three weeks before Father Kamber's death, the priest who was to replace me arrived from Croatia, I looked for the first opportunity to respond to repeated entreaties of my folks to visit my home. Since it is a long trip, I hoped to stay longer than the usual three weeks. I still keep the copy of the letter in which I begged the Archbishop to grant me two months leave of absence. To support my request, I pointed out that for the last one and a half years I worked daily, seven days a week, from about 7:00 a.m. to midnight or 1:00 a.m., except for time out for meals, and that in all that time I had not one single day off. He graciously granted my request, with no questions asked.

The priests' mandatory daily reading, or rather praying, of the breviary takes a little less than an hour. It is designed to sanctify the day. Ideally, the morning, daytime, evening and night prayers should be prayed at their proper times, and the fairly lengthy part referred to as "The Office of Readings" (with a passage from the bible and one from either writings of saints or Church documents) read at any time of the day. I rarely found time to pray the parts of the breviary at their assigned times. It is interesting how what must be done is done: by midnight the breviary was finished. During the Daylight Saving Time it was usually 1:00 a.m. The Church is a loving and generous Mother, and allows the priests to compute time for the purposes of breviary in any way that suits them best: Standard Time (also referred to as Mean Local Time: the same in all places of every time zone), Daylight Saving Time (one hour ahead of Standard

Time) or Real Local Time (it is just what its name says. E.g., in Oshawa midnight is at 12:15 a.m., in Toronto at 12:17 a.m.).

In the letter to the Archbishop I did not mention that I found it somewhat strange to pray late at night in one of the hymns for the morning prayer: "Now that the sun is rising, let us rise too, to praise the Lord..." Nor did I tell him that often it was quite a chore to finish the breviary by 1:17 a.m. I'd doze off and wake up repeatedly. Not knowing where on the page I had been, I'd repeat again and again passages of psalms or other writings. Nowadays, the time for finishing the breviary is not computed as strictly, nor is the obligation itself to pray it taken as seriously - for better and for worse - as it used to be.

Christmas 1968 remains indelibly imprinted in my memory.

It was Father Kamber's last Christmas, and health-wise he happened to be in one of his twilight periods: neither very sick nor very well. The day before Christmas we were both hearing Confessions many long hours: non-stop, except for lunch and supper, from sometime before noon until just before midnight. The confessionals had two small windows with trellis and sliding sound-proof wooden panel. It seemed almost like rowing a boat or paddling a canoe, very slowly but with alternating strokes: you closed the window on the left and opened the one on the right, then closed the one on the right and opened the one on the left, without any break. The priest's cubicle was lit, the penitent's behind the grille in darkness. No face could be discerned, only voices heard: now that of an old man or woman, now of a youth; an innocent child who had nothing else to confess than "I didn't always listen to mummy" may have been followed by an inveterate sinner who had been away from the Sacraments for decades. I may have had to rack my brain for proper advice or solution of a complicated problem of restitution. I was aware of my grave responsibility to give the most salutary advice or find the right solution, which more than once gave me real headaches. But the greater the misery, the more my heart went out to the sinner. I became vividly aware of the truth of Jesus' statement: "Just so, I tell you, there will be more joy in heaven over one sinner who repents than over ninety-nine righteous persons who need no repentance" (Lk 15:7).

In my heart there was such joy, too, and all the long hours of toil didn't bother me at all, in spite of the intermittent headaches or feelings of waking up from semi-consciousness. After all, I was only 42: in the best years of my life.

With midnight approaching, there were still penitents lined up outside on each side of the confessional, but we had to get ready for the midnight Mass. The pastor was to celebrate it in the church proper, I simultaneously downstairs in the large hall. Somehow I was able to push my way through the crowd gathered at the back of the church near the confessional, the vestibule and on the steps to the hall. The pastor's sermon was to have been heard also through the loudspeakers in the hall. All I'd have to do would be to sit comfortably in the chair and listen. Father Kamber was known to preach now and then for well over one hour, though he'd speed-up considerably the rest of the Mass (especially when it was still in Latin). He did not hesitate to deal concretely with matters political and Croatian. Once I brought up the subject, in the most diplomatic language I was able to muster. His answer was very convincing: "Jesus Christ spoke about fishermen and Pharisees and Jews and Samaritans, and their problems; in my place, he'd no doubt speak about Croats and their problems." Who could argue with that!?

As it happened, there was no connection between the pastor's pulpit upstairs and the loudspeakers in the hall. Something went wrong (which I should have anticipated, but was not yet fully aware of all the paragraphs of the famous Murphy's Law). I sat for a while, then preached a sermonette and continued the Mass. The pastor's sermon, too, turned out mercifully to have been one of his shorter ones (45 minutes or so?).

Midnight Mass over, we had a small snack with a little chat, and retired to get rested for the burdens of Christmas Day. There was no sign of any trouble brewing.

Around 2:00 a.m., just as I was about to slump into my bed, there was a knock on my door. The poor Father Dragutin stood there, slightly bent and holding with both hands his stomach: "Father, I think I have appendicitis. I don't know what to do."

"Let me take you to St. Joseph's hospital," I quipped. "If

it is really appendicitis, you have to go anyway. If not, the sooner we are back, the better." I didn't desire anything more than to be in bed as soon as possible. To my great relief he got ready at once.

In the emergency ward only a skeleton crew was on shift, for it was both night and Christmas. The doctors suspected kidney stones, which later turned out as the correct diagnosis. He had to drink some white stuff for the purpose of X-ray pictures. It took close to one hour before the nurse returned: "Sorry, but the pictures didn't turn out well; we have to repeat the procedure."

Father Kamber was lying on a stretcher parked in the emergency ward corridor. He was in severe pain and all the while holding tightly my hand: "Father, I beg you to stay with me; I must hold your hand to bear the pain."

What could I do? I couldn't extricate my hand from his and leave! Moreover, by now it was day, and soon there was the first of three more Christmas Masses to be celebrated. I was aware that more than one of the Slovenian priests in Toronto knew enough Croatian to take my place. I called Our Lady Help of Christians church: no answer. I called Our Lady of the Miraculous Medal church: no answer. I called again, and again: no answer. It didn't make any difference if everyone was still asleep or in church: there was just no priest available. Father Kamber had to let me go, no matter how reluctantly.

I celebrated the three Masses before midday, asking the people to pray for the pastor who was in hospital. Exhausted (do I need to say it?), I gulped down some food found in the fridge. The caretaker's family - all of them: Ludvik, Rosa and son Stephen - were away for Christmas Day with one of their relatives. I fell on my bed. No sooner did I hit the mattress, the telephone rang. There was no telephone in my little bedroom, which was the only room I had. Between it and the pastor's office was a kind all-purpose room. The only telephone on the whole second floor was in the pastor's office.

"How is Father Kamber?"

Dozens of times that afternoon and early evening I was raised from my bed by callers wanting to know the condition of their pastor. No sooner did I fall down than I had to get up again and again to answer the calls at the other end of the floor, for

241

there was no couch in the pastor's office to lay down.

Looking back over 20 years later, I think I deserved what I got then. In fact, they should have put me in jail; or at least in a mental asylum for a while. Surely there was more than one parishioner I could have called to answer the telephone that Christmas afternoon! Also, I would not work 16 and 17 hours day in and day out if I had the chance to go back in time to relive that period. True, it was a work of love and therefore I never found it really burdensome, especially since I was then in my best years of manhood. But there is a certain gift called common sense, and God's gifts were given us to be used, not abused or left unused.

Perhaps it would not be amiss to go back at this point and pick up another thread of the story about my "Croatian Connection."

The original Croatian Catholic church building in Toronto had been purchased from a Protestant congregation. It was quite decrepit and too small. During the 1962 New Year's party in the church hall underneath it a fire bomb was thrown into the mostly wooden building. It burned to the ground like tinder. To this day the arsonist has not been found. The pastor's enemies had a hey-day: for years there was no end of written articles, leaflets, pamphlets, and telephone calls stubbornly claiming, and "proving," that the pastor himself burned the church personally.

Most vicious attacks came from a fairly young Croatian hothead. Even before I heard of him, in my very first days in the parish, the Archdiocesan chancellor asked me with an enigmatic smile if I had already met the man. He offered no reason for the question, nor did I ask for one. Before long I became aware of the reason for the smile and why he said nothing more.

This man went so far as to assert that he helped personally his pastor to burn down the old church. Taking into account all the circumstances, I consider it possible, though by no means probable. I am not joking when I say that if he really did it, he deserves a big monument in front of the new, large and beautiful church. In order to help prevent any future bombings, it has no windows. However, it has enough skylights on its roof that it is brighter than most other churches. All said, without the fire the old wooden structure might still be there.

242

# MY CROATIAN CONNECTION

It was on the very occasion of the blessing of the new church by the Archbishop of Toronto, the Most Rev. Philip F. Pocock, on Sunday, June 19, 1966, that I arrived in the parish as assistant priest. The blessing was at 4:00 p.m., while I offered the last Mass at St. Bernard's, my former parish, at 5:00 p.m. Immediately after the Mass I left and arrived towards the end of the festive banquet in the large hall in the church basement: just in time for the dessert.

At the after-dinner speech time the Archbishop introduced me to the audience, and asked me to say a few words. The hall was packed, which made my considerable apprehension even more pronounced.

My first carefully chosen words were the popular greeting which is used by the faithful Croatian people even in today's secularized Western society instead of anything from "Good Morning" to "Good Night": *Hvaljen Isus i Marija* (Praised be Jesus and Mary).

Immediately after a loud *Uvijeke Hvaljen* (Forever Praised) in response, the whole crowd burst into a loud applause. I continued to point out how during the Second World War dozens of Slovenian priests, expelled by the Nazis, found refuge and warm hospitality by both the hierarchy and the general population in Croatia. Now I was glad to be able to do, hopefully, my little part to help repay that hospitality. Recalling St.Paul's statement that to the Jews he became a Jew and to the gentiles a gentile, in order to win them all or at least some for Christ (Cf 1 Cor 9:19 - 22), I added that to the Croats I want to be a Croat.

Almost instantly, my doors to the hearts of the Croatian people of Toronto opened widely, never to close again. Their welcome and acceptance was a *fait accompli.*

As recounted earlier, it was with more than a slight apprehension and reluctance that I answered the call to the Croatian parish. After all, it was a Croatian ethnic parish, and I am Slovene: so are all my ancestors, as far as I know. Add to this the stories I had heard about the fierceness of Croatian nationalism, the bombings of Yugoslavian consulates around the world by Croats, the macho character of the pastor...and you have a perfect recipe for fear and trepidation. "What does a slippery

Slovene have to do here?" I heard them say in my lively imagination. Certainly, every person must be valued on his or her own personal merits rather than on the basis of nationality or any other external criteria. There are good and not so good people in every nation under the sun, and the divide runs through every heart and soul rather than along rivers and mountain ridges. But Croats, generally, were looked upon in many quarters with considerably less than a favourable eye. Was not Croatia a satellite of Nazi Germany during the war? Were not Croats the bombers of Yugoslavian consulates in Toronto and elsewhere? Aren't they immigrants from the Balkans, the "powder keg" of Europe?

My experience with the Croatian people reinforced the lessons I had already learned years before: especially in Moscow, and even earlier in Germany. To sum up two or three of them as tersely as possible: there is some good and some bad in just about everybody of every nationality, although there may be variances of kind or degree on this point between individuals, and possibly even between nations as such. But at the deepest level of being, every human person is an image and likeness of God. It may be buried under many layers of junk, but it is there. And this image and likeness can be surmised or perceived only with the help of divine grace and faith (for which we must pray with a humble heart cleansed of sin), and only by intimate, loving, personal contact and meeting of souls. In this process we discover much less evil and much more good in every human being than anticipated. I learned this from experience again and again.

Almost at once I became aware what a wonderful person my first Croatian pastor really was. Ludvik and Rosa, the caretaker and housekeeper, became like father and mother to me, and their youngest son, Stephen, who was living with them, as brother.

Perhaps above all: I wish to emphasize in the strongest possible terms, that in all the six years and three months of my stay at Our Lady Queen of Croatia parish in Toronto, not one single Croat ever asked what was a Slovene doing in their Croatian parish. I have nothing but most cherished memories of this assignment: of the pastors, of Ludvik and Rosa and Stephen, and of the parishioners: men, women, old, young and children.

Of course there were difficulties, but as the ancient Romans already knew: "Where there is love there is no labour, or even the labour is loved."

Like every strong personality, Father Kamber had his enemies. He suspected that his defence of Mr. Artuković was at the root of most of the animosity towards him, and that it had its origin outside the Croatian community. Be that as it may, the most vitriolic verbal attacks came from the young hothead mentioned earlier. A self-styled super patriot, somewhat corpulent, he missed hardly any Croatian public event. On such occasions he always appeared with a large flag. He wrote countless leaflets and distributed them in front of the church. He would call in the middle of the night on the telephone: either whistling that I could hear it to my room on the other side of the floor, or cursing profusely and accusing the poor pastor of the most heinous crimes, or simply call and put down the receiver.

Father Kamber bought an old-fashioned tape recorder for no other reason than to catch and bring this gadfly to justice. I was present when the telephone rang. Father lifted the hearer. Knowing who was at the other end, he started to press buttons at random, so that a loud squealing noise came out of the machine, followed by the words from the receiver: "Record! Record!" That was the end of the recording adventure.

Once, when the pastor was away, Cardinal Stepinac's bronze bust disappeared from the square concrete pedestal in front of the church. It was found, with the screws that fastened it to the pedestal sawn through, in the neighbour's garbage bin. There must have been several culprits involved in the "work," for we found out that the bust could not be lifted by less than three strong men.

We also had to weather a long and very dangerous storm that blew in from outside the Croatian community. It was caused by the famous, or perhaps infamous, *Protocol.*

In 1946 the Archbishop of Zagreb, the Most Rev. Aloysius Stepinac, was sentenced in a kangaroo court to 16 years of imprisonment for trumped-up charges. The Vatican created him Cardinal, and the Yugoslavian government broke off diplomatic relations with it over the affair. In the second half of the 1960s the Yugoslavian government was eager to mend the fences, hoping for some relief of its political and economic troubles. The Vatican appeared (reluctantly?) willing to cooperate: the Church, too, hoped for some relief from the oppression and persecution. This was during the first stages of the new Vatican *Ostpolitik,* promoted vigorously by its Secretary of State, Agostino Cardinal Cassaroli.

It was a new ball game, so to speak. When the two parties finally came to some kind of agreement, they were at a loss what to call it: it was neither a treaty, nor a concordat, nor truce, nor any other of the traditional kinds of agreements. So they simply tagged it *The Protocol,* which the Oxford dictionary defines as an original draft of a diplomatic document, or formal statement of transaction. Regardless of what it really was, or wasn't, it immediately stirred up a storm in the Croatian community. That the Vatican would even negotiate with a Communist government appeared to many bad enough. Worse, it was widely believed that the real, sole beneficiary was the Yugoslavian government, while the people and the Vatican gained practically nothing. Worst of all was the real or imaginary fact that the Vatican dealt directly with the government in Belgrade, over the heads of the Croatian Catholic hierarchy. That was the most deadly sting of them all.

Most parishioners were gravely upset over the whole affair with *The Protocol.* They felt like drowning Cassaroli in a casserole of *minestra.* A group started a Croatian National Church, modelled on the Polish National Church. The latter has a nice church on Cowan Avenue in Toronto. The Croatian group began to gather in that church for Sunday worship. The grand design was to win over the bulk of Croatian Catholics in Toronto.

They invited me to a dinner in one of the homes, and offered me the honour of becoming their bishop. At first I thought it was a joke (a Slovene, bishop of the Croatian National Church? Come on, folks, wake up!). But they seemed so serious that even today I wonder whether they were really serious about it.

Father Kamber was very worried. He saw serious danger of a big schism. The redeeming factor in the situation was the fact that the principal promoter of the breakaway movement was - you guessed it right! - the aforementioned young man. Although a layman, at that time he began to wear clerical dress, complete with the Roman collar.

"Let us say nothing! Don't let us say anything about the breakaway group!" Father Kamber would urge me. "As long as he is the leader, we don't have to worry." Of course, there are times when one must speak up, but more often "speech is silver, silence gold"; or as a Slovenian proverb puts it: "Who keeps silence answers ten people."

Future events proved the wisdom of that approach. The whole thing fizzled out little by little. After my departure from the parish I heard, with a pleasant surprise, that the ringleader himself returned to the fold and became a devout parishioner. He, too, has since died. May he rest in peace.

The other storm was the outbreak of the serious disagreements between the bishop of Mostar in Herzegovina and the Franciscans. It hurt Father Kamber's priestly heart even more than the *Protocol* episode. Although it did not involve his own parish directly, this wound reaches deeper: to the very heart and soul of the Mystical Body of Christ, the Church, putting in jeopardy its unity. It is the very antithesis of Christ's fervent prayer for unity at the Last Supper (Jn 17:20-23). At the time of this writing, in 1992, the problem is still not solved. In all likelihood it will plague the Croatian Catholics for some time to come. On the occasion of a visit by the Archbishop of Ljubljana, who was at the time the Vice-President of the Catholic Conference of Yugoslavian Bishops, I asked him at a meeting with Slovenian priests about the state of "The Herzegovinian Question." He threw his hands up and head backwards, and replied with a bitter smile: "I think even Rome cannot solve this one."

It is an interesting story, but I am afraid it would take us beyond the scope of this chapter. Suffice it to say that a simmering situation boiled over when the bishop of Mostar took several parishes that had been served by Franciscans from times immemorial and sent in his own diocesan priests. In my humble opinion - for I do not know all the factors in this case - he acted lawfully but imprudently. Certainly he did not anticipate the dire consequences and the opposition of the people. There was, e.g., at least one case where they put a brick wall in the doors of a church to prevent the diocesan priest from coming in. There are theories about the bishop's motives. One is that he needed more income for the building of his cathedral (there was none in Mostar at the time). Another one is that he had too many diocesan priests. And there are no doubt others. Personally, I cannot think of any reason big enough to justify such immense damage to unity and peace.

Incidentally, the church in Medjugorje, now world-famous by reason of the alleged apparitions of Mary, is located in the diocese of Mostar, and still administered by the Franciscans.

In retrospect, God's Providence in sending the right kind of priests at the right time to the Croatian community in Toronto, is almost tangible.

The first one, a certain Father Hess, and possibly some others, began visiting their people soon after the Second World War. Then came Fr. George Vrdoljak. He exhausted himself toiling to establish the parish and buy the first church at 7 Awde Street in Toronto: the one that was burned down at New Year's 1962. Suffering from bleeding stomach ulcers, he died at a monastery in Austria in February 1969. His successor was Father Kamber. He had been pastor of a local church in Omaha, Nebraska, U.S.A., and accepted the invitation of the sickly Fr. Vrdoljak to come help and eventually succeed him as pastor. Like Solomon of old, who built the temple, he was destined to build the present imposing church (he liked to describe it as "masculine," while some of his opponents called it "a bunker"). It stands on the place of the old one and an adjacent house lot. The number is the same, but the street has since been renamed to Croatia Street. Unlike Solomon, though, he did not enjoy much peace. I cannot think of one single priest with his robust frame and character, and stamina to endure what he endured. Truly, he was the man for that place at that time. In view of his unusual health situation (described earlier in this chapter) he worked hard to get a priest from Croatia to assist and later succeed him. He also worked hard to get three or four religious Sisters from overseas for work in the parish. The priest arrived on June 7, 1969, Father Kamber died some three weeks later, on June 30. He had the joy and satisfaction to see the arrival of his successor,

Father Josip Gjuran (who was to have come to replace me as Father Kamber's assistant), while four Sisters, Servants of Infant Jesus, came from Croatia soon after Father Gjuran.

With the new church solidly in place, the time came to build on the foundations a strong Christian community of "living stones built into a spiritual house" (Cf 1 Pt 2:5).

Father Josip Gjuran was just the man for the task. He was born on August 4, 1922 in Ludbreg near Zagreb, and ordained priest in 1948. Before his arrival in Canada he was pastor of a small rural parish Sv. Jana near Karlovac, and dean (a kind of super pastor) of the parishes of the district. Like most other priests of that country at that time, he was savagely and unjustly persecuted by the civil authorities and loved by the people. He told me things done to him that people who never lived in similar circumstances would have a hard time to believe. Due perhaps at least in part to his gruesome experiences, he was not as ebullient as his predecessor, but more serious and restrained.

On his arrival I fetched him at Toronto Airport. On the way back we visited first Father Kamber in St. Joseph's Hospital who was, needless to say, all smiles. After a fairly long and optimistic conversation, our next stop was a visit to the church, next door to the rectory. He seemed full of awe, walking slowly down the aisle and looking up, down, left and right as if trying to know well every little detail of the church, in anticipation of a long stay. Indeed, at the time of this writing, in 1992, he is still the pastor there.

Having arrived near the altar he spotted on one side, at the back wall, a large cross with typically Croatian engravings in its dark wood.

"What is that?"

"That is the Bleiburg cross," I replied. There was no need to say more. Every Croat knows that Bleiburg is a town in southern Austria. In May 1945 large contingents of the Croatian army retreated there before the advancing Tito's partisans. Thousands were returned by the British back to Yugoslavia. Together with dozens of thousands of other Croatian soldiers, captured before they reached Austria, most of these miserables were summarily and without any further ado or process executed

249

(I think the proper word would be: murdered) and buried in abandoned anti-tank trenches and other mass graves in Slovenia and Croatia. Only lately the new civil authorities in (former) Yugoslavia admitted officially that these incredible things really happened. What makes them more heinous is the fact that they were perpetrated after the war was over. Taken together, they are referred to as "The Bleiburg Tragedy," and the people who perished "The Bleiburg Victims." The very mention of one or the other of these two phrases evokes strong emotions in the heart of every Croat.

Father Gjuran's reaction to my information that the cross was there in memory of "The Bleiburg Victims" was very typical of him.

He made slowly a step or two backwards, then moved his hands back to grasp the hand support in front of a bench. As it was too high for sitting, he leaned backwards on it. With an utmost serious expression on his face he looked for a while at the altar ahead of him, then at the huge, larger than life-size crucifix a little further to his right, hanging up on the sanctuary wall behind the altar. Finally, his head turned even further to the right. With an utmost serious expression on his face he gazed at the Bleiburg Cross standing there at the same wall. At long last he turned towards me and said slowly, distinctly and most solemnly, with slight emphasis on every single syllable: "I have come here to proclaim the Gospel."

Neither he nor I uttered one single word more on the subject on that occasion.

Only after the visit to the church we went to the rectory. Three weeks later, when Father Kamber died, he became my pastor. I remained his assistant more than three years, until he learned enough English. In fact, a third priest, Father Alexander Boras who arrived from Herzegovina, soon joined us.

I hope there is some kind of "statute of limitations" to allow my telling the following two little anecdotes without fear of prosecution.

A day or two after his operation at St. Joseph's Hospital in Toronto, Father Gjuran and I visited Father Kamber who had only a few days to live. He was in a secluded little room in a corner of the intensive care unit, quite vigorous looking and alert.

"I am a seriously ill patient," he said in a strong voice. "They found I have sarcoma, which is one of the worst kinds of cancer. You will notify right away Doctor (a Croat whose name escapes my memory) in London, England. Tell him to come as soon as possible to take care of me." After a short pause he continued: "I have a great desire for champagne."

We couldn't refuse the deathbed wish of our confrere. So we drove a few blocks to the nearest liquor store and fetched a bottle of champagne: the real stuff, imported from France - and very expensive. With the bottle hidden in a briefcase we took the elevator, sped down the corridor, through the intensive care unit into the little corner room. Father Gjuran disappeared into the washroom, while I remained with the patient.

Suddenly, there was a sound as of a minor explosion. I rushed to the washroom. What a sight - and smell! Delightful aroma pervading the air, champagne dripping from the ceiling, Father Gjuran, soaked in champagne, trying desperately to keep the volatile liquid in the bottle by pushing his thumb into its neck.

I rushed back to the bedroom, expecting nurses to rush in at any moment. Miraculously, nobody outside in the general intensive care area seemed aware of the happenings in that little corner room.

The patient tasted the wine (probably it was his first taste of the real champagne), and handed the glass back. On return to the rectory we finished off the bottle: not at once, but with reasonable moderation in a day or two. I found the contents quite drinkable, but in my view champagne's glory is somewhat inflated, to say the least.

Father Kamber had appointed me to be executor of his Last Will and Testament. As such, I was under serious obligation to sell all his possessions and divide the money according to the terms therein. Among the few possessions I found a very fine revolver, which became a problem of conscience: I couldn't sell it, and I couldn't not sell it. In the dilemma I consulted a priest who said: "Leave the revolver and the responsibility to me," both of which I gratefully did. To this day I have no clue what became of that item and I have no desire to find out. And while I mentioned the *dramatis personae* of the champagne incident, I am still afraid to disclose the identity of the priest in the revolver episode, any possible "statute of limitations" notwithstanding.

We got along quite well with Father Gjuran as my pastor, and later on with him and Father Boras. Even though, as pointed out earlier, Father Gjuran was much more serious, he nevertheless also had behind his stern appearance a good sense of humour.

Noting the rather high frequency of my outgoing telephone calls, he remarked once very philosophically: "Father, if you should end in hell, which God forbid, they will cut off all the telephone lines to your abode: that will be your greatest punishment. But if you go to heaven, you will have telephones all around." His last few words were accompanied by his hand moving slowly in a semi-circle from left to right in front of him as if tapping some six or eight invisible telephones one after the other.

Relatives and friends at home kept inviting me for a visit: "Please come visit us. When are you going to come? You need a break..." And friends in Canada urged me to go, too. So, with Father Kamber gone to his well deserved reward and his successor in charge, I found the chance and excuse to go. It was a double excuse: ten years of priesthood, and a letter of Archbishop Philip Pocock requesting a priest, which I took personally to the Archbishops of Zagreb and Sarajevo, and to the bishop of Mostar. On the way I visited also the home of Ludvik and Rosa Rajtek, the caretaker and housekeeper, and then admired the gorgeous cathedral of Djakovo. Angelo Roncalli (later Pope John XXIII) who travelled as Apostolic Delegate to Bulgaria, is supposed to have said that it is the most beautiful building between Venice and Constantinople.

From Djakovo I drove south, soon crossed the river Sava and found myself in Bosnia. I had the pleasure of staying overnight at the rectory in Doboj, not far south of Sava, where Father Kamber had been pastor at the beginning of the Second World War, as noted earlier. His successor was overjoyed to meet his predecessor's assistant. We chatted into the early hours of the morning with him and his mother who was his housekeeper. As time went on, he was getting by all appearances somewhat too big a dose of refreshments. I wish I could describe the expressions on the face of his good mother, as she looked alternately at him and at me, while her son was in a truly spirited mood. I had the feeling that it was a first-time experience for both of them.

Next day I celebrated Mass in the local church, with no incident. A mouse appeared from behind the tabernacle, stopped at a candlestick, looked for a short while at me as if surprised to see me there, and disappeared just as suddenly. I wouldn't call that an incident, but it was quite amusing.

Bosnia struck me as if it were another world. Sarajevo, the provincial capital, with its mosques and their minarets has a distinctly Muslim appearance, which was unfamiliar to me before.

Father Kamber belonged to the Archdiocese of Sarajevo until his death. The Archbishop and he were good friends. He received me very kindly and after our meeting said to me: "I will talk to the bishop of Mostar, and between us we will find a priest for Toronto: if for no other reason, out of *pietas* for the late Father Kamber."

From Sarajevo I travelled along the river Neretva where one of the most violent battles between the partisans and Germans took place during the Second World War, and stayed overnight at the chancery in Mostar. The Chancellor put at my bedside a large container of the most exquisite whisky, along with several small drinking glasses: had I drank all of it, I would have probably stayed there at least a week. As I didn't, I continued next day along the beautiful Adriatic coast, over the mighty Velebit, through the Plitvice National Park with its beautiful water cascades, and slept at the rectory in Sv. Jana, where Father Gjuran had been pastor.

Everywhere I was received with utmost hospitality and genuine friendliness.

My visit home in 1969 came to an end all too fast; soon the time came to return back to Canada. I remained at the Croatian parish until the fall of 1972.

As I was leaving my beloved Croatian people to return back to St. Bernard's church as associate pastor, they gave me a wonderful farewell. On my part, I promised to use every opportunity to do anything I can for them. Especially, to help correct the all-too-widespread adverse, untrue stigma on the Croats as such. It is hoped that this chapter will help fulfil my promise.

This does not mean that I am against anyone else. Due mainly to unfortunate circumstances of history, Croats and Serbs, generally speaking, just don't seem to be able to get along. It is unfortunate, for none of the two nations is less good than the other. I had many friends in the Yugoslavian Army from all the peoples that were part of that state, including Serbs. And I am very happy to count among them also Muslims from Bosnia. In Toronto, too, I have some Serbian friends, although not many, because I never served in any of their parishes.

Sometimes I think of how the French and the Germans used to be seemingly irreconcilable enemies. In 1971 France lay defeated; in 1918 Germany; in 1940 France; in 1945 Germany. But then, under the leadership of great statesmen, the two great nations began to cooperate, and now they are part of the very foundations of Europe. I hope that some day soon the Serbs and the Croats will take the same road and become the foundation of peace in the Balkan, the largest peninsula of Europe, called often in the past a powder keg.

The Croatian community in Toronto and vicinity has come a long way since the 1960s. In 1966 the one parish had a $215.000 debt. Due to hard work and sacrifices of priests, religious Sisters and lay people, it has now a surplus to help others. While the numbers of Croats did not increase very much, they now have also a thriving parish of Croatian Martyrs in Mississauga, one in Oakville, and a Croatian National Centre on a 160 acre property, owned and served by the Franciscan Fathers, in Norval: all within less than half hour's drive by car from downtown Toronto - outside the rush hours, of course.

The people served in the late 1960s by two priests in one parish, have now some four or five priests and about as many religious Sisters in two parishes. And all have more than enough work.

In my Last Will and Testament I expressed the intention to be buried in the priests' plot at St. Augustine's Seminary where I studied for the priesthood. The second choice, in case for some unexpected reason the first were impossible, is the Croatian area of the Assumption Cemetery near the Toronto Airport (Pearson International Airport).

Thus, I imagine, when the trumpet sounds and the dead will rise, my first greeting will be either *Dominus Vobiscum* or *Hvaljen Isus i Marija:* The Lord be with you (in Latin) or Praised be Jesus and Mary (in Croatian).

Chapter Four

# The Milan Intermezzo

"Come for a visit!"

"When are you coming to see us again?"

"It's been seven years since your last visit..."

These and such like questions and promptings were becoming more and more frequent in my correspondence with relatives and friends overseas.

The Romans of old already knew: a drop makes its way through a stone; not by force, but by incessant dripping.

Well, the drop finally made its way through the armour of my heart. The occasion of my 50th birthday was the last straw to give in to the unremitting persuasion.

In the first part of this book it was pointed out that water was not my element. I withstood seven voyages over the Atlantic very well: four westbound, three eastbound. And especially the very first one was quite stormy. By now there were no more passenger ships. Practically the only way to travel was by air, and I never flew.

My great desire had been to travel by train and boat: via western Canada and the Siberian Railway. More correctly, my great desire had been to stop in Moscow in order to see the site of our P.O.W. camp. Most of the wonderful people I knew some 30 years earlier, especially the unforgettable *bábushka,* were certainly long since gone to their eternal reward. *Bábushka's* daughter Valja was most likely still living, and little Yurushka probably had teenagers of his own! I would have liked to see also the famous Moscow subway, (referred to as *Metró*), as well as the Kremlin. Although living well over one year a few kilometres from these sites, I never had the chance to see them.

In Poland I would have made another stop: I yearned to see the area of my military exploits. In my case the word theatre, which is sometimes used in reference to an area of military operations, would be very appropriate: in view of my front-line adventures it has a special ring of realism to it.

A BOUQUET FOR YOU

Unfortunately, my Croatian travel agent in Toronto advised me that it was not possible to take that route. Years later I learned that it was possible, because a priest from Madonna House in Combermere, Ontario, took it on the occasion of one of his jubilees. He travelled all the way from Vladivostok to Moscow by the Trans-Siberian Railway. In retrospect, I suspected at first that the agent, with close connections with the Yugoslavian air line JAT, had his own "ulterior" motives in this case. However, he was a good man, and I travelled by Alitalia. Be as it may, the unfortunate finale is that in all likelihood I will never again see these places, so emotionally charged in my memory. Very reluctantly, I took the only other possible way: by air.

I planned to leave right after Easter, because priests are very busy just before this greatest solemnity in the Church year. However, at the time I was under great stress, due to a combination of overwork and strained personal relations in the rectory. My Archdiocesan superiors were aware of the situation and gladly allowed me to leave a good two weeks before Easter.

Late on March 30, 1976, the Jumbo jet took off from Toronto airport. After a short stop in Montreal we landed next day towards noon in Milan, Italy. It was my very first flight, quite smooth and uneventful. My plan called for staying overnight in a small hotel near the railway station, and continuing my trip home by train early next morning. There was no premonition of the impending sickness which struck like a bolt of lightning from clear skies.

It was about 11 o'clock in the evening. I was in the process of going to bed, when all of a sudden, in the interval of one beat, my heart went berserk. First, there was one very strong beat, followed by an abnormally long pause, followed by totally irregular pulse: rapid, slow, strong, weak. No pain of any kind. Only a terrible feeling of anxiety, impossible to describe, and a distinct awareness of impending death in full consciousness.

Nothing helped: lying down, turning around on the bed, sitting, taking a drink of water - nothing!

After a few minutes my pulse appeared returning to normal. But then two almost identical attacks followed. During the third one I became convinced that the end of my earthly life

258

was at hand. My past seemed telescoped into one single instant. Nothing temporal in it mattered any more, except any good deeds: a smile brought to a sad face, a consoling word, any little help given or kindness shown to someone in need. These flashed before the eye of my mind like objects over a countryside enlightened by lightning in the midst of the darkest night.

My room was on the second floor. As there was no fourth occurrence of the phenomenon, I wobbled, shaking, downstairs to the front office to call for medical help.

"How soon will the ambulance arrive?" I asked the clerk who made the telephone call.

*In una mezzoretta* (in about short half an hour).

"Well, translated into plain English, that probably means about three hours or so," I thought to myself. But in about 20 minutes the ambulance stopped in front of the hotel entrance. Soon we arrived at the hospital emergency area. The doctor on duty stethoscoped my heart beat, gave me a pill, and ordered the attendants to leave me on the stretcher on *parkeggio:* at the emergency corridor wall. Next morning, after a good night's sleep, I was wheeled further down the corridors to a room on the same floor.

The hospital has to be the largest one in Milan. I was told that it housed about 1,200 patients, served by God knows how many people in their various capacities, and two full time Catholic chaplains. Its long and unfamiliarly sounding name puzzled me: *Ospedale Fatebenefratelli Fatebenesorelle Ciceri Agnesi.* My self-taught Italian sufficed for the first three words: "Hospital Do-good-brothers Do-good-sisters." The last two of them remained a mystery until it was explained to me that the hospital, unmistakably quite old, had been donated by some ancient aristocratic Milanese families and named after them.

My room was on the right side at the very end of the corridor. Across from it was an identical one for women. Between the two, against the end wall, stood a large desk which served as nurses' station. On our side of it was the door to a kitchenette behind the end wall of the corridor. The common sitting room, complete with a TV set, radio, a long table with chairs in the centre and chesterfields along the walls, was further up the corridor, adjacent to the women's room.

Every modern hospital has various departments or wards: heart, cancer, surgical, etc. I have no idea to which my room belonged. All I know is that it was located on the ground floor. Because of that, the tall windows were half-way up milky, so that only the tops of surrounding buildings and the sky were visible. The traffic just outside the windows was quite noisy.

There were seven beds in the room, all with heads towards the walls: three on the right, three on the left, one straight ahead of the entrance door. Between it and that bed there was a fairly large space: big enough for parking the food wagon or the vehicle with medicines, or manoeuvre the X-ray machine which was brought in occasionally. Along the wall on the right and left of the door were small cupboards: one for each patient. My bed was in the near corner at the right, next to the cupboards. It was an ideal spot for the overview of the whole room. Moreover, sitting on that bed enabled one to see the kitchenette when its door was open, and even a part of the nurses' desk.

All my room-mates were older than I: at least in their 60s, some over 80. At my arrival a few had been there already several weeks, and one or two the second time around. All were firmly convinced that whoever was "favoured" with a visit by the X-ray team and its ominous machine, died in a few days or sooner. While I was there, that rule worked infallibly.

Three men died during my 13-day sojourn.

The first to go was a very old one. His bed was opposite the door. Whole nights he spent in a more sitting than lying position in his bed, supported by several pillows, head bent down, seemingly semi-conscious and almost continually calling in a feeble voice on the nurse for the night bottle: *Signorina, il papagallo! Signorina, il papagallo!* Turning to leave his bedside on one of the last visits, the doctor whispered more to himself than to anybody else, with a gentle downward gesture of hand: *Piéga giù* (he is bending down). When I touched his hand and front, they were all wet with ice-cold sweat. His life faded away very peacefully, like the flame of a dying candle.

The next one had his bed in the far right corner, with only

one patient between us. His wife often talked to me; now and then she even offered me an apple, grapes, candy, or other such goodies. Once she sat on the other side of her husband's bed, near the window, and we exchanged over the two beds between us a few thoughts about the mystery of suffering and the faith of our ancestors. "My dear mother, God bless her soul," she said, both hands raised over her right shoulder and as if to grab and pull down from the wall the crucifix hanging there, "used to say: 'I know that I am a sinner, but I will just grasp his pierced feet and sneak with him into heaven'."

This lovable woman always encouraged her husband, but he lost all hope of ever getting out of the hospital alive. At first he often walked out of the room and back, visibly dejected. His condition deteriorated fast, and his walks became less and less frequent. In a week or so he died. I had a feeling that his death was accelerated by his pessimism and loss of hope.

The death of the third and last one to die in our room during my stay touched me most of all. Only a day or two before my release he was brought to the bed next to mine. Except for me, 50 at the time, he was the youngest: perhaps in his early 50s. He was of dark complexion (from southern regions of Italy?), with a small black moustache and black brush-cut hair. Within hours of his arrival the feared X-ray machine appeared in the room. It stopped at his bed.

The first thing I noticed when I awoke next morning were some men in white, standing at my bed. I thought they came to examine the new patient. To my shock they were wrapping the dead body of my neighbour in white sheets...

The two chaplains deserve a special mention.

The senior one was unmistakably a Lombard, from northern Italy: thin, tall, white haired. He reminded me of Voltaire or St. John Vianney (the two famous Frenchmen were worlds apart in their mentality and ideas, yet had the physical appearance of twins). Regularly once every day he appeared at about the same time at the door in black cassock. He came only one or two steps over the threshold and stopped, waved gently to every individual patient and made a small sign of the cross towards him, saying nothing. During the whole short ritual he kept nodding his head and smiling. Then he turned around and was gone.

His assistant was quite different: a typical Franciscan, small, almost rotund. When he walked, he seemed to me like a barrel, covered by a brown Franciscan cassock, with a round bald head without a neck sitting directly on top of it. His movement was so smooth that he appeared to float rather than walk. The two short legs seemed to dangle from under the cassock back and forth just above the floor. Usually he showed up only to bring Holy Communion to anyone who wished to receive it, and for the administration of Sacraments of the Sick to those who fell seriously ill.

His performance of this later priestly duty was also quite unique. I never saw him talk to the patient, except perhaps at most for a few words; never help him make a good Confession or prepare for a worthy reception of Viaticum (Holy Communion in danger of death). Rather, he would come usually when the patient was fast asleep: as a rule he floated in like a ghost in the quiet of the night. He acted as if taking great care not to wake anybody up, especially not the patient about to be anointed with the oil of the sick. First he soaked his thumb in the oil stocks, like any other priest. Then, with eyes glued to the Ritual in his left hand, he stretched his right hand and fingers as straight as possible and in a strictly horizontal position over the patient's head. Nothing moved except the thumb. Turned vertically down from the palm of the hand, it made a gentle sign of the cross on the forehead only; there was no anointing of hands, which should be done if at all possible. Mission accomplished, the good Father floated away to the kitchenette, washed his hands at the sink, and was gone.

A truly remarkable and unique way to administer the Sacraments of the Sick! Was it Franciscan? His own? Or a case of *alla italiana?* One of the best ways to describe the nature of the *alla italiana* phenomena I can think of is to give an example.

On the wall up the corridor, near our room, there hung a fairly elaborate plaque, supposedly a "No smoking" sign. I wish I had written down its remarkable message. It began by quoting certain state laws and paragraphs, including their reference numbers. There were terrible threats for anyone who would presume to light a cigarette anywhere near that sign. Mercifully, the punishment for the crime was not quite capital. It did not state explicitly that "you will hang by the neck until you expire" or something like that, if one dare to break the law; but it came dangerously close.

A redeeming feature of this frightful law was its respect for certain things that I would call, for want of a more precise term, "extenuating circumstances." Peaceful surrender to lawful authorities would cut the heavy fine at least in half. Voluntary confession of the offence would further reduce the punishment, etc. Finally, if the culprit was not in a mood to respond to the summons within a certain length of time, or was very sincerely disinclined to deal with the matter, the case would not be pursued any further.

Regretfully, I did not write down the exact wording of the law just described. However, taken with a grain or two of salt, my description is essentially true to reality. The elderly roommate with whom I discussed this interesting matter added that he observed once two workers putting up a similar sign. Having completed the job, they sat down under it and lit their cigarettes. It was he who informed me that this kind of laws and the peculiar manner of their observance and enforcement was *alla italiana.* I suppose the good Franciscan's administration of the Sacraments of the Sick belonged to that category.

Every day in the hospital life was well organized: a happy blend of serious Teutonic (Lombard) orderliness and Romanic vivacious ease.

Every patient had a standard, scrupulously kept up-to-date temperature chart affixed at the foot of his bed. The day began with a visit of the medical team: a doctor and one or two nurses. They examined carefully the temperature graphs, comparing them with their records. They paid at least a short visit to every patient, one after another: usually beginning with the one across from my feet and ending with me. If they deemed it necessary, they also checked the pulse, listened to the heart beat, took samples of blood, gave pills, etc.

Soon after their departure, the breakfast wagon arrived. At all the meals - morning, noon and evening - much of the food was ladled out from large containers and brought to each one's bed. The rest of the day pretty much the routine of any standard hospital prevailed. Most touching was the evening visiting hour and the end of the day.

Visits were allowed in our ward only one hour each day: I believe from 7:00 to 8:00 o'clock in the evening.

All the visitors arrived and left at the same time: exactly at the beginning and the end of the hour. They walked into the room peacefully and quietly: wives, sons, daughters, sisters, brothers, children, grandchildren, friends. Quickly a circle formed around every bed, except for the area behind the head, because of the wall. If able, the patient would sit on top of the bed rather than with feet to one side or the other, in order to communicate better with visitors on all sides.

My bed was the only one without such a circle. But my position in the corner of the room gave me a most suitable place from which to observe and enjoy the beautiful sight of love and care - also typically *alla italiana* at its best. For not only the relatives and friends, but I, too, a total stranger, received many a friendly smile, greeting, a few kind words... and yes, now and then also an apple, chocolate bar, or candy.

When the hour was up, all the visitors all of a sudden left: calmly and peacefully, just as they had arrived. But not before giving their dear one a loving wave, and usually also a gentle hug or kiss.

With visitors departed, an almost total silence followed the quiet warbling of a minute or two earlier. The patients who were able to leave their bed usually remained sitting, at lest for a while, but now they were able to stretch their legs down one or the other side of the bed. Some wandered slowly around the room or out into the corridor, as if they were lost.

At exactly 9:00 p.m., beautiful music began to be heard from the corridor. At first hardly audible, it became gradually louder. It came from a P.A. system which, I was told, had been installed by the chaplain, and rarely used for any other purpose than at this time in the evening. The music was quite evidently carefully chosen for the occasion. As a rule, it was not strictly religious, yet very appropriate for a hospital, especially at bedtime: soothing and peaceful. Pietro Mascagni's famous *Intermezzo* from his *Cavalleria Rusticana,* imitating the bells of an evening Angelus, could be pointed out as perhaps the most characteristic sample of it.

After the music faded out, just as slowly and gradually as it began, a short allocution by the senior chaplain followed: encouraging, comforting. Prayer of the Angelus followed his message, then some more music. When that music faded away, the day was considered done.

What a wonderful program for a truly Christian and Catholic hospital!

May it be added here that Palm Sunday 1976 occurred during the time of my stay in that hospital. The chaplain brought to every patient a small, nicely decorated plastic bag with a real olive twig. I still keep mine, even though one or two of its leaves have crumbled, as a treasured souvenir.

Among the very fine medical personnel a nurse whose name escapes my memory, and a certain "Dottore Rivolta" were truly outstanding. Dr. Rivolta was almost always the leader of the routine morning visit team. He also visited more often than any other doctor the patients who needed one during other times of the day, or occasionally during the night. During my stay in Milan his own father died, I believe somewhere else in the city. While Dr. Rivolta appeared visibly sorrowing, he nevertheless lost hardly any time from his hospital work.

The nurse mentioned earlier seemed to have lived in our ward. At all possible times of day or night she was around: at her desk in the corridor, taking pulse or blood pressure, distributing pills, and helping the bedridden in any way they needed a nurse's help.

There were dedicated nurses, doctors and other members of the staff I met. But Dr. Rivolta and the anonymous nurse stand out in my memory: not only as consummate professionals in their respective fields, but very warm and lovable persons.

Inside the hospital one day followed another with little or no change in routine. Outside the springtime weather was very sunny and beautiful. Time passed, and in 13 days Dr. Rivolta judged me well enough to be discharged.

Eager and glad to be able to resume my way home, I took my few belongings, wished well to my room-mates and said goodbye to them. At the desk in the corridor I asked the good nurse whom I was to see next and where to pay my bills.

"You don't have to see anybody," she smiled, "and you have no bills to pay. Just get your train ticket and enjoy your visit home. *Buon viaggio. Arrivederci.*

I was speechless. Surely, I had some Blue Cross medical coverage for travel outside Canada. But at the least I expected a lot of red tape, and some extra bills for one thing or another. Yet there I stood, free as a bird to continue my trip home without any further ado. I arrived home on Holy Saturday, the very day before Easter: needless to say, to the joy and excitement of everybody, including myself.

During my sojourn in Milan the weather had been balmy, sunny and warm. So had been, I was told, in the Julian Alps. As soon as I arrived, however, it turned bad and stayed such for perhaps two or three weeks: much of the time overcast, with temperatures near the freezing point, and at least one fairly heavy snowfall. Worst of all, about 9:00 p.m. on May 6, 1976, a powerful earthquake shook the area. While in our vicinity there were no serious injuries or damage, except for cracks in the walls and some tumbled chimneys, things were much worse just across the mountains, in northeastern Italy. About 1,000 people died there, and damage was very extensive. As this event does not really belong to the main theme of this chapter, it should probably not be described here in greater detail. Suffice it to say that an earthquake is a very frightful experience.

My doctor in Slovenia, a former missionary Sister in Madagascar, whence she had to return due to climate and ill health, ordered me to abstain from pork, take the prescribed pills regularly, and rest three months. About half of that rest I spent at home, and about half in Canada. When I was landing in Toronto on August 3, 1976, on a sunny afternoon, I was glad to be back. While by the very nature of things one can have only one native land - and Canada is not mine - yet I felt almost like coming home. My priest friend, Fr. Larry McGough, kindly offered me room and board in his rectory in Oshawa: the very one where we served some 16 years earlier together as assistant priests. Now he was pastor there, and invited me to stay as long as needed. After a few weeks I was given a parish (St.Philip's in the south end of Oshawa), where I served over eight years as pastor.

I am almost certain that the 1976 visit home was my very last one, for it is my firm intention not to travel again over the ocean.

A lot more could be said about that trip and visit, and about my impressions and experiences in the land of my birth. But let what has been written suffice, for my chief purpose in writing this chapter was not to speak about the trip. Rather, it was to describe the life in an ideal hospital - if indeed any hospital can be ideal. Above all, it was to pay tribute and express my enduring profound gratitude for the hospitality and goodness of the visitors, patients and staff at the *Ospedale Fatebenefratelli Fatebenesorelle Ciceri Agnesi* in Milan, especially the unrivalled duo: Dr. Rivolta and the anonymous nurse.

May God bless them all.
*Grazie infinite!*

Chapter Five

# Priestly Fraternity

My first recollection of Fr. Lawrence T. McGough (he preferred to be called simply Father Larry) dates from the early spring 1952.

Having just arrived from Quebec in January, I intended to enter in September St. Augustine's Seminary in Scarborough, a borough or suburb of Metropolitan Toronto, to begin the seven-year course as student for the priesthood. In the meanwhile I hoped to work and study. About two weeks I looked in vain for work in the big city. Finally I found it in the Seminary itself. I worked mainly in the laundry, but as that was not a full time job, I also helped the busy Sisters of St. Martha with their chores, mostly in the Seminary kitchen or cleaning professors suites. Two evenings every week I also attended night classes in French and Latin in Meisterschaft's College in Toronto.

The bedding and personal laundry was not washed at the Seminary: we only separated all the items according to kind, counted, and packed in large bags. Then it was shipped to a large factory-like shop, called New Method Laundry, in Toronto. My main job was to sort it out upon its return and put in numbered compartments on the wall, for each of the more than 200 seminarians had his own laundry number written with indelible ink on every item. Just as on a certain day of the week all the students brought down to the basement to my laundry room their soiled laundry bags, so they came on a certain day to the wicket to pick up two clean sheets, a pillow case and their own personal belongings.

Although Larry McGough is six months my junior, he was in the spring of 1952 already a deacon: in his seventh, last year of the Seminary and about to be ordained priest in a few short months. From that time I have only one recollection of him. Only one, but very vivid: not unlike those "lucid intervals" we all have of our earliest days of childhood.

One day he came slowly down the laundry room: tall,

thin, bespectacled, with rich dark hair carefully groomed, and deep, kind eyes. His general appearance seemed to me quite ascetical, the rather serious face suffused by a barely noticeable smile. His hand on his chest was clutching the strings of the soiled laundry bag flung over the shoulder.

In the 1950s the seminarians and the workers at St. Augustine's Seminary were not supposed to converse or mix with one another. Thus, Larry and I may have exchanged at most a short greeting. I certainly never knew his name, and even though I probably saw him many times before his ordination and departure from the Seminary later that spring, I have no other recollection of him for the next several years.

Our next meeting occurred seven years later.

After my ordination to the priesthood on May 31, 1959, I got three weeks holiday. Soon after it I was sent to my very first appointment as assistant priest to St. Gregory's church in Oshawa. A week earlier I went to meet my pastor, but had no idea who was his other assistant. In fact, I probably did not know he had one. Having taken my few belongings to my allotted room on the third floor of the rectory, returning back I met suddenly a thin, tall priest on the landing of the steps between the first and second floor. At once I recognized him as the former seminarian with the laundry bag flung over his shoulder, for he had not changed very much. The only noticeable difference were a few extra pounds he evidently gained. We met and exchanged a few words; then he continued his way up to his room and I went downstairs.

These details may seem insignificant, even irrelevant. But for me they evoke fond memories of priestly brotherhood and fellowship.

A very well founded theory has it that first impressions are not only lasting, but decisively important. My first two and half years of priesthood were spent at St. Gregory's church in Oshawa, and they were very happy ones. Over 30 years later I still feel their beneficial influence for my life and work.

Our pastor was Father Paul M. Dwyer, a short time later honoured with the title Monsignor. One of the main traits, perhaps the main one, of his noble character was a genuine kindness. He was ordained priest in the very mother church of Christendom: St. John Lateran basilica in Rome. Having studied as a seminarian for some time in Rome, he seemed to have assimilated some of the more suave and easy-going Roman traits. That does not mean he was lazy: just very kind, suave and easy-going. Usually more is accomplished by an easy-does-it approach than by a lot of useless rushing.

Being the only priest in Oshawa at the time who could speak Italian, most of them came to "Padre Eduardo" for marriages, baptisms and other priestly ministrations. In matters ecumenical he was well ahead of his time. He excelled in public relations with the leaders in the community far beyond the Catholic sphere. Acting on behalf of the Archdiocese, he acquired a number of sites for future churches and Catholic schools. So much so that on the occasion of one of his anniversaries (or retirement?) his good friend and parishioner, Mr. Ernest Marks Q.C., a prominent lawyer, who acted as Master of Ceremonies, told an amusing story about it. By that time Father Dwyer was honoured in recognition of his merits with the title Monsignor.

The story has it that Monsignor Dwyer died. He made it as far as the pearly gate, but there he got stuck: St. Peter couldn't find him anywhere in his records.

"I'm sorry, Monsignor, but I cannot let you in," said the heavenly gatekeeper after long searches of his many files. "I looked for your name under all the relevant headings: no luck. Sorry."

The good Monsignor was petrified: quite seriously so, no play on words here!

"That means I have no chance?" he stuttered, shaking like a poplar leaf in the wind. "And I, I..."

In that seemingly endless moment his guardian angel appeared: suddenly, as if from nowhere.

"Dear St. Peter," the angel pleaded, "please, please don't give up the search. Try under the Real Estate Agents."

"Eureka! I've got it! I've got it!" exclaimed St.Peter, almost as soon as he opened the quite voluminous Real Estate Agents ledger. And Monsignor Dwyer went straight into heaven.

While he had been still active on this earth, Monsignor Dwyer was not only interested in real estate, but more so in real people, as already indicated. One of his high priorities was Christian education of youth. While I was his assistant, he worked very hard on the establishment of a Catholic high school in Oshawa. He succeeded in this noble endeavour, and in getting the Sisters of St. Joseph to staff the school. Not unexpectedly, the school was first titled St. Joseph's High School. Later it became known as Oshawa Catholic High School. Only after his death it became Paul Dwyer Catholic High School. I am convinced he well deserved this great honour.

As pastor, Paul Dwyer gave his assistants the greatest possible freedom of action. He never interfered with my priestly work, according to his explicitly stated policy: "I presume you know what you should do. Go ahead and do it!"

In the 1950s a pastor's assistant priest used to be called curate; today he is referred to as associate pastor. At St. Gregory's there were usually two curates, because the Catholic chaplaincy at the Oshawa General Hospital was entrusted to that parish. Thus, I was known as the junior curate, while the senior curate was Father Larry McGough. When I arrived at St. Gregory's he had already been there for some time; and he remained when two and a half years later I was transferred to Toronto.

While Father Dwyer was smooth, easy going, and somewhat disorganized, Father McGough was very "matter of fact" and decisive: a veritable paragon of good organization and efficiency.

My only earlier brush with Oshawa had been my train trip through it from Quebec to Toronto, way back in January 1952. I didn't even travel through it again until one week before going to begin my first priestly assignment. As I didn't recall ever meeting my first pastor before, a friend drove me from Toronto to get acquainted with him a week in advance of my permanent arrival.

At the city limits we passed a sign: "Oshawa 59,500." In 1992 the "City that motovates Canada" (an allusion to its huge G.M. plant) boasts about 125,000 inhabitants.

First I wanted to visit the church: mostly to say a fervent prayer for God's blessing on my first priestly assignment, partly to see the church where I would celebrate Mass, baptisms, officiate at marriages, etc. As soon as I stepped in, I felt at home.

# PRIESTLY FRATERNITY

There was something warm about the place, built in 1892 on the spot of an earlier wooden one, which had been there, I believe, since the founding of the parish in 1842.

The good pastor was having an afternoon nap. Mrs. Regan, the friendly housekeeper, bid me to wait in a small room near the pastor's suite on the second floor. After a long wait the door opened. We met, and one of his first questions was: "I understand your home is very near the Italian border: do you speak any Italian?" He seemed somewhat disappointed that I did not.

About a week later I moved in to stay. In the meanwhile I tried to learn from my classmates and others more about my first clerical boss. It was all good news: he was not bossy, and kind...and he always ladled out the soup to his curates, which was apparently somewhat unusual at the time. Soon I found out that he also cut the roast beef and handed it to us on plates.

An emergency sick call soon made me realize that I was in urgent need of a car. That I had not enough money to buy one I already knew all too well. In those days a curate's monthly income, besides free room, board and laundry, amounted to about $120.00: approximately half of it salary, the other half daily Mass offerings. A parishioner who owned a mechanical shop did lend me an old Chevrolet until I could afford my own car. But its steering wheel and brakes were in such shape that Fr. Dwyer considered it to be a suicide vehicle. I was not only endangering myself, but others, too: not least the generous seminarian from our parish who taught me to drive during his summer holidays.

The old Chevrolet was "not safe at any speed," as the saying goes. The bad experience with it made me reluctant to buy any second hand car. So, I made up my mind to get a new one that I could afford. About the cheapest at the time was the Volkswagen beetle, but even it amounted to about $2,200.00, which was beyond my means. And borrowing went against the principles of my youthful upbringing. Mother used to warn us: "You only have to start a debt, and it will grow by itself." I found myself in a real squeeze!

When my pastor became aware of my predicament, he offered to lend me $300.00, without interest. I was able finally to buy a brand new Volkswagen!

When at long last I was about to return the money, Father Dwyer just made a little gesture with his hand, and with a smile and a twinkle in his eye quipped: "Just put it in your pocket and don't worry about it!"

I am sure it was his own savings. Four or five months' salary! And just put it into my own pocket? Wow!

That was the kind of priest Father Paul Dwyer was. In two and a half years as his assistant, I remember only one episode in our relationship which could be considered negative; and even it was due to my own thoughtlessness.

Every weekday there was a Mass at 6:30 a.m. at the St. Joseph's Sisters residence: the Sisters taught in Oshawa Catholic schools and had to leave early. There was also a Mass at 7:30 and one at 8:00 a.m. in the parish church. While the two curates alternated on a weekly basis celebrating the earlier two Masses, the pastor always took the one at 8:00 a.m. His private thanksgiving after the Mass at his prie-dieu near the altar over, he returned to the rectory for breakfast. Having eaten, he remained regularly at the table for quite a while, holding and reading attentively the morning papers, taking once in a while a sip from his cup of coffee, and an occasional light draft from the smoking cigarette stuck gently between the first and second fingers of his right hand.

One morning I was probably delayed after the 7:30 a.m. Mass, so that I had my breakfast when the pastor was already buried in his newspaper. I felt the kind of embarrassment that occurs when both parties in a conversation feel they should say something but don't know what. My problem was that I didn't realize we were not engaged in conversation. On the contrary: talk was the last thing the pastor wanted at the time. So, even though I did not have something to say, I felt I just had to say something from time to time.

I should have seen it coming, for both his monosyllabic replies and quick looks at me over the paper were becoming ever more frequent and more quick.

Finally the cup of his patience ran over. He put the paper and the cigarette down, took a long, exasperated look at me and exploded: "Aren't you finished yet! Just go, go, go!" At every "go" he flung his palms forwards and upwards, as if throwing me symbolically out of the dining room. Moreover, every successive "go" was a little swifter and louder than the preceding one, and its accompanying swing of hands a little longer and higher. There was no need to throw me out: I was out of the dining room and up the stairs just as fast with my own effort.

How right was my mother: "As long as we live we learn, and still die stupid!"

This one unfortunate episode came and went like a little dark cloud on a sunny day over the sun. Perhaps it could be likened to a shade behind the picture of Father Paul Dwyer and our relationship: instead of obscuring, it rather enhances its serene beauty.

There is one other anecdote of happier memory which I would like to share with you, dear reader. It occurred towards the end of Monsignor Dwyer's earthly life.

Monsignor Paul Michael Dwyer was born on January 21, 1898, and died on March 19, 1976, on the very feast of St. Joseph, the patron of a happy death; Father John Maxwell Markle was born on February 16, 1927, and died on February 17, 1976, of heart illness: one month before his immediate predecessor, only 49 years old! I was at the time in Toronto, and returned to Oshawa for the funerals of both brother priests.

I believe it was the occasion of Father Markle's funeral. After the Mass the priests returned from the church to the adjacent sacristy, in single file. I was the last one. When I stepped through the rather narrow door, I looked to my right and behold: there sat Monsignor Dwyer, breviary in hand! He was obviously too weak to join the other priests in the church, yet still able to come to the sacristy. The moment I noticed him, he looked up from the book and straight at me, smiled, and beckoned with his finger to me to go to him. I thought he would ask me for a glass of water or some other little favour.

When I came to him, he pointed with his finger to the passage in the breviary which he just happened to read and said, slowly and with peaceful emphasis: "Frank, these lines are worth meditating on." Following with his finger along the lines of Psalm 90, he chose some and read them to me: "Lord...a thousand years in thy sight are but as yesterday when it is past, or as a watch in the night...The years of our life are threescore and ten, or even by reason of strength fourscore; yet their span is but toil and trouble..."

At the end of this last sentence he looked up at me and with an almost other-worldly smile exclaimed, to the extent his weakened condition allowed him to: "But mine, they were so full of joy, to overflowing!" Leaving the breviary still open and holding it in his left hand, he thrust in spite of weakness his right palm up at the word "full" as if to emphasize the fullness of joy.

I often remember fondly this truly unforgettable event. The good priest knew he was in his 79th of the biblical "fourscore" (80 years). He also knew he had terminal cancer of the liver. Yet, he was unmistakably "full of joy."

How could anyone forget something like that?

How could anyone forget such a priest!

Many years ago I read a book, translated from German and titled *Priestly Existence.* One of the objectives of the author was to point out the decisive importance of a priest's, - and, I'd say, anybody's - first assignment. He recounts real life stories to prove his point: some happy, some not so happy, but all quite interesting and informative. One can be affected for better or for worse, depending on the first assignment, or more truly so, the first pastor. And affected for life! I know a priest who had a rather troubled record. On one occasion he appeared to have been slightly under the influence of drugs or alcohol, which made him speak very openly about his past life. As soon as he began to describe the character of his first pastor, the cause of his later problems became quite evident.

I was truly blessed in this regard. God knew that I was at the time, due to my war and post-war experiences, to a certain extent still like a half-broken reed. Perhaps that is why I was launched into my priestly existence in a most favourable manner.

Not only was my first pastor a paragon of kindness and generosity: he also allowed me almost complete freedom of action. At the time that was still a rarity; nowadays, of course, the pendulum has swung too far to the opposite side.

There we were: Father Paul Dwyer, the pastor, Father

Larry McGough, the senior curate, and myself, the junior curate. It seemed as if we were a nearly perfect blend for a nearly ideal team to live and act in harmony for the good of each member and of the whole parish.

The pastor was like a good father, counsellor and guide, as it must be evident from what has been already said about him.

The senior curate, Father Larry, was a friend and like a brother to me. Even though six months my junior, he acted like a senior brother, and I respected him accordingly, for he was ordained priest seven years ahead of me.

My room at St. Gregory's rectory was on the third floor, next to his. When on the occasion of my arrival I stepped into it, he already had a long, neatly typed list of all the important names, addresses and telephone numbers waiting for me on my desk: local priests, parishes, hospital, doctors, nurses, and more.

On the weekly day off, Father Larry occasionally took me with him to visit his mother and family in Willowdale on the outskirts of Toronto. Now and then we visited the parish in Penetanguishene near Midland, a good two hours' drive to the north, where he served before coming to Oshawa. On the way back, late in the evening, we usually first prayed the rosary together. Then he would tell me to listen to quiet music, or simply lean back, relax, or just snooze.

By the time of my arrival at St. Gregory's, a kind of informal poker club had been in operation: a few of the most faithful couples in the parish and - you guessed it right! - Father Larry. Almost at once he introduced me to this wonderful group who accepted me as an equal and full-fledged member and partner. We met almost regularly every second Friday evening. As Friday was at that time a day of strict abstinence from meat, we played poker until the small hours of Saturday, nibbling on peanuts or potato chips. Everyone had a glass of pop, usually reinforced by some stronger substance, always ready to soothe a dry throat. With all the jokes (for the most part quite clean), laughter, and a good measure of honest-to-goodness bluffing all around, time just flew by, almost too quickly.

These poker parties were held on a rotating basis: every time at another member's home. When the rectory came on the row, the pastor, Father Dwyer, would also occasionally take part in the party. In fact, once in a blue moon he himself hosted a special poker night for priests only. The majority of participants were pastors. On one occasion they played for fairly high stakes. I joined in their games and almost lost my shirt, as the saying goes. Speaking about bluffing! I am tempted to say cheating, but I think that would be an exaggeration. It would also be a scandal, of course. Priests, cheating?!

The members of the regular poker group probably knew that for us curates money was no problem: we hardly had any worth mentioning. That is probably why the chips and the stakes were very low. There was no reasonable worry of losing or, by the same token, winning much. All that mattered was the fun - and, not least, the delicious meal. After the party one was perhaps two or three bucks richer or poorer. Do I need to spell out what was my usual fate? In any case, my monetary loss was always well compensated by good fellowship and good food.

The host - or more truly and precisely: the hostess - always had a delicious, usually somewhat exotic, meal ready for the *grand finale* at one or two o'clock Saturday morning. There was a great deal of variety from one place and one time to another: genuine "creativeness" at its best!

Prominent among the many laudable traits and customs of Father Dwyer was his attitude to and treatment of the "problem" of holidays. Almost every year he went, usually during the colder time of the year, for a month or two to Rome. He enjoyed the company of his many good friends there, some of whom were in the inner circles of the Vatican. His curates, in the meanwhile, enjoyed an even greater freedom than usual in the parish. Father Larry also always took advantage of the pastor's absence for cleaning up his large, massive desk. At his departure it was clogged by layers of newspapers, useless notes and other junk; on his return one could find only an odd pen or letter opener on it, besides the telephone, and perhaps a family photo or two.

Out of the goodness of his heart, Father Dwyer granted every year after Christmas one week off to his curates: first to the one, then to the other.

After the Christmas of 1961 I went for a week to my friends in Sutton, where I had stayed as seminarian two summer holidays (working in a dairy) in the mid-1950s. One day a lady in the town, a leading member of the Archdiocese of Toronto Catholic Women's League, called me on the telephone.

"Father, is it true that you are being moved from Oshawa?" she asked point blank.

"You have to be kidding!" I replied. "I never heard a single word about it. And got no letter, either."

"Well," she persisted, "I understand it's true."

My first reaction could perhaps best be described as amusement. I thought it was one of those rumours that crop up now and then. But then I began to have second thoughts; so I called St. Gregory's rectory, just in case. To my considerable astonishment I learned it was true.

This manner of learning of one's transfer seems almost bizarre. I can think of at least three factors, though, which make it less incredible. First, the investigative and detective skills of some women should never be underestimated. Secondly, in those days priests (especially curates) were not consulted about their placements or transfers. At most, one's pastor might have been consulted, or at least notified about it beforehand. And lastly, I must have forgotten to leave at the rectory any note regarding my whereabouts.

My week off had to be cut short. Stepping into my room, an empty envelope lay on my desk, with the inscription neatly printed in a printing shop: "My going-away gift to Father Frank," or something to that effect. Father Larry had it printed, in all likelihood before I learned about my transfer, for a special offertory at next Sunday Masses. When the time to leave arrived, it was also he who moved me, lock, stock and barrel (in pedestrian English: me and my junk) to my new parish: St. Bernard's in northwest Toronto.

Priests assisting pastors used to be called curates; now they are referred to as associate pastors. I served in that capacity five outstanding men: Fathers Paul Dwyer in Oshawa, Austin Marshman, Charles Kamber and Josip Gjuran in Toronto, and Philip Kennedy in Brampton: some 15 years altogether. Their personalities differed considerably, but everyone of them was a genuine spiritual father and brother in Christ to me. And everyone, each according to his talents and qualities, had an influence on my priestly life and work. Much the same could be said about the associate pastors with whom I have been associated in one way or another: Fathers Lawrence McGough, Alfred Quesnelle, Charles Wigglesworth, Alexander Boras, and Ermanno Bulfon.

I hope they, too, were enriched, at least a little, by their association with me. Especially I pray this were true of the one whom I could call perhaps my "Benjamin": Father Bob O'Brien. In 1988 he spent eight months of his last year before ordination to the priesthood with me at St. Joseph's parish in Beaverton as Seminarian Assistant. He was my helper, but the main purpose was a kind of internship: practical experience for the future work.

To everyone of these fine men I owe something for the happiness of my life as priest. Of course, there are inevitably crosses and trials in every life and in every vocation; my priestly life had its fair share of them. Yet I can say sincerely that I would not exchange it for anything else in this world. The meaning and purpose of sharing in the one and only priesthood of Jesus Christ, and the goodness of so many people, both Catholics and others, contribute greatly to make "the yoke easy and the burden light" (Cf Mt 11:30).

There is no group of people known to me where fraternal charity and mutual support, generally speaking, are stronger and more genuine than among priests. Nowhere can you hear more hearty laughter than at their gatherings. I owe so much to many of them: to the pastor of my native parish who baptized and guided me through the first conscious years of my life in Christ in my youth; to the Rector and the professors at the College of St. Stanislaus Kostka; to Msgr. John Ingoldsby, the Rector of St. Augustine's Seminary, (as well as the staff and the Sisters of St. Martha); to Dr. Jakob Kolarič, the pastor of Our Lady Help of Christians (Slovenian) parish in Toronto; to the pastors and others whom I mentioned earlier; and to all whom, regretfully, I would certainly miss if I tried to mention everyone by name.

The fields are vast and the harvest ripe, but labourers all too few (Cf Mt 9:37-38). The scene of St. Paul's vision in Troas comes to mind: "And a vision appeared to Paul in the night: a man of Macedonia was standing beseeching him and saying, 'Come over to Macedonia and help us'" (Acts 16:9). Cries for help are coming nowadays from all directions; they reverberate around the globe. Usually they are disguised - drug abuse, vandalism, rebellion, boredom, immorality, suicidal tendencies, etc. - for those crying are not even aware of what is really hurting them. A child lost in the woods may have some idea that the absence of mummy or daddy is the cause of fear and crying; so many youths, and others, today do not realize that the absence of God from their lives is the root cause of their unhappiness: "For yourself have you made us, O God, and our hearts are restless until they rest in you" (St. Augustine).

"How beautiful upon the mountains are the feet of him who brings good tidings, who publishes peace..." (Is 52:7). Nobody could be more suited to "publish" peace than the priest who pronounces the words spoken by Jesus in the Sacrament of Penance and Reconciliation, upon confession of sins by a repentant sinner: "Through the ministry of the Church may God give you pardon and peace. And I absolve you from your sins in the name of the Father, and of the Son, and of the Holy Spirit." Who could bring better news? Who could grasp better the truth that there is "more joy in heaven over one sinner who repents than over ninety-nine righteous persons who need no repentance" (Lk 15:7)? For the priest, himself a sinner, knows both the joy of being forgiven, and the joy of being an instrument, a channel of God's mercy and forgiveness.

In our times, there is an acute crisis of faith and morals in the Western world. Some go so far as to claim that this is already a post-Christian era: an era of new paganism, much worse than the ancient one. There are not enough true and dedicated bearers of glad tidings, both priests and others.

At the same time, however, "The harvest is plentiful, but the labourers are few; pray therefore the Lord of the harvest to send out labourers into his harvest" (Mt 9:37-38). There are still saints and martyrs, and countless plain, ordinary good people, saving the world from the ultimate disaster. And yes, there is hope for the future: there are many young people just as eager and zealous to work and make sacrifices for everything true, good, and beautiful as in any other age in the past. Indeed, with the help of a little realistic optimism, one can sense the first stirrings of a new spring in the Church and in the world.

In these circumstances, my only temptation to regret is that the shadows of my life's day are getting longer; it is almost sundown time, and the harvest fields crying for labourers. Why just temptation rather than regret? Because nobody can claim the privilege of living two lives, either one after another or simultaneously. I thank God for the one and only one I have. Could I live it over again, there are some things both of commission and omission that I would hopefully not repeat. But my vocation in life? I would chose the same one!

Chapter Six

# Maelstrom and Meadow

Even a cursory bird's eye view of the history of humanity presents a bewildering, disconcerting spectacle.

Our knowledge of prehistoric times is, naturally, very sketchy. Yet the sad story of Cain and Abel takes place at the very beginning of the human race: in the very family of our first parents. Significantly, it is a story of fratricide: Cain murdering his own brother Abel.

As far as the written history is concerned, both the biblical and secular sources are full of accounts of man's inhumanity to man. True, in both these sources there are many examples of heroism, virtue, greatness, and of genuine holiness. Yet accounts of wars, greed, hatred, murder, violence and sins of every imaginable variety far outnumber those of self-sacrificial love and goodness.

St. Augustine wrote, in the beginning of the 5th Century A.D., that not even lions and dragons have ever waged among themselves the kind of wars which men have fought (*City of God,* Bk XII, Ch 23). What would he say today, after Verdun, Dresden, and Hiroshima...?

As a boy, I laughed when my choleric uncle, a veteran of the First World War, talked about his experiences and then added, in desperation and perhaps somewhat shaken faith: "I'll throw images of saints out of my house and put in their places pictures of lions and bears." Today, I don't find his picturesque language quite so funny: he had a point, albeit expressed somewhat bluntly.

Generally speaking, the whole human history seems to be a history of mutually self-inflicted torture and horror.

The Swedish Academy of Sciences has allegedly studied it, starting with the earliest written records, the Sumerian wedge writings: a period of some 5,600 years.

It is shocking to learn that in all this long period of time the study was unable to find more than 292 years without war.

Some wars devastated entire nations. Some lasted several

decades. It is estimated that there were approximately 3,064,000,000 victims. The apex of violence, or rather the rock-bottom, has been reached precisely in our own supposedly most enlightened and progressive 20th century A.D. The two World Wars alone are estimated to have taken some 65,000,000 lives, not to mention countless other minor and major internecine conflicts, both international and revolutionary.

On top of it all: what about the literally hundreds of millions of real human lives sniffed out in the last few decades by what the Second Vatican Council (1962 - 1965) branded as an "unspeakable crime"- abortion?

And there are, at the time of this writing, still several years of this century left: more than enough for humanity to commit the "unthinkable crime" - a global nuclear holocaust! Or stumble into an A.B.C. (Atomic, Bacterial, Chemical) war. Very appropriately the prospect of a nuclear war has been designated as M.A.D. (Mutual Assured Destruction).

We are indubitably unable to save ourselves from our own breathless stupidity. It is high time for all to exclaim with the apostles in the midst of the storm on the sea: "Teacher, do you not care if we perish? "(Mk 4:39), and pray and work for peace.

Jesus himself used many parables or stories in his discourses. The evangelist St. Mark goes so far as to say that "he did not speak to them without a parable" (Mk 4:34). This gives me the nerve to try one, too. Call it parable, allegory, dream, daydream, plain blarney, whatever. Here it is.

I had the vision of having reached on a long journey, late one summer afternoon, the edge of a not very high plateau. Having just struggled somewhat uphill through bushes and thorny bramble thickets, the path now seemed clear "for miles and miles," as one could have put it before the advent of the metric system. The exact nature of the seemingly endless plain ahead was not yet discernible, yet as far as one could see, the path across it looked very romantic. It was smooth, narrow, winding its way amidst rich fields of wheat, oats, flowers, and buckwheat fields galore, before it went out of sight in the distance. I took first a long glance over the whole vast expanse of breathless beauty. Then my eyes returned to graze on the lush buckwheat field in bloom just a few steps ahead. Every cluster of buckwheat blossoms had one or more butterfly, bee, or bumble bee. They were swinging on the pink clusters, hopping from one to another, busily gathering honey.

Every stalk of grass on the edge of the sunbathed plain swayed peacefully in gentle breeze. The pure air was saturated with inebriatingly mellow aroma of buckwheat in bloom.

The ground where I emerged from the bushes was still slowly rising for a short distance, but far, very very far away beyond the plain, rising as it were from a hardly discernible veil of mist, was a mountain range. The mountains looked low from the vast distance, but in reality they were evidently gigantic. Their snow-capped peaks were shining in a bright silvery glow, suffused with a hardly perceptible touch of red, in the setting sun.

"That's the big goal of my journey," I said to myself as in a state of mild inebriation, "to reach the top of the highest peak, no matter how long it takes or how steep the path. The good Lord will help me, and then show what lies beyond."

Have you ever experienced one of those sudden, violent summer storms, when the day turns almost to night, pierced only by blinding strikes of lightning with almost simultaneous peels of thunder? Winds rise to near hurricane force, rain comes down in torrents, and hail that turns rich wheat fields and blossoming buckwheat into barren wastelands. Such storms occur usually after very hot, muggy spells when pure, cold air masses clash with the hot, humid ones.

This time the storm rose after pleasant weather. And it was much more sudden and more violent than any I had ever experienced before.

It started with an ominous calm before the storm. Then, in a very short time, everything turned dark. Momentarily the darkness was split with lightning, followed by thunder. Their succession became ever more frequent, the closeness between every lightning and its thunder also ever closer to one another. Soon they became blinding; and deafening, not unlike the so-called "down fire" of artillery, or a nocturnal air raid on a helpless city.

I should have probably returned, and sought shelter among

the bushes. For some unexplained, and indeed inexplicable reason, I charged forwards into the field. Torrential downpour mixed with hail turned the ground into a sea of mud. As the level of the field seemed very slowly but surely lower the further I advanced, so was the level of water and mud, mingled with hail, becoming ever higher.

What drove me on was the hope of reaching some small tree, or at least shrub, under which to find a modicum of shelter in the furious storm. Meanwhile, I protected my head against the hail by a wicker basket. Fortunately I had it with me: to carry in it a large wedge of rye bread and some extra pieces of clothing and footwear. These I tucked under my elbow, and put the basket on my head as if it were a helmet.

Hoping against hope for the storm to blow over, I pushed on. But while thunder and lightning up in the skies became slightly more distant, the situation on the ground was going from bad to worse. The mud, already up to my waist, began to reach up to the shoulders. I had the distinct feeling that I was loosing the ground under my feet. At times I had to walk literally on my toes, with mouth and nose lifted upwards, in order not to become submerged and drown.

At this point it began to dawn on me that the sea of mud was really not stationary. I began to feel rather than know that it was more like an immense stew-like stream, the more stinking the further one got into it. All over its vast expanse there were widely scattered red and black patches: unmistakably some of fresher, some of already rotten blood. The ugly mass was moving very slowly but inexorably in a generally leftwards direction.

To my horror my feet began to bump into what felt like human skulls, bones and even corpses. Then low and behold: the bloated body of a child appeared nearby. Was it dead or still fighting for breath of life? I'll never know, for before I could reach for it, it drifted away. What I do know is that soon after more and more corpses appeared strewn all over, as far as the eye could see in the flashes of lightning. Were they men? Women? Old or young? Children? Dead? Alive? It was impossible to discern clearly.

One thing was certain: some were dead, others still alive but dying. For now and then the unbearable stench of rotting or roasted human flesh struck the nostrils, while the ears perceived out of darkness the agonizing groans of drowning human beings.

In all likelihood the human groans and shrieks were mixed with sounds of berserk animals such as pigs, cows, dogs, and many other kinds. It was hard to distinguish between the human bodies and sounds and those of animals.

Certain cries were peaceful, almost pleading: strangely reminiscent of the hurrahs of young Russian soldiers charging uphill and dying in the hail of heavy machine-gun fire in the early morning dawn of that awful August day way back in the year of the Lord 1944. The most frightful of them all were the unmentionable blasphemies spewing out of distorted mouths of evidently evil men and women perishing in despair. Perishing and yet, even in this blood-curdling predicament, on their very way to the nether regions of temporal and possibly eternal damnation, trying to tear the very flesh from one another's bodies.

When a huge green snake with angry fiery eyes and needle-sharp pair of fangs surfaced, jaws wide open and hissing menacingly, practically in front of my very nose, I almost flipped. Only the buoyant effect of the stream saved me from flopping flat on the ground.

In a word: things went from bad to worse; from horrible to unbearable, approaching the indescribable.

I was tempted to give up the struggle for survival. I thought I'd die of fear, anyway, sooner rather than later.

At this point I got the feeling that a voice was calling through the dark. It seemed more like an inner voice rather than a sound audible by ears. Actually, it sounded more like two voices: one lower, the other distinctly feminine. Both were coming from the same area: several degrees to the left from the direction in which the ugly stream was moving.

I turned a little more left, so as to move with the stream, cupped the ears with my hands, and listened.

The voices were gone. It had to be wishful thinking. Or hallucinations?

But now they appeared again, more clearly than before.

This time there was no doubt: yes, it was my dad and mum calling my name. Carried over the vast expanse by the howling winds, its only vowel long and drawn out, it came through unmistakably: "Franc! Franc!" Just as long ago when it called me to lunch from the forests up the mountains or from work in the fields.

With the desperation of a drowning person I mustered all the failing strength of my whole being, trying to move more and more leftwards as I was carried on by the flow. I yearned to reach the area whence the voices originated. It seemed next to impossible, but the effort was not in vain. After what seemed half of eternity the stream was becoming distinctly slower and shallower. Before too long I was able to crawl, then glide on my stomach over the soggy ground. Finally I reached a very steep and very high rock. I took a short rest at its foot. Then I looked up its heights in the twilight. They seemed forbidding, yet not absolutely impassable. I started climbing resolutely, not once glancing dawn into the dark precipice but only up, and up: looking for safe footholds to grab them by hands and pulling myself up to stand on.

After a seemingly endless and most exhausting climb I suddenly reached the grassy top, and collapsed.

Having come again to myself, I was able to see that I was almost at the tip of a promontory. On three sides the almost vertical, rugged crags descended down into the dark below. Towards the mainland the promontory became wider and wider, and slowly rising. But one could still not see very far, because the twilight either just began or was just ending: it was impossible to guess whether night or day was at hand.

By now the hail had stopped. The rain abated. The wind fell. The rumbling thunder and lightning was moving farther and farther away over the nightmarish stream far below.

There was no tangible sign of my parents' presence, yet I just knew with my whole being that their prayerful love was mysteriously somehow all around me.

Completely exhausted, hungry after days of no food, with my few possessions lost, yet as happy and grateful as I could be, I took again the road under my feet. I walked from the promontory towards the mainland, but always keeping slightly to the right. The grassy ground rose very gently, so I had to walk a little uphill, all the while looking for somebody or a house where

I could find something to eat. I passed through a short and heavy downpour. But it was very refreshing, for it washed away all or at least most of the ugliness reified that still saturated every thread of my clothing and clung to my skin. Then, in matter of minutes, the dark clouds moved in the direction from which I just came, and a beautiful full moon appeared. After a while it became very clear that it was early morning rather than late evening, for it was getting slowly brighter.

A building of sorts appeared on the horizon. It was a log house. I aimed straight for it. Near an old linden tree on the courtyard there was a round well with a crankshaft and bucket to draw water. For quite a while I leaned on the well, pondering whether or not to knock on the door at this early hour. The parching thirst, joined with stomach-biting hunger, tipped the scales of my mind: I knocked gently.

It took quite a few minutes before a most lovable old lady opened the door just enough to peep out, no doubt wondering who would wake her at such an ungodly hour. She seemed a little scared, yet she greeted me with a charming smile.

"I'm very sorry, lady, to wake you up," I apologized, "but I'm starving. I have come a long way and have not eaten for days."

"Please do step in," she interrupted me, "you poor young one. I'm old and poor myself. But we'll find something for your empty stomach. Meanwhile, lie down on the bench here behind the door and have a little rest." That, at least, was the gist of her words, for she spoke a foreign language. But it was obviously one of the Slavic family of languages, like my mother tongue. So I understood some of it, and her gestures and smile spoke more clearly than any words could.

In minutes I was sound asleep. When I awoke, the meal was ready: a bowl of hot cabbage soup, with a large piece of rye bread next to it, and a bowl of milk.

That was the most tasty, royal meal in my life!

We chatted a little: more in gestures than words. Then she gave me a medium-sized can of milk, a big loaf of rye bread, some home-churned butter, and a whole little bag of dried hazelnuts. "This is for the road," she said, "go in peace and God be with you. I'll pray that we meet in heaven some day." I thanked her from my whole heart for her generosity, and said goodbye.

Before leaving the courtyard, I turned back. She was still standing on the threshold. We waved again to each other. Then I turned and left between some plum trees, through the yard gate, and into the wide open fields, to continue my journey.

After a few hundred metres of walk sideways and up the slowly rising slope, not far from where it appeared to become level, there was a bush. Sitting down under it, with hands around my knees, I looked down the gently falling field. The sight far ahead and farther to the left reminded me spontaneously of the passage from Genesis: "And Abraham went early in the morning to the place where he had stood before the Lord; and he looked down toward Sodom and Gomorrah and toward all the land of the valley, and beheld, and lo, the smoke of the land went up like the smoke of a furnace" (Gen 19:27-28).

In the far distance huge, dark-grey, frightful clouds filled the whole field of vision. They rose from the ground far up into the skies, reminiscent of the diabolic mushroom-like clouds over Hiroshima or Nagasaki back in August 1945. You saw their photographs, I'm sure. The only difference was that this cloud, though much larger, did not look like a gigantic mushroom at all, for it had no stem. All was just one dark, dense, wildly churning mass: like a mass of thick ash-coloured wool, evolving rather fast from its inner regions balls of more curling wool of a dark-grey ashen or lead hue. The curling, churning balls were here and there momentarily but constantly lit up by a reddish glow as if by fierce lightnings from within.

Little by little, as by an intuition, I began to realize that the whole vast area under the spine-chilling panorama was in reality not a stream but rather an immense whirlpool. While things at its edges hardly moved at all, the speed picked up in direct proportion to the closeness to the centre. There speeds and conditions were nothing less than fantastic, and there was a direct connection with the nether regions. Really, the whirlpool was not unlike a mini-galaxy: not a beautiful, cosmic one, but the very opposite of everything true, good and beautiful.

I went through the fringes of the ugly whirlpool and lived. How could I thank God enough for it?

Sitting under that hazelnut bush, I had an internal vision of the infernal maelstrom. I already began to describe it for you, but I changed my mind: because it would take too long, for it is really indescribable, and because it may bring you nightmares. Yes, I even got the gut feeling that letters would burn through the very writing paper. Or make it burst in flames.

Before getting up, the profound, consoling words of St. Paul came to my mind: "I consider that the sufferings of this present time are not worth comparing with the glory that is to be revealed to us. For the creation waits with eager longing for the revealing of the sons of God; for the creation was subjected to futility, not of its own will but by the will of him who subjected it in hope; because the creation itself will be set free from its bondage to decay and obtain the glorious liberty of the children of God. We know that the whole creation has been groaning in travail together until now; and not only the creation, but we ourselves, who have the first fruits of the Spirit, groan inwardly as we wait for adoption as sons, the redemption of our bodies" (Rom 8:18-24).

With breast swelling to overflowing with that faith and hope I got up, invigorated and full of confidence, turned around and continued my journey.

With a song in my heart I almost frolicked up the short remaining stretch of the gentle slope: keeping always slightly to the left and trying not even to look to the right. With eager anticipation I pressed towards the horizon: delightfully impatient because a mysterious hope was welling up in my whole being that better, wonderful things were waiting beyond it.

A few more steps, and an immense plain appeared before me in all its breathtaking, heavenly beauty.

The sun was just rising at the other end of it in all its majestic glory.

I happened to find myself on a more or less narrow plateau full of variegated flowers, the breezy air filled with their exotic fragrance.

Beyond the plateau, in the general direction of the rising sun, the ground sloped downwards: hardly perceptibly, but very, very far. Then it turned gradually into an immense flatland, as long and wide as the eye could see. In the seemingly almost infinite distance, towards the horizon on the far side, it appeared to rise again ever so gently. Far, far away, ahead and to my right, the plain also rose for a very long distance slowly towards the foot of the mountains. Because of distance they seemed rather small, but in reality they were quite obviously no less than gigantic. Their higher regions were covered with virginal snows, glistening with a silvery glow in the morning sun.

I stood as enchanted for a long time, drinking with all my five senses, even more with my powers of imagination and intellect, indeed - and perhaps above all - with my whole heart and very soul the beauties displayed before me. I drank them to inebriation and ecstasy.

No genius could possibly describe adequately the indescribably beautiful scene, no painter depict it on canvas. How could then this lowly writer hope to give justice to his description of it! Just as the unaided human eye cannot perceive things below the red or above the violet extremes of the visible spectrum, so also there are limits for a mortal tongue's ability to describe the depths of sorrow or the heights of delight beyond certain limits. For that reason he will not even try, except for a few sketchy remarks.

Having as it were awakened from a daze, I sat down and enjoyed a snack. Basking in the now near-noonday sun tempered by the gentlest of breezes blowing from the plain, I had the feeling of being on a meadow in the garden of Eden, such as "no eye has seen" (1 Cor 2:9).

The air was filled with the scent of blooming buckwheat and other aromas most pleasant to the nostrils.

Refreshed and invigorated by the tasty meal, I got up and continued my journey with uplifted spirit and light step: almost as if walking on the moon, but on a ground that was level or just discernibly tilted to my advantage.

I struck a barely recognizable path winding its way among meadows adorned with exotic flowers, and large fields of various grains, but predominantly buckwheat in bloom. Way back beyond these meadows and fields were lovely villages. In the middle or at the edge of each there stood a white church with its high steeple pointing heavenwards: like a shepherd in white robes, with a staff, and ewes or little lambs huddled around him. Every village was surrounded by blossoming orchards. In the foreground, just before the orchards, lay long fields of wheat or rye, swaying in the peaceful wind in such a way that it seemed as if waves began at the extreme left of the field, then followed one another slowly all the way to its other end. Their crests were of a notably deeper green than the ebbs between.

Almost before I realized it was "toward evening and the day is now far spent" (Lk 24:29). The song of birds and the sounds of crickets, grasshoppers, and a myriad of other little creatures ceased gradually. With the sunset most of them also seemed to have retired, to rest from the work done and gather strength to give glory to their Creator next day, each in one's own special way. The wind fell to practically zero velocity. One had the feeling that the first beginnings of dusk were almost at hand. Almost tangible peace was descending all over the land, and into my whole being.

Carried by a most gentle zephyr, the sound of a church bell from far, far away reached my ears: on account of distance feeble, yet "as clear as the bell." In a few seconds another of a slightly higher pitch joined in. Then a third, quite low, and more of them: from very far and a little nearer, from left and right, from all over the vast land. Everyone had a different tone, so that their ringing sounded strikingly like the accompaniment to the melody of Schubert's *Ave Maria:* one tune flowing into and blending harmoniously with the other of a slightly lower or higher pitch.

There could be no doubt: it rang the Angelus.

Spontaneously the inspired verse of the psalmist came to my mind: "Blessed is the nation whose God is the Lord" (Ps 33:12), and in spirit I joined in the prayers of the unknown blessed people.

Just as the bells joined in the chorus one after another, so also they stopped ringing one after another, until finally the last solitary one very far away, with perhaps the deepest tone of them all, also fell silent. Before long the moon was high up over the horizon, shedding its soft silvery light all over the land. I sat down under a hazelnut bush near the path, ate a light meal, and fell asleep almost as soon as my head hit the folded jacket serving

# A BOUQUET FOR YOU

as pillow. The sun was already high, with some beautifully shaped clouds moving slowly here and there over the blue skies, as I woke up from a most refreshing and invigorating sleep. After thanking God for the good night, asking Mary to pray for me, washing in the little creek, and eating a hefty breakfast of thickly buttered rye bread and milk, I continued my journey.

This next day was pretty much like the first one. I kept more or less to the right, so as to skirt the villages in a huge, left-veering but not quite completed semi-circle, then turning again more rightwards to continue in about the same direction as before reaching the area of villages.

An other-worldly, indescribable peace seemed to lay over the enchantingly beautiful, sun-bathed plain. But it was not a bogus, dead peace. Rather, it was a peace full of bubbling life. Not only was there luxuriant vegetation everywhere, but also sounds of crickets and birds in the air, and bees, butterflies and many other kinds of little creatures. In late afternoon groups of people could be seen in far distance; they were certainly returning home after the work in the fields. And after the sunset sounds of music and songs could be heard: some more like folk dancing tunes, others more like sacred songs.

Some mysterious, unexplainable emotion kept me from entering any of the villages. At nightfall a gentle rain was falling and I sought shelter on the back porch of a solitary house that stood, surrounded by a garden full of fruit trees and lush flowers, somewhat out of the nearest village. The voices of adults and children were heard from inside; although I couldn't discern the words, it was clear that they were praying the family rosary, just before bed time. Then the light went out and a peaceful quiet enwrapped the whole place.

Just before leaving the area of villages to set out over the wide open, very gently rising plain towards the far distant mountains, I arrived near a group of children at play on a meadow. Some noticed me. A few boys and girls ran towards me and a girl clasped firmly her hands around my knees. She threw her head backwards and with an angelic smile looked for a little while straight in my eyes, saying nothing.

She had beautiful brown eyes. I had the feeling that I was

294

seeing reflected in them the innocence of my own youth of long ago. An indescribable beauty was in these innocent eyes, and heaven itself seemed reflected in their mysterious, endless depths.

The girl then extended her hands wide and upwards. I bent down and she put them gently around my neck for a few moments, her cheek pressed softly to mine. Then she turned and frolicked away to rejoin her playmates on the meadow. Her companions who stood near us smiled, waved to me, and followed her. I also turned and continued my journey, sleeping overnight under a small hazelnut bush.

Next day the plain with the villages got farther and farther away behind me, while the mountains seemed to grow higher and higher.

Finally I reached them and entered one of their valleys. Having trod for several hours a path along the lively murmuring stream, I reached its end: or beginning, depending on one's point of view.

I sat on a little hillock. I had an unusual appetite, so first I enjoyed a bigger than usual meal. Only then I began to assess my situation.

The valley was fairly wide. Even its bottom must have been quite high over the sea level, for the air seemed rarer than on the plains. It was certainly notably cooler. On all three sides towering, steep, breath-taking heights loomed skywards, almost up into the fast moving clouds. Way up, at the far end of the valley, was the lower edge of a giant glazier. The creek that ran through the valley originated from under its massive ice. For a long time I was deliberating what to do next day: for the mountains appeared impassable even for a mountaineer with the best equipment, let alone for me who had none.

When the reddish, breath-like glow of the sunlight on the highest peaks faded away, I laid me down to rest, as usual. During the night, though, I woke up, because it was quite chilly.

The whole of nature lay in deep silence: I could hear every beat of my heart.

The very dark blue sky was so full of bigger and smaller, brighter and less bright stars, and clusters of stars, that nobody could count. And the Milky Way, like a thin veil, or breath on a cold window pane, was arched from one end of the firmament to the other.

In the mountainside there was a cave: a deserted lair of a bear? Or not so deserted? I didn't speculate long. Whatever it was, it looked like an ideal protection from cold drafts descending down from the glaziers. I gathered some dry leaves and turned the cave into a cosy bivouac. Then I laid down and covered myself with my jacket from the shoulder to the ankles.

Whether still awake, half asleep, or in a dream, I do not know; "whether in the body or out of the body I do not know, God knows" (2 Cor 12:2): all I do know is that my whole journey appeared in a mysterious manner, yet vividly, before the eyes of my mind. At the same time, not unlike the sound of hardly audible background music, I recalled the words of the poet: "Heaven is above you and hell below. And life, in between, scoops with its cup for you now from the woes underneath, now from the raptures above."

When the image of the playing children appeared, the words of another poet surfaced, as it were, imperceptibly from my subconsciousness. He was not only poet, but saintly bishop and candidate for beatification. In his poem *The Home of Joy* he describes his search for happiness: "O my dearest joy, where is your home? Tell me where you dwell, my heart's darling. Over hills and dales I am running after you, yearning to see and embrace you." He is looking for joy among dancers, drinkers, gamblers...everywhere. No luck: all in vain.

At last he finds its trail. Galloping and out of breath he arrives on the meadow behind a village: "Look! There is joy, entertaining the children and playing with them: there is its home!"

But the poet soon wakes up to the bitter truth: there is no way to return to his childhood. It has passed into eternity, never to come back again.

Yet there is no need to whine or despair: "One joy is still waiting for me: in the most beautiful land where everyone is young. No suffering can find its way into that land. Only there is the home of true joy."

As if hearing it whispered over my shoulder in unspoken words, my whole being suddenly became deeply aware of some of the main lessons from a passage in the Book of Deuteronomy: "See, I have set before you this day life and good, death and evil. If you obey the commandments of the Lord which I command you this day, by loving the Lord your God, by walking in his ways, and by keeping his commandments and his statutes and his ordinances, then you shall live and multiply, and the Lord your God will bless you in the land which you are entering to take possession of it. But if your heart turns away, and you will not hear, but are drawn away to worship other gods and serve them, I declare to you this day, that you shall perish..." (Deut 30:15-18).

At this point it occurred to me that even Moses, the great leader of his people from slavery, was denied entry into the Promised Land, because he had not been fully faithful to God at all times. He could see it from Mount Nebo in the Abarim Mountains, but he died before entering it.

I thought to myself that Moses at least saw the Promised Land, albeit only from a distant mountain. My heart seemed to draw me on and up the mighty mountains: perhaps up there I could sit down on a grassy slope near the top, look back, and admire the distant, peaceful land which I skirted on my way? And which, it occurred to me now, resembled in at least some of its aspects "the holy city Jerusalem coming down out of heaven from God" (Rev 21:10). Perhaps I could then make a few more steps and suddenly have displayed before my eyes, as in my youth on the top of the Karavanke mountains, a whole beautiful new world deep down on the other side? But I just knew, in the heart of my heart, that I would never be able to reach the forbidding heights before me.

What lay beyond those mysterious peaks? Only God knows; but that must suffice. Instinctively I felt - I was sure! - it was "the land where true joy is at home, and everybody is young." The land where "Eye has not seen, ear has not heard, nor has it so much as dawned on man what God has prepared for those who love him" (1 Cor 2:9). The land where "nothing unclean shall enter it" (Rev 21:27). I knew in the very heart of my heart that that blessed land was what was still ahead: beyond the lofty horizons, waiting for me.

And for you.

But it is the land that no sinful, mortal flesh may see, let alone enter.

I also knew that the journey behind me was my past life, with the maelstrom and the meadow an image of the world. Granted, the reality is not quite as sharply "bifocal," for the images from the two poles are often blended, in real life. And I believe that when everything is taken into account, those of the meadow predominate. But this was a vision: a spiritual vision, for which I thank God, and which I would like to share with you, to the best of my ability.

The more frightening images of beasts, fires, apocalyptic riders and other horrors from *The Book of Revelation* could certainly describe the realities of recent history better than this parable. Its author speaks about "the great winepress of the wrath of God" (Rev 14:19); in his visions he saw horses with heads "like lions' heads, and fire and smoke and sulphur issued from their mouths" (Rev 9:17), locusts "like horses arrayed for battle" (Rev 9:7) - and more. Much more!

God, in his boundless munificence, seems to give different vision to different eyes and minds.

How wonderful! How merciful! For if it weren't so, how could people find their spouses to admire, love and marry? Everyone would want the same one!

And so, the author of *The Book of Revelation* was given greater gifts, and a different way to describe things. Unlike his writing about the visions in exile on the island of Patmos, mine is not literally inspired by God. But the parable of the talents (Mt 25:14-30) teaches that what matters is not how many gifts one has, but rather how well does one use them for the benefit of the Master and his dear ones.

My parable tries to express the horrors of the Maelstrom and the raptures of the Meadow to the best of my ability, even though it cannot do justice to either. They cannot be expressed, I believe, in non-inspired human language. And the angelic is beyond the powers of us mortals.

In a nutshell: the *Parable of the Maelstrom and Meadow* is a vision: a spiritual vision, in which is reflected the world as it is. But with a little intuition one can discern in it also how it should be.

And how it could be.

And how it would be, if only we would listen: if only we would listen to God, and turn our swords into ploughshares, and our spears - from atomic submarines, tanks and bombers to pens and tongues - into pruning hooks (Cf Mi 4:3).

It has been said that the opposite of love is not hate but fear. We fear the unknown. Therefore, we must strive to know one another: our minds and hearts must meet. For example: how wonderful that lately thousands of people, with their priests and bishops, from the three neighbouring dioceses in the three states in the area of my homeland, representing the three great families of European nations (Germanic, Romanic, Slavic) come annually on a rotating basis for one day to one of the Marian shrines to meet and pray as one family of God! Things like this will foster reconciliation and peace in the world more than all the armies.

True peace and true love are inseparable. Both begin at home, but should not end there. Let them spread, like ripples caused by a pebble dropped into a tranquil pond, to ends of the world and beyond, to the very shores of eternity.

Let there be peace in the world.
Yes, and let it begin with me!

"Lord, make me an instrument of your peace!
Where there is hatred - let me sow love;
Where there is injury - pardon;
Where there is doubt - faith;
Where there is despair - hope;
Where there is darkness - light;
Where there is sadness - joy.
O Divine Master,
Grant that I may not so much seek
To be consoled - as to console;
To be understood - as to understand;
To be loved - as to love;
For it is in giving that we receive;
It is in pardoning that we are pardoned;
It is in dying that we are born to eternal life."

A Prayer of St. Francis of Assisi.

TRIGLAV 2864m

JULIAN ALPS

ITALY

RJAVINA
2542m

KRMA

RADOVNA

BLED